Cooking Up
an Italian Life

Cooking Up an Italian Life

$\backsim$

Simple Pleasures of Italy
in Recipes and Stories

Sharon Sanders

pergola
WEST

Center Valley, Pennsylvania

PergolaWest
PO Box 314
Center Valley, Pennsylvania 18034-0314
http://www.pergolawest.com; info@pergolawest.com

Publisher's Cataloging-in-Publication
(Provided by Quality Books, Inc.)
Sanders, Sharon.
    Cooking up an Italian life : simple pleasures of Italy in
recipes and stories / Sharon Sanders ; illustrator, Linda Holt
Ayriss ; photographer, Walter Sanders. — 1st ed.
    p. cm.
    Includes bibliographical references and index.
    LCCN: 00-106383
    ISBN: 0-97029-813-7

    1. Cookery, Italian. 2. Italy—Description and travel.
3. Italy—Social life and customs. I. Ayriss, Linda. II. Sanders,
Walter, 1948- III. Title.

TX723.S26 2001   641.5945
                                   QBI00-837

⌣

FRONT JACKET PHOTOGRAPHS: Clockwise from bottom right: a greengrocer
in the Mercato Centrale, Florence; the lake town of Como in
Lombardy; Arista, Roast Pork with Rosemary and Garlic *(page 172);*
a cheese vendor in Montepulciano, Tuscany; country houses
overlooking an olive grove in Tuscany.

BACK JACKET PHOTOGRAPH: Window on Borgo Allegri, Florence.

To Emma and Tess,
who are doing a fine job of raising me

Acknowledgments

Writing a book is like moving to an unfamiliar place. No matter how carefully you have planned, the change is jarring. The terrain is alien. Every day is a challenge to adjust.

If you're lucky, you'll meet new companions who help along the way. If you're blessed, old friends will ease your transition, too. I have been living in this new place—this book—for more than a year and have been lucky as acquaintances became friends and blessed as longtime friends grew closer.

Thanks to . . .

Virginia Van Vynckt, for her steadfast guidance through the treacherous terrain of publishing.

Faith Hague, for presenting this book to the world in a beautifully designed package.

Susan Figliulo, *qui aiutami a trovare la mia voce*, and made me laugh, too.

Linda Holt Ayriss, whose lovely illustrations breathe *la vita Italiana* into these pages.

Patrizia Bracci, M.A., of Muhlenberg College, for expert counsel on Italian language usage. *Grazie mille*.

Piero Antuono, M.D., who literally went out of his way early and often, to check on Italian usage, facts, and sources.

Carol A. Berman, for sharing wine choices that transform daily meals into celebrations. Cheers!

Nanette Bendyna, for meticulously grooming the text and creating the index.

Barbara Gibbs Ostmann, for immeasurable assistance with the international conversion information. And to Norene Gilletz, CCP, with ready answers on Canadian measures.

Anna Baldesi Gaggio, a true Italian country cook, who is so generous with her gifts.

The family of Marcello and Marisa Gori for their kindness to *stranieri*.

Loriano and Gabriella Pallini for so very many wonderful meals at Trattoria Benvenuto.

David Joachim, superb counselor and friend.

Mycologists Kathie Hodge, Ph.D., of Cornell University, and Francisco Camacho, Ph.D., of the University of California at Berkeley, for sharing their time and expertise in answering my questions about *Boletus*.

Susan McQuillan, R.D., who once challenged me to develop complete meals with only five ingredients. Ever since, I have tried to distill recipes to their essence.

Walter Sanders, for his evocative cover photographs, beautiful stories, and, more important, for sharing his life's adventure with me.

Emma and Tess Sanders, who are good eggs and smart cookies.

The countless home cooks, bakers, cheesemakers, vintners, restaurateurs, greengrocers, fishmongers, and butchers in Italy, from whom I've learned so much about cooking and living.

The recipe samplers who graciously shared their time, taste buds, and thoughts. Real people with full schedules—a dentist, a neurologist, a magazine editor, a nurse, a market researcher, two farmers, two mothers of five, several librarians, and so many more—all of whom cook because it enriches their lives: Linda and Piero Antuono, Marcia Bittner, Bonnie Beck, Gary Borman, Allison Collins, Loretta Costa, Jerry Delaney, Ellie Denuel, Melanie and George DeVault, Kristen Morgan Downey, Jeanine Faust, Gail A. Fenstermaker, Cindy Freid, Mimi Gilbert, Mary Gillespie, Donna Gilreath, Deborah Hill, Ann L. Hunsicker-Morrissey, Susan and Rich Kaeser, Janet Kenealy, Carolynne, Will, Ted, and Harry Kent, Diane Koch, Harriet Kohn, Diane Laughlin, Susan Leo, Dot Lick, Laura Mandel, Claire McCrea and Peter Moore, Robin Metzger, Ann Michael and David Sloan, Debbi Pereira, Laura Piazza, Karen Randolph, Rita Rife, Delia and Mark Ritzmann, Melinda Rizzo, Martha and Michael Sanders, May May Tchao, Sue Trinkle, Loretta Wursta, Melanie Wursta, and Lisa Zajdel.

"Then the pernicious charm of Italy worked on her, and, instead of acquiring information, she began to be happy."

E.M. Forster
A Room with a View

Contents

Prologue

Are we truly what we eat?

I eat Italian.

Yet, sadly, no matter how much pasta, porcini, and prosciutto I consume, I *still* am not Italian. For years now, I've had to overcompensate for this genetic shortcoming.

My motivation in wanting to "be" Italian is complicated—and it has a history. If the story were a film, I would want a director with a deft touch for quirky material, perhaps Jonathan Demme or Nora Ephron.

To produce the movie, I'll need a brilliant screenwriter and money. To get the big bucks, my screenwriter no doubt would have to do a verbal tap dance before some arrogant Hollywood executive, like the one played so deliciously by Tim Robbins in Robert Altman's *The Player*.

STUDIO EXECUTIVE: "What's your pitch?"

SCREENWRITER: "Young woman from coal country. Central Pennsylvania—northern Appalachia, really—beautiful scenery, zilch opportunity. Dad works in the mines; mom's raising five kids and farming the family plot. No one ever leaves.

"But this girl is different. Think Sissy Spacek, in the early scenes of *Coal Miner's Daughter*—she's uncertain, yet she yearns for more."

STUDIO EXECUTIVE: "Sounds heavy. Is it funny?"

SCREENWRITER: "Very funny. And with heart. See, she takes a tour to Italy. The ruins, the art, the food, the crazy Italians living in the moment—it completely *transforms* her. Think Helena Bonham Carter in *A Room with a View*."

STUDIO EXECUTIVE: "Risk-taking is good. Is there romance?"

SCREENWRITER: "Is there *romance?* The tour stops in Florence and she falls head over heels for a rascal from Chicago. Imagine the irony—she could've gone for an Italian. Turns out this guy helps her break free of her provincial upbringing. Think Julian Sands in

A Room with a View—remember how he inspires Helena Bonham Carter? Same thing here: The guy's love gives her the self-confidence to pursue a career as a food writer."

Studio Executive: "What about conflict? In *A Room with a View*, the girl's afraid to be her own woman, so she rejects Julian Sands and gets engaged to that prig—who was it?—oh, yeah, Daniel Day-Lewis."

Screenwriter: "Conflict! Sure! The boyfriend is used to playing the field. The girl knows he's the one but he's not so sure. Plus, it's the early '70s, with social upheaval—the Vietnam War, Watergate. We can weave in plenty of period texture—young foreign expats hanging out in Florentine clubs. Neil Young and Cat Stevens on the soundtrack."

Studio Executive: "I like it. Turbulent times, internal character flaws keeping the lovers apart."

Screenwriter: "Yeah, and there's a happy ending. When these two get married in a Renaissance chapel in Florence, there won't be a dry eye in the theater."

Studio Executive: "So, it's *Coal Miner's Daughter* meets *A Room with a View*—with humor . . . conflict . . . romance . . . *and* a happy ending."

Screenwriter: "Don't forget the food: location shots at open air markets, cheese shops, bakeries, trattorias, wine festivals. This girl is nuts about Italian cooking. The audience will drool."

Studio Executive: "Sounds appetizing. Work up a treatment and get back to me. What's your title?"

Screenwriter: "I call it *Cooking Up an Italian Life*."

Taking Time to Smell the Pasta

Basics

Stories

M

any people believe there is only one Italy. This is incomplete. Another Italy exists, for those who know where to look.

The Kingdom of Two Italys

Italy, the country, is easy to spot on a globe. The boot-shaped peninsula jauntily steps away from Europe into the Mediterranean, a jolly topographical metaphor for the Italians' propensity to set their own course. The other Italy, the state of being, is vast, invisible, endlessly seductive. Because its borders are malleable in time and space, it is eternally accessible and you need never leave home to go there. Travel no farther than your kitchen, where you'll find many of the necessities for preparing your passport.

To access the magic of this Italy in an immediate, intimate way, simply boil up a package of dried Italian pasta. Drain the pasta; lean forward; inhale its moist fragrance. You'll detect a subtle aroma of grain, with honey-like overtones from the semolina wheat. Close your eyes and let the sweet steam envelop you.

Now toss the pasta with voluptuous olive oil, spicy basil, juicy tomatoes. The fragrance is overwhelming. You lift the big bowl, carry it to the rustic table where you will share this meal with *amici simpatici*, "genial friends." Someone pours crisp, cool white wine from Orvieto. Bougainvillea cascades above, filtering the last blast of evening sun. Nearby, the crumbling walls of an ancient stone parapet stand sentinel. Nothing bad can happen here. *La vita é bella*. "Life is beautiful."

Cook Italian, Be Happy

Few things make me as happy as Italian food. It stimulates and satisfies my senses. Italian food brings grace notes to my life, so I try to play that tune every day. I'm motivated by the gustatory results, of course, but I also cook for other reasons: the pleasures of working with my hands and of connecting with something genuine, to name just two.

In this collection of recipes and stories, I've tried to capture the simple pleasure that cooking and sharing Italian-style meals brings to me. I also, here and now, let you in on a secret: It's far more gratifying to prepare simple meals at home than to eat out or carry in.

What's that I hear? The harried chorus chanting: *no time, no time, no time!* Do you have time to hug, to laugh, to sing? If you do, you have time to feed yourself well.

Restaurant food and factory-created meals are fine once in a while. But to grant them sovereignty over such an intimate act as eating is no way to live. These emperors simply have no clothes.

L'insieme: *The Whole Thing*

In Italy, *l'insieme* has many nuances. My friend Piero explains it like this: "At the literal level, l'insieme is togetherness, wholeness, entirety, unity—the end result of many diverse parts which result in a final 'thing' or 'insieme.' When a girl and a boy *stanno insieme*, it means they are going out together. A transformation is implied, an interaction, often hidden or unpredictable, which bears a result that may be unexpected."

It is my hope that in this book, the recipes stanno insieme to help you prepare wonderful meals. More important, I hope the stories and asides inspire you to create some space in which to savor those meals.

The recipes here aren't flashy; they don't jump from the page saying "look at me" with the relentlessness of a four-year-old starved for attention. These are dishes designed insieme, to work together as part of the whole.

The pantry (page 254) is consciously selective, yet its contents yield surprisingly varied meals. The ingredients here will get used up instead of sitting on the shelf. Balsamic vinegar appears in salads, in marinades, even in biscotti. Pine nuts, available in reasonable quantities and price from the bulk food bin, may be sprinkled on pastas, cooked chicken, salads, or desserts. Extra-virgin olive oil bought in the most economical size will be gone long before it spoils; it is used liberally because it makes *everything* taste better.

Any well-stocked supermarket will carry the ingredients you need to

> "I think sometimes that it is almost a pity to enjoy Italy as much as I do, because the acuteness of my sensations makes them rather exhausting..."
>
> The Letters
> of Edith Wharton

maintain an intelligent, integrated pantry. This is the secret to meals that come together when there's "nothing" to eat: Pizza with Caramelized Onions and Ripe Olives (page 55), Polenta-Pesto Casserole (page 114), Cannellini Bean Salad (page 104), and more.

Seasonal recommendations frequently accompany these recipes as a gentle nudge to re-connect with nature. Serve the Pork Chops Ossobuco-Style (page 164) in January and Rotini in Tomato Basil Sauce (page 71)in July and you will feel the rightness of things.

My cooking style respects the essentials of Italian cooking. It is based on freshness, high-quality ingredients, and authentic essentials, such as real Parmesan and extra-virgin olive oil. Yet it allows latitude about ingredients, techniques, and equipment. Corn on the cob is not eaten in Italy, but I would be foolish to exclude it from my table in August.

Wine, another food that's essential to the enjoyment of Italian-style dining, is also on my table. Wine makes good food taste better and great food taste fabulous. Dotted throughout the meal recipes, you'll discover wine educator Carol A. Berman's recommendations on felicitous food and wine pairings.

> "Be Italian, you rapscallion . . . live today as if it may become your last."
>
> Saraghina
> the Broadway
> musical Nine

All Recipes Lead to Home

Throughout the far-flung Roman Empire, all roads led to the capital. In this book, almost all the recipes lead to home and good meals. Seven chapters consist of recipes that are in themselves complete meals. Many of these meals are contained in a single dish. Other meals include recipes or instructions for a salad, vegetable, fruit, or other accompaniment.

Ingredient lists and directions for each meal appear on the same page, to consolidate and streamline planning, shopping, and cooking.

Most of the meals serve four to six. Dietitians are fond of controlled portions, but in truth, some eaters have big appetites and some have small appetites. Four light eaters will benefit from extra portions, to be saved for lunch or the makings of a brand-new meal.

The central recipe in each meal also makes an excellent main course for weekend meals or special occasions. For entertaining, when other courses are added to the meal, these recipes usually will serve six to eight. To choose a starter and dessert, turn to "Appetizers and Desserts for Special Meals."

As you get comfortable with the book, you may want to dip into "Capturing Summer Flavors for All Meals." Perhaps you grow basil in patio pots. You may make and save your own fragrant pesto. If you take your children to pick strawberries at a local farm, take a few minutes to cut and sweeten some of the fruit to freeze for *sorbetto.* Your off-season indulgence will be doubly sweetened with summer memories.

The basics boxes, scattered throughout the book, take you further into the art of Italian cooking. If you're curious about baking rustic bread or making fresh egg pasta with your own hands—not because you have to, but because you want to—the directions are here, waiting for you.

Thinking Outside the (Recipe) Box

How did humans survive for hundreds of thousands of years until the modern era, when recipes are formulated in measures as precise as $1/8$ teaspoon? I'm not an anthropologist, but I'm guessing that people learned to cook by watching experienced cooks at work. They then practiced

> "The world is loveable when the world is Rome."
>
> *Barbara Grizzuti Harrison*
> Italian Days

> "The meat sizzles in the warm spring air. 'Che profumino,' I say politely. Which is to say 'great smell,' though you only need to compare the lyricism of 'profumino' with the prose of 'smell' to appreciate how differently the Italians feel about such things."
>
> *Tim Parks*
> An Italian Education:
> The Further Adventures of an Expatriate in Verona

I Brake for Italians

I don't actually own a bumper sticker announcing "I Brake for Italians," but the national decal of Italy—a bold black capital "I" on a white oval field—*is* on the rear of my station wagon.

The vanity sticker is a souvenir from a gas station in Parma and it's one of many objects, talismans really, that enable me to feel close to Italy. I treasure these articles, most inconsequential, some substantial, all meaningful.

As I type, the noble head of Michelangelo's *David* gazes from the mouse pad, a kitschy memento from a *tabaccheria* in Siena, where I shopped with my daughters on a scalding June day.

Gold earrings reproduced from an Etruscan design are tucked away in my jewelry case. Archaeologists don't know much about this ancient people, who lived in what is now central Italy, but I can see from these baubles that the Etruscans knew how to accessorize.

An enlargement of a photograph my husband shot on a long-ago summer afternoon aboard the ferry to Elba hangs on the bathroom wall, one in a cluster of water pictures. I'm always soothed by this glimpse of the slate waters of the Tyrrhenian Sea and the sun glinting warmly off the stones of Fort Stella in Portoferraio. Mentally stepping into the image, I'm back on the deck, exulting in my escape to a more carefree time.

My beautiful handbag, crafted of green Florentine leather, is as smooth as an Italian playboy's pickup line. I reserve it for those occasions when I absolutely must present *la bella figura*.

A rosemary plant always graces my summer herb garden, though it is never the same specimen from year to year. I tend the thing religiously, praying for a miracle that will cause it to flourish like the rosemary hedges in Tuscany. By November, I am forced to acknowledge my folly. Like me, the rosemary would rather be in Italy than in the chilly clime of Zone 6 on the USDA plant hardiness map.

To console myself at this and other trying times, I head indoors to leaf through the pages of *Italian Style*, a coffee table tome I have practically come to inhabit. I never tire of strolling through the grand rooms, spacious terraces, and lush gardens that are home to designers, artists, and assorted nobles. These people have taste to burn.

Italian Style sits on a shelf with its own kind, a bevy of glossy lifestyle tomes that serve as wish books for Ital-infatuated foreigners like me. Curious how the titles run together: *The Most Splendid Ancient Hill Towns of Undiscovered Italy Hidden Beneath the Mediterranean Sun.* Some of us just can't get enough of this particular fantasy: Perfection exists, and it's just over that hill, past the cypresses, beyond the grove of olive trees.

Without a doubt, my most tenuous "Italian" purchase was an expensive jacket that I bought in Chicago. I wasn't even shopping for a coat, but the fabric—a faux antique gold silk overlaid with brocaded ribbon—captured my fancy. It echoed the Renaissance design of the stationery that's in all the paper shops in Florence.

As I ogled myself in the mirror, fantasizing that I was Sophia Loren circa *Marriage Italian Style*, the salesclerk appeared. I take pride in the invincibility of my armor against sales tactics, but this stranger, with her Euro accent and continentally chic appearance, found my chink and let the arrow fly. "You look sooo *ee-tal-i-an* in this coat," she murmured as I helplessly handed over my charge card. At home, I laughed out loud when I noticed the "Made in China" label.

My most life-enhancing "Italian" possession is as solid as it is evocative: the pergola over our patio. My dictionary says a pergola is "an arbor or passageway with a trelliswork roof on which plants are grown . . . from the Latin *pergula*." My meaning is not so easy to articulate. From the kitchen window, my daily view of the world is of three sturdy white columns framing flower gardens. Even when no one is in it, my pergola is a setting for contentment, a space to savor the moment.

When we share a meal under the pergola on a balmy evening, I allow myself to break for Italian time. I'm secure with those I love. Sometimes neighbors come over to share a glass of wine. We talk. We laugh. I savor a whiff of lavender on the breeze. I am smug in my secret: I don't need to live in Italy to live like an Italian. ↜

until they gained experience and other people watched them cook. And so it went.

As a food writer, I have been trained to write recipes with exact amounts, exact directions, and exact cooking times so that anyone who can read may duplicate the dish *exactly*. I have come to see this as a two-edged sword. What is meant to be hand-holding can instead be confining. Following written recipes to the last dot on each "i" complicates a natural, fluid process. In the kitchen, I rely on technique combined with all six senses: sight, touch, taste, hearing, smell, and—most important—common sense.

Flexibility is a key ingredient in cooking well. The results often improve when you lighten up. So follow your own preferences and inclinations. The lemon you buy may not be as tart as the one I used; you could need a little more lemon juice to suit your taste. Your medium onion may be larger than mine; if you like onions, by all means use it all. In a cheese sauce, I appreciate the spicy undertone of grated nutmeg, but you may think it tastes like eggnog. If so, lose the nutmeg. You are *in control*. (And can you say this with certainty about anything else in your life?)

Go ahead. Make these dishes your own. You'll please yourself and me, too. Desserts, of course, are another story. Exact measurements do make a difference in the chemistry of baked goods, so remember to use nesting cups for dry ingredients and pouring cup measures for liquids.

> "As at most boarding schools, Downe's standard fare seemed to consist of a collapsed suet pudding. . . . With my mouth in my mind, I would dream of Agostino's delicate fritti misti or Adelina's tortelloni. I nearly wept with longing."
>
> *Kinta Beevor*
> A Tuscan Childhood

They Sure Make a Big Deal out of a Peach

My daughter Tess used to think she didn't like peaches. But when she was nine and visited Italy, she changed her mind. We bought some lush peaches at the most charming *frutta e verdura*, "fruit and vegetable shop," I had ever seen. The shop exterior was, appropriately, painted exactly the rosy blush color of a ripe peach. Folk art paintings of fruits and vegetables graced the windowpanes.

As we strolled by, the scent of peaches beckoned us, like those visible aromas that tickle the characters' noses in cartoons. Inside the shop, the lettuces, radicchio, scallions, strawberries, cherries, onions, and peaches were arranged in an edible tapestry that would have impressed Martha Stewart.

Within moments Tess was in heaven, sweet golden juice dripping down her chin, eating a wondrous peach out of hand.

A day or two later, as we finished our midday meal at a family-run trattoria—not a fancy place at all—I wasn't surprised when Tess ordered a fresh peach for dessert.

The waitress returned with a plate, a knife, and a fork, laying the cutlery carefully at Tess's place setting.

"What's this for?" Tess asked.

"Italians cut the fruit and eat it from a plate," I explained. "They treat a ripe peach with the respect it deserves."

Next, the server brought a clear glass bowl filled with cool water.

"What's this for?" Tess asked.

"Italians clean the fruit just before eating it so none of the luscious flavor is washed away," I answered.

Finally, the waitress presented the ripe peach, in full regalia, nestled in a linen-lined basket.

Tess blinked with amazement and grinned widely. Now she understood: "They sure make a big deal out of a peach!" ↜

These recipes were developed with ease of preparation in mind, keeping the number of ingredients to a minimum. With variations and tips, however, I have offered ideas for deliciously expanding on the basics.

Un Regalo: *A Gift*

Any meal, whether a humble pizza or a luxurious Florentine T-bone steak, is as special as you make it. The evening meal can be a daily oasis if you want it to be.

Sit down at the table to dine, not just to eat.

Turn off the TV or radio, which will divert your eyes or ears from the pleasures at hand.

Light some candles. As the flame warms your spirit, you'll actually feel yourself start to relax. It's primal—a safety around the hearth that we humans crave.

Give yourself *un regalo*, a gift: Take time to smell, savor, and share the pasta.

> *"To eat good food is to be close to God."*
>
> Chef Primo
> Big Night

Soup and Egg Meals

Recipes

Stories and Basics

Soups and egg dishes make perfect suppers—lighter meals ideal for winding down the day. Both are simple to prepare and soothing to eat.

In Italian homes that maintain the custom of a big lunch at midday, the evening meal often is simply *una minestra*, "a soup," or *delle uova*, "some eggs," accompanied by good bread from the *panificio* and followed by ripe fruit from the *frutta e verdura*.

Soups fall into two broad categories, quick-cooking and long-keeping, and each offers its own kind of convenience. Soups based on canned broth or frozen homemade broth take only minutes to prepare. Chicken Noodle Soup with Spinach and Basil and the Beans, Greens, and Sausage Soup prove that a complete meal can be cooked in less than thirty minutes.

On the other hand, soups that call for many ingredients or are prepared using homemade broth will take longer to cook but actually benefit from advance preparation. When a minestrone is cooled after cooking and then refrigerated or frozen, the flavor will develop a complexity that just isn't there immediately after cooking.

Even more than soup, eggs are the original convenience food: inexpensive, versatile, readily available, quick to cook, easy to digest, and relatively long-keeping. Eggs, in short, are just the ingredient to keep in the refrigerator for sandwiches, pasta sauces, main-course salads, or accompaniments to glorious seasonal vegetables.

One of the best-known Italian egg dishes, probably because of its versatility, is the frittata. This flat omelet, filled with chunks of cooked fish, meat, poultry, vegetables, or cheese, is a natural for supper or brunch. When seasoned with an assertive filling, such as Gorgonzola cheese or roasted peppers with capers, a frittata adds both style and substance to an antipasto buffet. ↫

One taste of this soup whisks me to rural Tuscany—a bargain compared to airfare. Anna Maria Gaggio showed me how to make this dish in the kitchen of her Tuscan farmhouse, using fresh porcini.

Porcini Mushroom Soup
↬ Spinach, Orange, and Red Onion Salad

Soup:

1	ounce dried porcini mushrooms
2	cans (14$\frac{1}{2}$ ounces each) chicken broth, divided
$\frac{1}{3}$	cup olive oil
1$\frac{1}{4}$	pounds white or brown mushrooms, sliced
4	cloves garlic, minced
1	tablespoon minced fresh rosemary leaves
$\frac{1}{4}$	teaspoon crushed red pepper
$\frac{3}{4}$	teaspoon salt
4	cups water
1	can (14$\frac{1}{2}$ ounces) diced tomatoes, drained
4 to 6	slices (1 inch thick) toasted rustic bread
$\frac{1}{2}$	cup (2 ounces) grated Parmesan cheese

Salad:

1	bag (6 ounces) baby spinach leaves
2	navel oranges, halved and sliced
$\frac{1}{2}$	small red onion, sliced
2	tablespoons olive oil
$\frac{1}{8}$	teaspoon salt

I recommend using canned reduced-sodium broth or salt-free Chicken Broth (page 39). If you use regular canned broth, you may want to omit the salt.

↬

Those who prefer a sharper salad may add a splash of red or white wine vinegar.

To prepare the soup: Place the porcini and 1 cup of broth in a microwaveable glass measuring cup. Cover with plastic wrap, leaving a vent. Microwave on high for 3 minutes, or until bubbling. Set aside for 10 minutes to soften.

Meanwhile, warm the oil in a large pot over high heat. Add the white or brown mushrooms, garlic, rosemary, red pepper, and salt. Cook, stirring, for about 5 minutes, or until the mushrooms start to give off liquid. Turn off the heat.

Drain the porcini through a fine sieve lined with a coffee filter. Save the broth. Rinse the porcini and chop. Add the porcini and their soaking broth, the remaining chicken broth, water, and tomatoes to the pot. Cook over medium-low heat for 20 minutes for the flavors to blend.

Place a slice of toasted bread in the bottom of each soup bowl. Ladle the soup over the bread. Sprinkle with the Parmesan.

To prepare the salad: While the soup is cooking, place the spinach, oranges, and onion in a bowl. Drizzle with the oil. Add the salt. With the back of a spoon, press some of the orange slices to release their juice. Toss.

Serves 4 to 6

arancia

Fresh rosemary is preferable to commercially dried leaves, which often are sharp as needles. Home-dried leaves (page 242), which crumble more readily than the commercially packaged rosemary, are also good to use. When you buy a bunch of fresh rosemary for a recipe, it makes sense to dry the remaining branches so they don't go to waste. Two teaspoons of dried rosemary may replace the fresh.

Hunting for Porcini

My youthful encounters with wild mushrooms did little to prepare me for Italian porcini. The fungus of my childhood is the puffball (*Calvatia gigantea*). Every year at summer's end, dozens of these absurd orbs ballooned in the grass of our front yard in central Pennsylvania. My dad picked piles of puffballs and proudly lugged them into the kitchen, where my mom sliced and seasoned them, dipped them in flour, and hauled out a cast iron skillet to fry them in homemade lard. Thank goodness for the pork fat. If those puffballs had any flavor, they were keeping it to themselves.

Years later, I tasted fresh porcini (pronounced pohr-CHEE-nee) and my appreciation of wild mushrooms was drastically, permanently upgraded. It was autumn at a country restaurant in Tuscany. The cook cleaned one just-picked *fungo porcino*, removed its stem, drizzled the saucer-sized taupe cap with fruity extra-virgin olive oil, seasoned it with salt and the wild herb *nepitella*, and grilled it over a wood fire. He served the mushroom alone on a plate, which made it seem really special.

I bit into the juicy flesh. It tasted like meat from the earth—complex, rich, and woodsy. The body was substantial yet tender. Truly this was a mushroom so exciting, it deserved to be called wild.

I learned that porcini, which means "piggy," probably is a reference to the stubby appearance of the mushrooms. Porcini belong to the genus *Boletus*, of which the most sought-after are the *B. edulis*, which grow under fir trees, and the *B. aereus*, found under oaks. The marvel of these fungi is the symbiotic relationships they have established with the trees. The tree and the mushrooms actually exchange nutrients that enable each to flourish.

Neither farmers nor scientists have yet discovered how to cultivate *B. edulis*. In an age when botanical engineers can splice a single gene from one plant into another, porcini remain one of nature's closely held secrets.

Into the Woods

A few years after my first porcini, I set out with Mario Gaggio, an accomplished *fungaiolo*, "mushroom hunter," into the woods surrounding his home east of Florence. I felt privileged to be invited. Serious mushroom hunters guard their locations fiercely.

Mario apprenticed with an experienced fungaiolo and, ever since, has been refining his skills, which rest on an exquisite sensitivity to nature. Porcini thrive when hot, dry weather in August is followed by autumn rains.

In September and October, Mario sets out before dawn almost daily to scout his prime locations. "He doesn't remember faces," says his wife, Anna, "but he remembers the trees." Each day Mario studies the way the sun falls through the branches of firs, chestnuts, oaks, and pines. He says the ground must boil for a white mold called *la muffa* to form in these sunstruck patches.

If it does, and if all else goes well, within two weeks porcini magically appear. Then timing is crucial. The mushrooms must be gathered in their prime; if porcini grow even a bit too large, they will quickly rot.

For all his expertise, Mario is always at the mercy of nature. Some years, the porcini just don't come. Or, capriciously, they won't appear where they previously grew.

Lately, whenever I wince at the cost of a tiny cellophane packet of imported dried porcini, I find myself thinking of Mario patiently treading the Tuscan forest. There nature works her magic and resourceful humans reap the benefit in an eternal dance of delicate balance.

May the secret life of porcini remain shrouded under the trees, forever cloaked in mystery. ↪

I created this dish with prime late-summer tomatoes on a cool, rainy September day that announced "fall is on the way." This soup soothes, yet the flavors are fresh—a meal that spans the seasons.

Fresh Tomato and Potato Soup

4   medium-large red-skinned potatoes, peeled, cut into chunks
1   can (14½ ounces) chicken broth
2   cups water
1   bunch scallions, white and light green parts, sliced
6   fresh plum tomatoes, peeled and chopped
½   teaspoon salt
¼   cup chopped fresh flat-leaf parsley
¼   cup (1 ounce) grated Pecorino Romano cheese

In a large pot, combine the potatoes, broth, and water. Cover and cook over medium-high heat for 10 to 12 minutes or until the potatoes are softened. With a potato masher or the back of a large spoon, mash the potatoes until small chunks remain. Add the scallions, tomatoes, and salt. Reduce the heat to medium-low. Cover and cook for 5 minutes, or until the tomatoes are softened. Add the parsley. Remove from the heat for 5 minutes. Sprinkle each serving with Pecorino Romano.

SERVES 4 TO 6

Add a small minced fresh hot chile to this soup for a more spirited rendition.

To make a more substantial meal, stir in chopped ham or cooked chicken with the tomatoes.

This recipe may be doubled to make use of end-of-season tomatoes. It freezes well.

When a chunk of Parmesan is grated down to the rind, I toss it into a plastic bag in my freezer. I add it to the soup pot, where it softens and adds a rich supporting note to the vegetables.

Minestrone ⌒ Rustic Bread

½	cup olive oil
1	large onion, chopped
1	celery heart, chopped
2	large carrots, chopped
3	large cloves garlic, minced
3	dried bay leaves
1	tablespoon dried thyme leaves
1	can (14½ ounces) diced tomatoes, with juice
2	cans (15½ ounces each) cannellini beans, rinsed and drained
2	cans (14½ ounces each) chicken broth
3	cups water
6	ounces kale, torn or chopped
1	cup dried elbow macaroni
	Salt and ground black pepper
¼	cup (1 ounce) grated Parmesan cheese

Rustic Bread

Heat the oil in a large pot over medium-high heat. Add the onion, celery, carrots, garlic, bay leaves, and thyme. Cook, stirring, for 10 minutes. Do not allow to brown. Add the tomatoes, beans, broth, and water. Bring to a boil. Reduce the heat to low. Cover partially and simmer for 45 minutes, or until the vegetables are softened.

Add the kale and macaroni. Season with salt and pepper to taste. Cover partially and simmer for 5 minutes. Remove from the heat and set aside for 10 minutes. Remove and discard the bay leaves. Sprinkle each serving with Parmesan.

Serve the bread on the side.

SERVES 4 TO 6

Great Northern beans may replace the cannellini beans. Any small dried pasta may replace the macaroni.

⌒

If you plan to freeze the minestrone, cook the vegetables for only 35 minutes. Omit the pasta. Cool the soup and pack in plastic containers for the freezer. To serve, heat the thawed soup gently in a saucepan. Add the pasta and simmer for 5 minutes. Remove from the heat and set aside for 10 minutes.

⌒

Wine
Cirò from Calabria. The gaglioppo grape in this red wine possesses soft, full flavors and perky acidity to pair and play with tomatoes and the subtle sweetness of Parmesan.

⌒

This soul-sustaining meal is based upon common ingredients from northern Italian mountain cooking.

Cabbage and Rice Soup with Bacon ⌁ Glazed Apples with Dried Cherries

Soup:

8	ounces sliced bacon
2	leeks, white and green part, sliced
2	carrots, thinly sliced
1	cup fruity white wine
1	head savoy cabbage, thinly sliced
3	cans (14$\frac{1}{2}$ ounces each) chicken broth
1	cup medium or long-grain rice
2	dried bay leaves
	Salt
1	teaspoon ground black pepper
1	egg

Apples:

1	tablespoon butter
$\frac{1}{4}$	cup sugar
1	teaspoon vanilla extract
4	Golden Delicious apples, peeled, cored, and quartered
$\frac{1}{4}$	cup dried tart cherries

I recommend using canned reduced-sodium broth or salt-free Basic Broth (page 38). If you use regular canned broth, you may want to reduce the salt.

⌁

Johannisberg Riesling is a good choice for the wine.

To prepare the soup: Place the bacon slab on a cutting board. Cut crosswise at $\frac{1}{2}$-inch intervals. Separating some of the pieces, scatter the bacon in a large pot set over medium heat. Cook, stirring, for about 5 minutes, or until crisp.

Remove the bacon with a slotted spoon to a paper towel-lined plate. Pour off and discard all but 1 tablespoon of bacon drippings. Add the leeks and carrots. Cook, stirring occasionally, for about 5 minutes, or until golden.

Add the wine. Increase the heat to high. Bring to a boil and cook for about 5 minutes, or until reduced to about $\frac{1}{4}$ cup. Add the cabbage, broth, rice, bay leaves, and $\frac{1}{2}$ to 1 teaspoon salt. Bring to a boil. Reduce the heat to medium-low.

Cover partially and cook for 20 minutes, or until the rice is tender. Add the pepper. Remove and discard the bay leaves.

Beat the egg in a medium bowl. Gradually add 1 to 2 cups of broth skimmed from the soup. Add the egg mixture to the pot. Cook, stirring constantly, for about 2 minutes, or until the soup thickens slightly. Season with salt to taste.

Sprinkle each serving with the reserved bacon.

To prepare the apples: While the soup is cooking, preheat the oven to 375°F. Put the butter in a 12 x 8-inch baking dish. Place in the oven for about 5 minutes, or until the butter melts.

Remove the dish. Add the sugar and vanilla. Stir with a fork to combine. Add the apples and cherries. Toss to coat.

Bake for 12 to 15 minutes, stirring occasionally, or until the apples are tender when pierced with a knife.

SERVES 4 TO 6

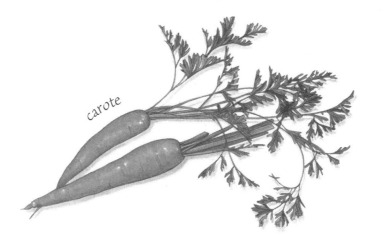

carote

Savoy cabbage, which comes in heads of loose, crinkled leaves, has a mellower flavor than regular cabbage. A medium head of green cabbage (about 1 pound) may replace the savoy cabbage.

Other baking apples such as Rome Beauty, Baldwin, Empire, Gravenstein, Northern Spy, Cortland, Fuji, Greening, Pippin, or Granny Smith may be used. The baking time among types may vary slightly.

I use dried cranberries when I don't have dried tart cherries. A sprinkling of chopped toasted walnuts or Caramelized Almonds (page 213) is good over the tender baked fruit.

Chicken Noodle Soup with Spinach and Basil

<table>
<tr><td>8</td><td>ounces dried wide egg noodles</td></tr>
<tr><td></td><td>Salt</td></tr>
<tr><td>3</td><td>tablespoons olive oil</td></tr>
<tr><td>3</td><td>cloves garlic, minced</td></tr>
<tr><td>1</td><td>pound skinless, boneless chicken breasts, cut into thin strips</td></tr>
<tr><td>2</td><td>cans (14$\frac{1}{2}$ ounces each) chicken broth</td></tr>
<tr><td>4</td><td>cups water</td></tr>
<tr><td>1</td><td>bag (6 ounces) baby spinach leaves, stems removed</td></tr>
<tr><td>$\frac{1}{2}$</td><td>cup fresh basil leaves, torn or cut into slivers</td></tr>
<tr><td></td><td>Ground black pepper</td></tr>
<tr><td>$\frac{1}{4}$</td><td>cup (1 ounce) grated Parmesan cheese</td></tr>
</table>

Bring a covered large pot of water to a boil over high heat. Add the noodles and
2 teaspoons of salt. Stir. Cover and return to the boil. Uncover and cook at a
rolling boil, stirring frequently, for about 7 minutes, or until tender but firm. Drain
and rinse; set aside.

Return the pot to the stove. Add the oil and garlic. Cook over low heat for
about 2 minutes, or until fragrant. Add the chicken. Cook, stirring, over medium
heat for about 4 minutes, or until the chicken is opaque.

Add the broth, water, and $\frac{1}{2}$ to 1 teaspoon salt. Cook for about 5 minutes, or
until hot. Do not boil. Stir in the spinach, basil, and the reserved noodles. Remove
from the heat to sit for 5 minutes. Season to taste with pepper. Sprinkle with
Parmesan at the table.

SERVES 4 TO 6

aglio

I recommend
using canned
reduced-sodium
broth or salt-free
Chicken Broth
(page 39). If you
use regular
canned broth, you
may want to omit
or reduce the salt.

When you have
pesto on hand,
this dish comes
together quickly.
Reduce the
olive oil to
2 tablespoons and
omit the garlic
and fresh basil,
then add
3 tablespoons of
purchased pesto
or homemade
Basil Pesto (page
234) with the
broth.

Turkey breast
cutlets may
replace the
chicken breasts.
The spinach may
be replaced with
kale leaves, stems
removed and
leaves thinly
sliced.

The hearty flavor of this soup belies its brief cooking time.

Beans, Greens, and Sausage Soup
↜ Seedless Red Grapes

12	ounces mild or hot Italian sausage, casings removed
3	large cloves garlic, minced
1	tablespoon rubbed dried sage leaves
3	cans ($15\frac{1}{2}$ ounces each) cannellini beans, rinsed and drained
3	cans ($14\frac{1}{2}$ ounces each) chicken broth
4	cups water
1	cup dried elbow macaroni
1	bag (6 ounces) baby spinach leaves, stems removed
1	tablespoon balsamic vinegar
$\frac{1}{8}$	teaspoon salt
$\frac{1}{4}$	teaspoon ground black pepper
	Grated Pecorino Romano cheese
	Seedless Red Grapes

Any small dried pasta may replace the macaroni.

Crumble the sausage into a large cold pot. Cook over medium-high heat, turning occasionally, for about 3 minutes, or until browned. Remove with a slotted spoon; set aside. Pour off and discard any drippings. Add the garlic and sage. Cook for about 1 minute, or until fragrant. Add the beans, broth, and water. Increase the heat to high and bring just to a boil. Scrape up the browned bits at the bottom of the pot.

Reduce the heat to medium-low. Cover partially and simmer for 15 minutes.

Transfer about half of the beans, and enough broth to cover, to a blender or food processor. Purée and return to the pot. Add the macaroni and the reserved sausage. Simmer for about 5 minutes, or until the pasta is al dente. Stir in the spinach, vinegar, salt, and pepper. Sprinkle with Pecorino Romano at the table.

Serve the grapes after the soup.

SERVES 4 TO 6

Beef and Cauliflower Soup with Gemelli ⤳ Bartlett Pears

*This soup may be
made in stages.
The beef, carrots,
and garlic may be
cooked, then
cooled and
refrigerated for up
to 3 days before
continuing with
the recipe.*

⤳

*Gemelli, which
means "twins," is
a small dried
pasta consisting
of two intertwined
rods. Rotini,
elbow macaroni,
or another small
pasta may replace
the gemelli.*

1	boneless beef chuck or top round steak (about 2 pounds)
10	cups water
1	can (14$\frac{1}{2}$ ounces) beef broth
2	carrots, cut in 2-inch lengths
2	branches fresh rosemary
3	large cloves garlic, peeled
$\frac{1}{3}$	cup olive oil
2	leeks, white and light green part, sliced
1	medium head cauliflower, cut into small florets
	Salt
$\frac{1}{2}$	teaspoon ground black pepper
1$\frac{1}{2}$	cups dried gemelli

Bartlett Pears

In a large pot, combine the beef, water, broth, carrots, rosemary, and garlic and cook over high heat until almost boiling. Reduce the heat to medium-low. Cover partially and simmer for about 1$\frac{1}{2}$ hours, or until the beef is very tender.

Remove the beef and carrots. Set aside for 10 minutes. Slice the carrots. Cut the beef into thin slices across the grain; set aside.

Meanwhile, strain the broth through a fine sieve into a large bowl. Remove and discard the rosemary. Smash the garlic with the back of a spoon and add to the broth; set aside.

Return the pot to the stove. Warm the oil over high heat. Add the leeks. Cook, stirring, for about 5 minutes, or until softened. Add the cauliflower. Cover and cook, stirring occasionally, for 5 minutes. Add the reserved broth, 1 teaspoon salt, and the pepper. Cover partially and simmer for 10 minutes. Stir in the gemelli. Cover partially and cook for about 8 minutes, or until the gemelli is al dente. Add the reserved beef and carrots. Taste and adjust the seasoning.

Serve the pears after the soup.

SERVES 6 TO 8

A composed salad makes an easy meal for any season. The ingredients may be adjusted according to what's on hand in the pantry.

Hard-Cooked Egg and Vegetable Salad with Parmesan Dressing

6 to 8	eggs
4	medium-large red-or-white-skinned potatoes
1/2	cup olive oil
3	tablespoons red or white wine vinegar
2	teaspoons Dijon mustard
1/4	cup (1 ounce) grated Parmesan cheese
1/2	teaspoon **each** salt and ground black pepper
1	head romaine lettuce, ribs removed, leaves torn
1	can (14 ounces) artichoke hearts, drained
1	carrot, shredded
1/3	cup (2 ounces) ripe olives, pitted
1	small red onion, sliced and rinsed

Bring a saucepan of water to a boil over high heat. With a large spoon, lower the eggs into the water one at a time. Reduce the heat until the water simmers rapidly but does not boil. Cook for 10 minutes. Drain and place the eggs in a bowl of ice water.

Meanwhile, cut the potatoes into 2-inch chunks. Place in a single layer in a microwaveable container. Cover with waxed paper. Microwave on high for 10 minutes, or until tender. Remove and set aside to cool slightly.

In a large bowl, whisk the oil, vinegar, mustard, Parmesan, salt, and pepper. Add the lettuce, artichoke hearts, carrot, olives, onion, and potatoes. Toss to combine. Peel the eggs and cut in lengthwise quarters. Place atop the salad.

Serves 4 to 6

When the first asparagus comes to market in the spring,
I make a meal of it with this dish.

Eggs and Asparagus with Parmesan Sauce
∽ Rustic Bread

To brown the
sauce, preheat the
broiler. Place the
cooked eggs in a
broiler pan coated
with no-stick
spray. Drizzle with
the sauce. Broil
4 inches from the
heat source for
3 to 4 minutes, or
until golden. With
a pancake turner,
carefully lift the
eggs and place
over the
asparagus.

2	tablespoons flour
$\frac{1}{8}$	teaspoon ground nutmeg
4	tablespoons water, divided
2	cups whole or 2-percent milk
$\frac{1}{2}$	cup (2 ounces) grated Parmesan cheese
5	tablespoons olive oil, divided
2	pounds asparagus, ends trimmed
	Salt and ground black pepper
2	tablespoons plain dry bread crumbs
6 to 8	eggs
	Rustic Bread

In a saucepan, whisk the flour with the nutmeg and 2 tablespoons water.
Gradually add the milk, whisking until smooth. Cook, whisking, over medium heat
for about 4 minutes, or until the mixture boils. Remove from the heat and stir in
the Parmesan. Cover and set aside.

Heat 4 tablespoons of oil in a large sauté pan over medium-high heat. Place
the asparagus in the pan. Cover and cook for 3 minutes. With tongs, turn the
asparagus. Add 2 tablespoons water to the pan. Cover and cook, turning the
asparagus occasionally, for about 5 minutes, or until the asparagus is tender.
Season with $\frac{1}{4}$ teaspoon each salt and pepper. Sprinkle with the bread crumbs.
Turn the asparagus to coat with crumbs. Remove the asparagus to a platter or
individual dinner plates. Set aside.

Wipe the pan with paper towels. Add the remaining 1 tablespoon of oil. Warm
over medium-high heat. Gently break eggs into pan. Season lightly with salt and
pepper. Cover and cook for about 2 minutes, or until the yolks are just set. Place
the eggs over the asparagus and drizzle with the reserved sauce.

Serve the bread on the side.

SERVES 4 TO 6

During my years at the Chicago Sun-Times, restaurant reviewer Pat Bruno devoted an annual column to the Italian Egg and Pepper Sandwich, a popular Lenten item at Italian beef stands.

Egg and Pepper Sandwiches

¼	cup olive oil
2	green bell peppers, sliced
1	large onion, sliced
1	teaspoon dried oregano
½	teaspoon salt, divided
¼	teaspoon ground black pepper
6 to 8	eggs
¼ to ½	teaspoon crushed red pepper
4 to 6	large Italian bread rolls or Kaiser rolls, split

In a large skillet, preferably nonstick, warm the oil over medium-high heat. Add the peppers and onion. Cover and cook, stirring occasionally, for about 6 minutes, or until golden. Add the oregano, ¼ teaspoon salt, and black pepper. Place the pepper mixture in a bowl; set aside.

Preheat the oven broiler.

Set the skillet over medium-high heat. Break the eggs into the pan. With a fork, pierce the yolks, but do not beat. Season with red pepper and ¼ teaspoon salt. Cook, stirring occasionally, for about 3 minutes, or until set. Remove from the heat. Place the rolls, cut side up, on a baking sheet. Broil 6 inches from the heat source for 1 to 2 minutes, or until golden. Place the eggs, peppers, and onion on the rolls.

SERVES 4 TO 6

In late summer, sliced ripe tomato is a wonderful addition.
For a richer sandwich, place slices of mild provolone, Tuscan Pecorino, or Fontina cheese on the rolls before broiling.

peperoni

Making Broth

Brodo. The Italian word for "broth" sounds substantial. Broth is the base that provides the underlying character for soups, risottos, stews, and many other preparations.

When I have the time and inclination, I simmer a batch of Basic Broth and store it in the freezer. Even when my stockpile is ample, I tend to save it for special dishes, such as *tortellini in brodo*, which deserve to float in the real thing. For daily cooking, I rely on canned reduced-sodium chicken broth.

For a vegetarian broth, I'll sometimes reconstitute dried porcini mushrooms in water. I prefer this to canned vegetable broth, which I find overly sweet and unnatural tasting.

To make Mushroom Broth, process ½ ounce of dried porcini in the food processor until finely chopped. Add this coarse mushroom powder to 4 cups of boiling filtered or bottled water, stir, and set aside for 30 minutes. Strain the mixture through a fine sieve, to screen out the large mushroom pieces; then strain it again through a fine sieve lined with a coffee filter or clean cheesecloth, to screen out the considerable sediment. The mushroom broth may be stored in the refrigerator for up to a week. Just don't mistake it for iced tea, as I once did.

Basic Broth

MAKES ABOUT 8 QUARTS

The ultimate Italian broth is the cooking liquid left over from a *bollito misto*, or "mixed boil," an elaborate main dish preparation of various meats, fowl, and vegetables. The rich broth from a bollito is often served alone as a first course. This simplified recipe calls for both beef and chicken to yield a full-flavored, versatile broth.

1   broiler-fryer chicken (about 3½ pounds), split in half
1   beef chuck roast (about 2½ pounds)
1   beef shank (about 1 pound)
1   large onion, quartered
2   carrots, cut into 3-inch lengths
1   celery heart, cut into 3-inch lengths
4   dried bay leaves
    Stems from 1 bunch fresh flat-leaf parsley
2   tablespoons dried thyme
8   quarts water

Combine the chicken, chuck roast, beef shank, onion, carrots, celery, bay leaves, parsley stems, thyme, and water in a 12-quart pot. Place over high heat and bring almost to a boil. Reduce the heat to medium-low so the liquid simmers gently but does not boil. Skim off and discard any foam. Partially cover and cook for 4 hours.

Allow to cool. Remove the solids to a large shallow pan. Ladle the broth through a fine sieve lined with a coffee filter into a large pot or bowl. Discard the solids. Refrigerate the broth, uncovered, for about 12 hours. Lift off and discard any fat that hardens on the surface.

To freeze the broth: Ladle the cold broth into 1- or 2-cup plastic freezer containers. Place in the freezer for several hours, until solid. Pop the frozen broth out of the containers and place in resealable plastic freezer bags. Store in the freezer for up to 6 months.

For pure-tasting broth, start with bottled or filtered water instead of chlorinated tap water.

Don't salt the broth because it is a neutral base that may be used in soups, sauces, stews, grain dishes, and more.

Variation

Chicken Broth: Replace the beef chuck roast and beef shanks with a second broiler-fryer chicken (about 3½ pounds), split in half.

MAKES ABOUT 8 QUARTS

Egg, Ricotta, and Spinach Tart ⤳ Pineapple and Red Grape Salad

Tart:

3	tablespoons butter
¼	cup plus 2 tablespoons plain dry bread crumbs
¾	cup (3 ounces) grated Parmesan cheese, divided
1	small onion, minced
1	bag (6 ounces) baby spinach leaves, stems removed
1	carton (32 ounces) whole-milk or part-skim ricotta cheese
6	eggs
¼	teaspoon salt
⅛	teaspoon ground nutmeg

Salad:

1	peeled and cored fresh pineapple
1½	cups red seedless grapes
1	tablespoon lemon juice
1	tablespoon sugar

⤳

Wine
Sparkling
Prosecco *from Veneto, named for its grape, is fresh and lively, yet finishes dry with an earthiness and acidity that bring it all home.*

⤳

To prepare the tart: Melt the butter in a large sauté pan. Remove from the heat. Place 1 tablespoon of the melted butter in a small bowl. Use ½ tablespoon melted butter to rub over the bottom and 1 inch up the sides of a 10-inch springform pan. Dust the pan with the bread crumbs. Shake excess crumbs into the bowl with the butter. Add 2 tablespoons of the Parmesan. Toss with a fork; set aside.

Place the sauté pan over medium heat. Add the onion to the butter remaining in pan. Cook, stirring, for 2 minutes. Add the spinach. Cover and cook over high heat for 1 to 2 minutes, or until it wilts. Drain any liquid. Set aside.

Preheat the oven to 350°F. In a bowl, beat the ricotta, 2 of the eggs, salt, nutmeg, and the remaining Parmesan. Spoon into the pan. Top with the spinach mixture. With the back of a tablespoon, make 4 oval indentations, radiating from the center like flower petals, in the ricotta mixture. Break 1 egg into each indentation. Sprinkle with the reserved crumb mixture.

Bake for about 45 minutes, or until set. Remove tart to a rack to cool for at least 30 minutes before removing sides of pan.

To prepare the salad: While the tart is baking, cut the pineapple into 8 long strips. Cut the strips into chunks. Place the pineapple and any pineapple juice in a serving bowl. Add the grapes, lemon juice, and sugar. Toss to mix.

Cover and refrigerate, stirring occasionally, for at least 30 minutes.

SERVES 4 TO 6

uva

For brunch, I often drape thin slices of prosciutto on the plate with a wedge of tart. Or, sometimes I add 1 cup of diced thick-cut cooked ham or salami to the ricotta mixture before baking.

To serve as part of an antipasto buffet, the tart may be chilled for several hours after cooling and then sliced into thin wedges.

Frittata with Peas and Scallions
⤳ Pan-Fried Oregano Potatoes

Potatoes:

4	tablespoons olive oil
5	medium-large red or white-skinned potatoes, unpeeled, cut into $1/2$-inch chunks, patted dry
$1/2$	teaspoon dried oregano
$1/4$	teaspoon salt

Frittata:

8 to 12	eggs
$1/2$	cup cold water
$1/2$	teaspoon **each** salt and ground black pepper
6	tablespoons olive oil
1	bunch scallions, white and light green part, sliced
1	cup frozen petite peas
$1/2$	cup (2 ounces) shredded Fontina cheese

To prepare the potatoes: In a large skillet with an ovenproof handle, preferably nonstick, heat the oil over medium-high heat. Add the potatoes and stir to coat with oil. Cook, without stirring, for 5 minutes, or until until browned on the bottom. Reduce the heat to medium. Sprinkle with the oregano. Cook, stirring occasionally, for about 12 minutes, or until well browned. Remove to a platter; season with the salt.

To prepare the frittata: Meanwhile, in a bowl, beat the eggs, water, salt, and pepper.

Preheat the oven broiler (see note). Add the oil to the potato skillet and heat over medium heat. Add the scallions and cook for about 2 minutes, or until fragrant. Add the peas and stir. Pour on the egg mixture. Sprinkle with the Fontina. Reduce the heat to medium. Cook for 3 to 4 minutes, lifting the edges of the eggs as they set to let uncooked egg run underneath. When the bottom of the frittata is set, place the skillet in the broiler 4 inches from the heat source for about 3 minutes, or until the frittata is puffed and golden. Serve the potatoes on the side.

SERVES 4 TO 6

I like to finish cooking a frittata under the broiler in a nonstick cast iron skillet with a flame-resistant handle. The frittata may also be flipped in the pan and cooked completely on the stovetop. Agile cooks may take a large round platter, such as a pizza pan, and place it atop the skillet. Armed with heatproof mitts, firmly grasp the skillet and the platter. Turn the skillet over so the frittata rests on the platter. With a deft motion, slide the frittata back into the skillet to cook for about 2 minutes. More cautious cooks may want to cut the frittata into wedges and flip each wedge with a pancake turner.

A frittata is tasty served at room temperature,
as well as hot from the skillet.

Cheese Frittata with Tomato Basil Sauce ∽ Rustic Bread

Frittata:

2	tablespoons olive oil
8 to 12	eggs
$\frac{1}{2}$	cup water
$\frac{1}{4}$	teaspoon **each** salt and pepper
$\frac{3}{4}$	cup (3 ounces) shredded provolone cheese

Sauce:

2	tablespoons olive oil
2	cloves garlic, minced
1	can ($14\frac{1}{2}$ ounces) diced tomatoes, with juice
$\frac{1}{4}$	cup slivered fresh basil leaves
$\frac{1}{4}$	teaspoon **each** salt and ground black pepper
	Rustic Bread

When I have locally grown tomatoes, I use 12 plum tomatoes (about 2 pounds), peeled and chopped, in place of the canned tomatoes. Tuscan Pecorino or Spanish Manchego cheese may replace the provolone.

To prepare the frittata: Preheat the oven broiler (page 42).

In a large skillet with an ovenproof handle, preferably nonstick, heat 2 tablespoons oil over medium-high heat. In a bowl, beat the eggs, water, salt, and pepper. Pour into the skillet. Cook for 3 to 4 minutes, lifting the edges of the eggs as they set to let uncooked egg run underneath. When the bottom is set, sprinkle with the provolone. Place in the broiler 4 inches from the heat source for about 3 minutes, or until the cheese is golden and bubbly. Slide onto a platter or cut into wedges and put on plates. Set aside.

To prepare the sauce: Return the skillet to medium-low heat. Add the oil and garlic. Cook for about 1 minute, tipping the pan to moisten the garlic, or until fragrant. Add the tomatoes. Increase the heat to medium high. Cook, stirring occasionally, for about 5 minutes, or until slightly thickened.

Add the basil, salt, and pepper. Spoon partially over the frittata wedges.

Serve the bread on the side.

SERVES 4 TO 6

Browned onions are sweetly pungent—one of the most satisfying flavors in all of food land.

Caramelized Onion Frittata
∽ Fennel Salad ∽ Rustic Bread

Salad:

1	medium bulb fennel
2	tablespoons (½ ounce) grated Parmesan cheese
1	tablespoon olive oil
2	teaspoons red or white wine vinegar
¼	teaspoon ground black pepper

Frittata:

3	tablespoons olive oil
2	medium-large onions, sliced
¾	teaspoon salt, divided
8 to 12	eggs
½	cup water

Rustic Bread

To prepare the salad: Cut the stalks from the fennel bulb. Reserve some of the dill-like leaves; discard the stalks. Cut the fennel in lengthwise quarters. Cut out and discard the core sections. Cut the quarters into thin slices. Chop the leaves. Place in a bowl with the cheese, oil, vinegar, and pepper. Toss to mix; set aside.

To prepare the frittata: In a large skillet with an ovenproof handle, preferably nonstick, heat the oil over medium-high heat. Add the onions and ½ teaspoon salt. Cover and cook, stirring occasionally, for 5 minutes. Reduce the heat to medium-low. Cover and cook, stirring occasionally, for 6 to 8 minutes, or until well browned.

Meanwhile, preheat the oven broiler (page 42). In a bowl, beat the eggs, water, and the remaining ¼ teaspoon salt. Pour into the skillet on top of the onions. Increase the heat to medium. Cook for about 4 minutes, lifting the edges of the eggs as they set to let the uncooked egg run underneath, or until the bottom is set. Place the skillet in the broiler 4 inches from the heat source for about 3 minutes, or until the frittata is puffed and golden.

Serve the bread on the side.

SERVES 4 TO 6

finocchio

Bread and Pizza Meals

Recipes

Stories and Basics

Bread, not pasta, is the staple food of the Italian peninsula. Throughout Italy, at home and in restaurants, *il pane*, "bread," accompanies every meal. The standard *pane e coperto* fee charged at every trattoria pays for the table itself and for the bread that arrives moments after the patrons are seated.

Through the meal, plain bread—never buttered!—provides a neutral accompaniment to the various courses. It's eaten with antipasti: spicy *salumi*, pungent cheeses, olives, and vegetable relishes. Chunks of bread sop up the flavorful last drops of soup, rich juices from roasted meats and fowl, sauce from seafood stews. Bread even captures the pungent liquid puddle at the bottom of the salad plate.

Most home cooks buy fresh bread every day, but they also make appetizing use of leftover bread. *Crostini* (page 202), small slices of toast, are topped with anything from extra-virgin olive oil to elaborate spreads made with meats and vegetables. *Panzanella* is a salad of dry bread cubes born again with juicy tomatoes, cucumbers, and onions.

Bread also provides the base for many savory street snacks, or *merende*, which are eaten mid-morning or late afternoon, purportedly to quell between-meal hunger pangs. Actually, these breaks for *un panino*, a small roll filled with meat or cheese, are an excuse to socialize and sip red wine at a bar or *vini*, a wine and snack shop that's literally a window open to the street.

Outside of Italy, these simple bread dishes make delightful meals. Of course, the most famous version of Italian bread is pizza, which is nothing more than a hot open-faced sandwich. From its birthplace in Naples, pizza went on to conquer the peninsula and then the world.

Pizza variations are many. The turnover called calzone, which means "trouser leg," is a hot meal enclosed in a pocket of dough. At room temperature, a calzone becomes a convenient portable lunch or picnic food. Chilled and sliced, many *calzoni* make wonderful antipasti. ↩

Few dishes cut through the torpor of a sweltering day like this refreshing end-of-summer salad.

Bread Salad with Tomato, Cucumber, Onion, and Basil

8	ounces rustic bread, cut into $^1/_2$-inch-wide slices
$^1/_2$ to $^3/_4$	cup olive oil
2	tablespoons red or white wine vinegar
$^3/_4$	teaspoon salt
2	medium-large fresh tomatoes, coarsely chopped
$^1/_2$	English cucumber, peeled, coarsely chopped
1	small red onion, coarsely chopped and rinsed
$^3/_4$	cup loosely packed slivered fresh basil leaves
	Ground black pepper

If using home-made Rustic Bread (page 50), half of a loaf is the right amount for this recipe. Many commercial loaves weigh 12 ounces, which means you'll use about two-thirds of the loaf. Bread that is a day or two old and too dry to eat works fine for this dish; add a bit more cold water to reconstitute.

A smattering of chopped fresh chile pepper makes a spunky addition.

Toast the bread in a toaster, toaster oven, or oven broiler. Cut into $^1/_2$-inch cubes; set aside to cool.

In a large bowl, whisk $^1/_2$ cup oil, vinegar, and salt. Add the tomatoes, cucumber, onion, basil, and bread. Toss and set aside for 15 to 30 minutes at room temperature. Press the salad occasionally with the back of a spoon so the tomatoes release their juice. Taste a bread cube. If it seems too dry, drizzle with up to $^1/_4$ cup more oil or a few tablespoons of cold water. Season generously with pepper.

SERVES 4 TO 6

pane rustico

This dish combines two Tuscan favorites, tuna salad and panzanella, *a bread salad moistened with garden vegetables and olive oil.*

Bread Salad with Tuna and Capers

8 to 10	ounces rustic bread, cut into 1/2-inch-wide slices
1	bunch scallions, white and green parts, chopped
3 to 4	tablespoons red or white wine vinegar
1/2	teaspoon salt
1/2	cup olive oil (approximately)
1	can (12 ounces) water-packed tuna, drained and flaked
1	large tomato, cut into thin wedges
2	ribs celery heart
3 to 4	tablespoons drained capers

Toast the bread. Cut into 1/2-inch cubes; set aside. Reserve 2 tablespoons of the dark green scallion stems.

In a large bowl, whisk the vinegar and salt. Add the oil and whisk to combine. Add the tuna, tomato, all the chopped scallions except reserved stems, celery, 3 tablespoons capers, and bread. Toss and set aside for 15 to 30 minutes at room temperature. Toss occasionally. Taste a bread cube. If it seems too dry, drizzle with a bit more oil or a few tablespoons of cold water. If too bland, add up to 1 tablespoon vinegar and 1 tablespoon capers. Sprinkle each serving with scallion stems.

SERVES 4 TO 6

If using home-made Rustic Bread (page 50), half of a loaf, or slightly more depending on how many servings you want, is the right amount for this recipe. Many commercial loaves weigh 12 ounces, which means you'll use most of the loaf. Bread that is a day or two old and too dry to eat works fine for this dish; add a bit more cold water to reconstitute.

Sometimes, I serve this salad on a bed of torn lettuce leaves.

A sprinkling of crushed red pepper adds some color and heat.

Making Rustic Bread

I wish I could invite you to step into my kitchen and make bread. Working the dough, shaping the loaves, inhaling the wheaty aroma—all this is a relaxing experience. And the payoff is enormous: bread that tastes wonderful, a source of pride for the baker, and satisfaction for the people who share it.

Many traditional breads in Italy taste so good because they are leavened with a *biga*: a spongy mixture made from flour, water, and some commercial yeast. This sponge ferments at room temperature on its own, for a few hours or as long as two days.

If you mix a biga in a 4-cup glass measuring cup or clear glass bowl, you'll be able to see its bubbling action throughout the process. You'll also give the mixture the room it needs to expand to three times its original volume. Cover it with plastic wrap and tuck it inside a microwave oven or an unlit range oven for 12 to 48 hours. The thick mixture will bubble up and rise, and then fall slightly. At the end, it will look like pancake batter.

To make bread dough, you mix the sponge with flour and water, adding salt for flavor. Knead the dough on a lightly floured surface for 4 to 6 minutes, or until the dough is resilient. Even novice bakers will sense when the dough has been sufficiently kneaded: It feels alive.

At this point, you may set aside the dough to rise—just once, or as often as three times—punching it down between rises. You might even cover the bowl tightly and leave the dough in the refrigerator for several hours. Because a slow rise provides more time for complex flavors to develop, bread made this way will taste even better.

Any all-purpose flour is suitable for the following recipe. It contains a small amount of whole-wheat flour for color and flavor, but the recipe will work perfectly well with all-purpose flour alone. Filtered or bottled water is best if your tap water contains chemicals that might add off flavors. Active dry yeast, not instant dry yeast, is specified here because its slower rise results in a better flavor.

If you're a novice, you may want to prepare bread by hand this first time. The experience will be more pleasurable, and educational, as you feel how soft and moist this dough should be. But the recipe will also work in a food processor or electric mixer fitted with a dough hook. A plastic dough scraper makes quick work of cleaning the bowl. Bake the bread on heavy baking pans that don't buckle with the heat. If you have a ceramic baking stone, preheat it and bake the loaves directly on it for a crisper crust. After the baked bread is cool, store it in a brown paper bag for a day or two.

If you choose to double this recipe to make 4 loaves, add only 1 tablespoon of salt for the double-batch recipe. And doubling is an excellent idea: It's barely more work and you'll have extra loaves to store in the freezer.

Rustic Bread

MAKES 2 LOAVES (ABOUT 1 POUND EACH)

Sponge:

1	package (1/4-ounce) active dry yeast (2 1/4 teaspoons)
1/2	cup warm bottled or filtered water (105°F to 115°F)
3/4	cup all-purpose flour

Dough:

1 1/2	cups warm bottled or filtered water (105°F to 115°F)
1	cup whole-wheat flour
2	teaspoons salt
3 to 3 1/2	cups all-purpose flour
	Cornmeal

To prepare the sponge: In a medium bowl, combine the yeast and water. Stir to dissolve. Add the flour and beat to make a batter. Cover tightly with plastic wrap. Set aside in a draft-free spot for 12 to 48 hours.

To prepare by hand: Scrape the sponge into a large mixing bowl. Add the water, whole-wheat flour, and salt. Beat with a wooden spoon to make a batter. Adding about ½ cup at a time, incorporate 2½ cups of all-purpose flour, mixing well after each addition.

Measure the remaining 1 cup of flour. Dust a work surface with 1 tablespoon of the flour and pour the rest in a mound alongside your work surface. Turn the dough onto the work surface. Clean the bowl with a plastic dough scraper. Clean hands and scraper with flour. Lightly dust the dough with a little of the remaining flour. Using the dough scraper, turn the dough over on itself until its outer surface is no longer sticky.

Knead the dough, dusting the work surface as necessary, for 4 to 6 minutes, or until the dough is springy. All of the flour may not be needed. Coat a large bowl with no-stick spray. Shape the dough into a ball, and place in the bowl. Coat with spray. Cover with plastic wrap; set aside to rise at room temperature for about 1 hour, or until doubled.

Scatter 2 to 3 tablespoons of cornmeal on a large baking sheet. Punch down the dough. Divide in half. Allow to sit for 10 minutes. On a lightly floured work surface, use lightly floured palms to press each dough half into a rectangle, about 12 by 6 inches. Starting at one long end, roll into a tube and pinch the ends to seal. Rub the loaves all over with flour. Place the loaves on the prepared baking sheet. Dust the loaves with flour. Cover with plastic wrap and set aside to rise for about 1 hour, or until doubled in size.

Meanwhile, preheat the oven to 425°F.

Bake the loaves for 25 to 30 minutes, or until they are well-browned and an instant-reading thermometer registers 200°F in the center of each loaf. Remove to a rack to cool.

To prepare in a food processor: Place the sponge in a food processor work bowl fitted with a plastic or metal blade. Add dough ingredients and process according to recipe directions.

To prepare with an electric mixer: Place the sponge in the large bowl of an electric mixer fitted with a dough hook. Add dough ingredients and beat according to recipe directions.

To freeze the bread: Cool completely, then cut into slices 1 inch thick. Wrap tightly in plastic wrap, then in aluminum foil.

To thaw the bread: Unwrap the bread and discard the plastic wrap. Separate the slices and place them on the foil. Place in a pre-heated 350°F oven for about 10 minutes, or until warm. This method produces a crisp crust.

Variations
Cheese Bread: After pressing the dough into two rectangles, sprinkle each with ½ teaspoon minced fresh rosemary (or crumbled dried oregano, thyme, or sage), plus ½ cup shredded Gruyère, Fontina, Tuscan Pecorino, or provolone cheese, mixed with 2 tablespoons grated Parmesan cheese.
Olive Bread: Work ½ cup pitted, slivered ripe olives into the dough during the kneading.
Rustic Bread Rolls: Before the last rising, shape the dough into 16 small or 8 large ovals. Place on a baking sheet dusted with cornmeal. Dust with flour. Cover with plastic wrap and set aside to rise for about 45 minutes, or until doubled. Bake in a preheated 425°F oven for about 15 minutes, or until the rolls are well browned.

Ham and Sun-Dried Tomato Strata
↪ Mango with Marsala and Toasted Pine Nuts

Strata:

12	ounces rustic bread, cut into ½-inch-wide slices
1	bunch scallions, white and green parts, sliced
1	tablespoon butter
¼	cup sun-dried recipe-ready tomato strips
6 to 8	ounces thick-sliced cooked ham, cut into small chunks
1	cup (4 ounces) shredded Fontina cheese, divided
3	eggs
3 to 3½	cups milk
½	teaspoon **each** salt and ground black pepper
⅛	teaspoon ground nutmeg

Mango:

2 to 3	ripe but firm mangoes
¼	cup Marsala wine
	Sugar
2	tablespoons pine nuts, toasted

Bread that is a day or two old and too dry to eat works fine for this dish; add a bit more milk, if needed, to moisten adequately.

To prepare the strata: Coat a 13 x 9-inch baking pan with no-stick spray.

Toast the bread and cut into ½-inch cubes. Place in the prepared pan; set aside. Reserve 2 tablespoons of dark green scallion stems in a small dish. Cover with plastic wrap and refrigerate.

In a small skillet, melt the butter. Add the remaining scallions. Cook, stirring, for 1 minute. Add the tomatoes. Stir and cook for 1 minute, or until the scallions are softened. Spoon over the bread. Sprinkle with the ham and ¾ cup of the Fontina. Toss to combine.

In a mixing bowl, beat the eggs with a fork. Add 3 cups milk, salt, pepper, and nutmeg. Beat just to combine. Pour over the bread mixture. Press down gently with the back of a spoon. Sprinkle with the remaining ¼ cup Fontina. Cover with plastic wrap and refrigerate for at least 30 minutes or as long as 12 hours.

Preheat the oven to 325°F.

Remove the plastic. Squeeze one of the top bread cubes. If it's not squishy, add the remaining ½ cup of milk.

Bake for about 40 minutes, or until the cheese is golden and the center is hot. Sprinkle each serving with the reserved scallion stems.

To prepare the mango: Peel the mangoes and slice. Place in a bowl with the Marsala. Sprinkle with sugar to taste. Cover and refrigerate, stirring occasionally, for 1 hour. Sprinkle each serving with pine nuts.

SERVES 4 TO 6

For a meat-free strata, omit the ham.

Dark rum may replace the Marsala wine.

pomodori pelati

Even in New Orleans, I make the Italian connection with a mammoth muffaletta sandwich from the Central Grocery on Decatur Street. This sandwich is an antipasto assortment tucked into a bread loaf.

Antipasto Sandwich

A few tablespoons of hot giardiniera or peperoncini makes a vibrant addition to the olive salad.

~

Delicatessen roasted peppers may be used. Crusty buns may replace the bread.

$^1/_2$ cup chopped pitted green olives

$^1/_2$ cup olive oil

2 tablespoons drained capers

$^1/_2$ teaspoon dried oregano

$^1/_4$ teaspoon ground black pepper

$^1/_4$ teaspoon crushed red pepper

1 round or oblong loaf (16 ounces) rustic bread

6 large lettuce leaves

2 red or yellow bell peppers, roasted and peeled

4 ounces sliced ham

4 ounces sliced mortadella

2 ounces sliced Genoa salami

4 ounces sliced provolone cheese

In a bowl, combine the olives, oil, capers, oregano, black pepper, and red pepper. Stir and set aside.

Slice the loaf in half. Lay both sides on a work surface, cut side up. Pick out some of the bread from the center of each half. (Reserve and dry for bread crumbs; page 247.) Drizzle the oil from the olive salad on both pieces of bread. Spoon half of the olive salad on the bottom of the loaf. Top with the lettuce, peppers, ham, mortadella, salami, and provolone. Top with the remaining olive salad. Cover with the top of the loaf. Press down. Cover with a heavy skillet or other weight. Set aside for 10 minutes, for the bread to absorb the dressing, before cutting with a serrated knife.

SERVES 4 TO 6

*Ripe olives that are dry-cured in olive oil and/or
salt are meaty, pungent, fruity, and chewy. Their texture
is very different from softer brine-cured ripe olives.*

Pizza with Caramelized Onions and Ripe Olives
↬ Cantaloupe Wedges

	Pizza Dough (page 62)
1	tablespoon cornmeal
¼	cup olive oil
2	large onions, sliced
¼	teaspoon salt
¼	teaspoon dried oregano
½	cup dry-cured ripe olives, pitted
1	medium ripe cantaloupe, cut into wedges

Prepare the Pizza Dough. Coat a 14- or 15-inch round pizza pan with no-stick spray. Sprinkle with the cornmeal; set aside.

Punch down the dough and place on a lightly floured work surface to sit for 5 minutes. With lightly floured hands or a rolling pin, pat or roll into a 15- or 16-inch circle. Transfer to the prepared pan. Fold the edges to make a rounded border. Cover with plastic wrap and set aside for about 15 minutes, or until slightly risen.

Preheat the oven to 450°F.

Place a large sauté pan over high heat. Add the oil and heat. Add the onions. Stir. Cover the pan and cook for 2 to 3 minutes, or until the onions start to brown. Stir. Reduce the heat to medium. Cook, stirring occasionally, for about 10 minutes, or until browned. Add the salt and oregano.

Spread the onions over the prepared crust. Sprinkle with the olives.

Bake for about 15 minutes, or until the crust is golden. Remove to a cooling rack for 5 minutes.

Chill the cantaloupe during dinner and serve after the pizza.

SERVES 4 TO 6

↬

*Wine
Salice
Salentino, a
red wine from
Puglia. The
negroamaro
grape is earthy
and ripe with a
dry finish. It's
perfect with
the natural
sweetness of
onions and the
pungency
of olives.*

↬

Pizza with Fresh Tomatoes and Basil
ᔰ Greens, Cucumber, and Red Onion Salad

Pizza:

Pizza Dough (page 62)
1	tablespoon cornmeal
2	tablespoons olive oil
2	large cloves garlic, minced
4 to 6	fresh plum tomatoes, sliced, patted dry
	Salt
¼	cup tightly packed slivered fresh basil leaves
¼	cup (1 ounce) grated Parmesan cheese
½	cup (2 ounces) shredded Gruyère cheese

Salad:

1	small cucumber, peeled, sliced
½	small red onion, sliced
	Salt
3	tablespoons olive oil
1	tablespoon balsamic vinegar
⅛	teaspoon ground black pepper
1	bag (6 ounces) mixed leafy greens

parmigiano-reggiano

To prepare the pizza: Prepare the Pizza Dough. Coat a 14- or 15-inch round pizza pan with no-stick spray. Sprinkle with the cornmeal; set aside.

Punch down the dough and place on a lightly floured work surface to sit for 5 minutes. With lightly floured hands or a rolling pin, pat or roll into a 15- or 16-inch circle. Transfer to the prepared pan. Fold the edges to make a rounded border. Cover with plastic wrap and set aside for about 15 minutes, or until slightly risen.

Preheat the oven to 450°F.

Place the oil and garlic in a small microwaveable bowl. Cover with waxed paper and microwave on high for 1 minute, until fragrant. With the back of a spoon or a pastry brush, coat the crust with some of the oil. Lay the tomatoes over the crust to the edge. Season lightly with salt. Add layers of the remaining garlic oil, basil, Parmesan, and Gruyère.

Bake for about 16 minutes, or until golden and bubbly. Remove to a cooling rack for 5 minutes.

To prepare the salad: While the pizza is baking, place the cucumber and onion in a bowl; sprinkle with ½ teaspoon salt. Cover with ice water; set aside for 10 minutes.

In a large bowl, whisk the oil, vinegar, pepper, and the remaining ⅛ teaspoon salt. Tear the greens and add to the bowl; set aside.

Drain the cucumber and onion. Rinse well under cold running water. Add to the salad bowl. Toss just before serving.

SERVES 4 TO 6

Pizza with Asti

Late on a rainy May night in Florence, a man and a woman dine quietly in a nearly deserted tourist pizzeria on Borgo San Lorenzo. They share a *quattro stagioni*, the "four seasons" pie topped with artichoke, mushrooms, olives, and ham. A bottle of Asti rests in an ice bucket next to the table.

The sparkling dessert wine would surely be the educated palate's last choice of wine to enjoy with a pizza. But there are times when dining decisions turn on much more than an appropriate pairing of wine and food.

Hours before the Asti, I had awoken in nervous anticipation at the Pensione Tornabuoni. This hotel, close to the Ponte Vecchio on one of the most stylish shopping streets in Florence, was a splurge—although, in truth, the once-elegant Tornabuoni was well into its Norma Desmond phase. Still, the height of the ceilings was awe-inspiring; a troupe of trapeze artists could have performed comfortably in the upper reaches of our room.

It was May 1978, and Walter and I had returned to Florence. Our fledgling tour company subsidized the expenses, granting us our self-indulgent wish to marry in the very church where we had met four years earlier. My sister, Barbara, was on hand. Walter's best friend, Tony, arrived from the States the day after the ceremony. (Other relatives and friends celebrated with us back home at parties that summer, extending a wedding into a seasonal festival.) As Barbara helped me pull back my long dark hair and pin it up with fragrant gardenias, I began to feel curiously calm. It was almost as if I were floating in that drafty old *pensione* room, gazing down on the nuptial preparations.

We hopped into a cab for the short ride up the Lungarno to the church of Santa Croce. The intermittent rain subsided as our friends greeted us with sunny words. *"Una sposa bagnata é una sposa fortunata."* "A wet bride is a lucky bride." Did Italians invent the art of spin or simply perfect it?

That afternoon remains a swirl of images. We posed for photographs in the courtyard of the Pazzi Chapel, the finest jewel in Renaissance architect Brunelleschi's crown for the ideal city. As I look now at the black-and-white pictures, I see a couple in their late twenties, looking a bit giddy. She's wearing too much makeup and her spike heels pitch her forward to a slight, teetering angle. He's got a head full of chemically induced curls and wide-legged trousers that trigger a flashback to Peter Frampton. How would Brunelleschi reconcile his artistic vision with the sight of these 1970s fashion victims?

The ceremony was scheduled for early afternoon in the exquisite Medici

Chapel, which is graced by Andrea della Robbia's enameled terra cotta altarpiece, the *Madonna with Child Between Angels and Saints*. Under this masterpiece, Padre Franchi conducted the ceremony in Italian. I was a bit apprehensive about understanding everything, so my future husband whispered this advice: "When there's a lull, just say 'sì.'"

Family and friends, both Florentine and American, filled the pews. Also attending were a couple Walter had met on a ferry from the island of Elba just a few days earlier. I have no idea who these people were or where they are now, but the album they gave us remains a treasure. Its leather cover is embossed with Botticelli's *Birth of Venus*, it bears our initials stamped in gold leaf, and, of course, it is filled with wedding photos.

After the ceremony, we celebrated in the Franciscans' recreation room. A long wooden table was adorned simply with a white linen cloth, big bunches of wild flowers, and trays of assorted savory pastries from Calamai, our favorite pastry shop. For days, I had been anticipating the *pasta sfoglia*, puff pastry rounds stuffed with cheeses, spinach, and tomatoes, followed by tiny tarts of fresh fruit and berries atop pastry cream and crisp cookie crusts. Instead of giving our guests little net bundles of sweets as souvenirs, we passed out long-stemmed roses tied with notes thanking them for sharing our day.

Walter and his *ragazzi*, the "boys" he had worked (and mostly played) with for five years in the Leather School behind Santa Croce, indulged in mock regret about their lost good old days. Goodbye to all that.

Suddenly, it was late. We were back in the cavernous room at the Tornabuoni in jeans and tees. We were feeling slightly stunned and we were ravenous. We hadn't eaten a bite since breakfast cappuccino and pastry. We had been too busy smiling. In fact, our cheeks ached from so much smiling.

It was too late for a decent meal at a trattoria, so we walked the wet cobblestones and found an open pizzeria. We ordered a pizza quattro stagioni. We were glowing with love, I suppose, or perhaps our 18-karat gold bands glinted tellingly in the light. Whatever the reason, the waiter asked if we were newlyweds. No sooner had we affirmed than he scurried behind the bar, returning with a bottle of Asti and an ice bucket stand, which he set up with an appropriate flourish. The wine was gratis, he insisted, peppering us with *tanti auguri*, "many good wishes."

Pizza with Asti on my wedding night? No marriage of food and wine was ever so brilliant. ✍

I sometimes grill the vegetables a day ahead when the coals are hot from cooking another meal on the barbecue kettle. With the vegetables ready in the refrigerator, this pizza comes together really quickly.

Double-Crusted Pizza with Grilled Vegetables

    Pizza Dough (page 62)
1   **tablespoon cornmeal**
2   **small zucchini, cut lengthwise into $1/4$-inch strips**
1   **red onion, cut into $1/4$-inch rounds**
3   **fresh plum tomatoes, cut lengthwise into $1/2$-inch slices**
    Olive oil
1   **cup (8 ounces) part-skim ricotta cheese**
2   **eggs**
1   **tablespoon cold water**
1   **cup (4 ounces) shredded Gruyère cheese**
$1/2$ **cup (2 ounces) grated Parmesan cheese**
2   **red, yellow, or orange bell peppers, roasted, peeled, cut into strips**
$1/2$ **cup packed torn fresh basil leaves**
    Salt and ground black pepper

Prepare the Pizza Dough. Coat a large baking sheet with no-stick spray. Sprinkle with the cornmeal.

Punch down the dough. Transfer to a lightly floured work surface. Divide into 2 balls.

Prepare a charcoal or gas grill.

Place the zucchini, onion, and tomatoes in a single layer on a tray. Drizzle or mist lightly with oil. Turn to coat all sides.

Grill the zucchini, onion, and tomatoes in batches on a portable grill rack on a charcoal or gas grill, stove-top grill, or large ridged grill pan until browned on each side. The zucchini takes about 6 minutes, the onions and tomatoes about 5 minutes. Set the grilled vegetables aside.

Place the ricotta in a small bowl. Beat in 1 egg. Place the remaining egg in a small bowl with the cold water. Beat.

Preheat the oven to 400°F.

Roll or pat 1 dough ball into a 14 x 12-inch rectangle. Place on the prepared pan. Brush the surface with some of the egg-water mixture. Sprinkle with one-third of the Gruyère and Parmesan. Top with the zucchini, onion, tomatoes, peppers, and basil to within 1 inch of the edges. Season with salt and pepper to taste. Cover with the ricotta mixture and the remaining Gruyère and Parmesan.

Roll or pat the remaining dough into a 16 x 14-inch rectangle. Place over the vegetables. Bring the edge of the bottom piece of dough up to overlap the top piece by ½ inch. Pinch the edges securely to seal. Brush with the remaining egg mixture. Pierce the top in several places.

Bake for about 30 minutes, or until golden. Remove to a cooling rack for 10 minutes.

SERVES 4 TO 6

zucchina

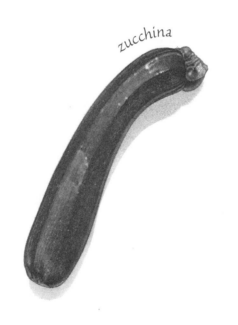

A portable round or rectangular grill rack takes the frustration out of grilling cut vegetables. The rack, often made of porcelain-coated steel, has holes set close together, so food won't fall through but smoke and heat can reach the food. If you don't have a portable rack, punch holes at 1-inch intervals in a rectangular low-sided disposable aluminum drip pan or double thickness of aluminum foil.

Making Pizza Dough

Every so often, in a long-term relationship, it pays to stand back and look at your partner with fresh eyes. A change in perspective might reveal hidden facets, new charms, even create some excitement.

So it is with pizza. We love pizza. We know pizza . . . or think we do.

Pizza charms us with its simplicity—it's nothing more than a disk of yeast bread topped with naturally sweet tomato sauce, herbs, and melted cheese—and its spontaneity—it bakes quickly in a hot oven to produce a crisp but tender crust.

Recapturing the original magic of pizza is easy, right in your own kitchen. You can have pizza made from scratch, even for weeknight meals, by planning ahead. You may make the dough in the morning and refrigerate it for a slow rise. Or make several crusts on a weekend and freeze them to bake (no need to thaw) for a really quick weeknight meal.

Even for a cook who has never made yeast dough, this recipe is foolproof. Allow yourself a relaxed atmosphere the first time you make it—maybe a lazy Sunday afternoon. Make several batches so you get the feel of the dough. Resist the urge to add too much flour; this will dry out and toughen the dough.

After some practice and advance preparation, you'll be pleased to see that it's true: Homemade pizza is within your reach, any night of the week.

Pizza Dough

MAKES ONE 15-INCH ROUND PIZZA CRUST,
OR 6 CALZONI

1$\frac{1}{4}$	cups warm bottled or filtered water (105°F to 115°F)
1	envelope ($\frac{1}{4}$ ounce) active dry yeast (2$\frac{1}{4}$ teaspoons)
1	tablespoon olive oil
3 to 3$\frac{1}{2}$	cups flour
$\frac{1}{2}$	teaspoon salt

To prepare by hand: Coat a large bowl with no-stick spray; set aside. In a glass measuring cup, mix the water and the yeast to dissolve. Pour into another large bowl. Add the oil and 1 cup flour. Beat until smooth. Add 1 cup flour and the salt; beat until smooth. Add 1 cup flour. Stir until the mixture forms a clump.

Place the remaining $\frac{1}{2}$ cup flour on a work surface. Push most of the flour to the side. With a dough scraper, lift the dough onto the surface. Sprinkle lightly with flour. With the scraper, fold the dough several times to get rid of surface stickiness. With your hands, knead for 5 to 6 minutes until the dough is resilient. Use additional flour only to prevent surface sticking. Some flour may remain. Place in the prepared bowl. Coat lightly with no-stick spray. Cover with plastic wrap. Set aside to rise for about 45 minutes, or until doubled in size.

Punch down the dough. Shape into a ball and transfer to a work surface. Let sit 5 minutes. Shape, add toppings, and bake according to recipe directions.

To prepare in a food processor: In the bowl of a food processor fitted with a plastic or metal blade, process the ingredients according to recipe directions.

To prepare with an electric mixer fitted with a dough hook: Make the dough in the large bowl of an electric mixer fitted with a dough hook. Add and mix the ingredients according to recipe directions.

To freeze pizza dough after the first rise: Punch down the dough and shape into a ball. Coat well with no-stick spray. Place in a freezer-quality plastic bag. Squeeze out all air and close tightly. Store in the freezer for up to 1 month. To thaw, place in the refrigerator overnight. With scissors, cut away the plastic bag. Place the dough on a lightly floured work surface. Shape according to recipe directions.

To freeze the unbaked pizza crust: Roll or pat the dough according to recipe directions. Place on pizza pan dusted with cornmeal. Cover tightly with plastic wrap, then wrap in aluminum foil. Store in the freezer for up to 1 month. To bake, remove from the freezer (no need to thaw). Remove wrappings. Top and bake according to recipe directions.

An instant-reading thermometer may be used to gauge the temperature of the water for the dough.

Baking pizza directly on a preheated ceramic stone produces a crisper crust because it simulates the intense sustained heat of a brick pizza oven. It may take some practice to successfully slide the pizza onto the stone with a wooden peel, or pizza paddle, dusted well with flour. Pat or roll the pizza dough on a well-floured surface. Add the toppings. Dust the paddle with flour. Slide the paddle under the pizza, then slide it off onto the preheated pizza stone. To remove the pizza from the oven, use the paddle again.

Choose extra-virgin olive oil and Parmigiano-Reggiano *cheese for the fullest flavor on this unique pizza.*

All-Cheese Pizza ⤳ Apple-Orange-Raisin Salad

Pizza:

  Pizza Dough (page 62)
1 tablespoon cornmeal
3 large cloves garlic, minced
2 tablespoons olive oil
$^1/_2$ cup (4 ounces) part-skim ricotta cheese
$^3/_4$ cup (3 ounces) shredded Gruyère cheese
$^1/_4$ cup (1 ounce) grated Parmesan cheese

Salad:

4 Gala apples, cut into chunks
2 navel oranges, cut into chunks
2 tablespoons raisins

To prepare the pizza: Prepare the Pizza Dough. Coat a 14- or 15-inch round pizza pan with no-stick spray. Sprinkle with the cornmeal; set aside.

Punch down the dough and place on a lightly floured work surface to sit for 5 minutes. With lightly floured hands or a rolling pin, pat or roll into a 15- or 16-inch circle. Transfer to the prepared pan. Fold the edges to make a rounded border. Cover with plastic wrap and set aside for about 15 minutes, or until slightly risen.

Preheat the oven to 450°F.

Place the garlic and oil in a small microwaveable bowl. Cover with waxed paper. Microwave on high for 90 seconds until bubbly. Remove and set aside, covered, for 10 minutes.

Drizzle some of the oil from the garlic oil over the crust. Spread with the back of a spoon. Mix the remaining garlic oil with the ricotta. Dollop on the crust. Spread with the back of a spoon. Sprinkle with the Gruyère and Parmesan.

Bake for about 15 minutes, or until the cheeses are golden and bubbly. Remove to a cooling rack for 5 minutes.

To prepare the salad: While the pizza is baking, combine the apples, oranges, and raisins in a bowl. Press some oranges with the back of a spoon to release juice. Cover and refrigerate.

SERVES 4 TO 6

These pies taste equally good served hot or at room temperature.

Chicken, Spinach, and Cheese Calzone
∽ Bartlett Pears

       Pizza Dough (page 62)
1   tablespoon cornmeal
2   tablespoons olive oil, divided
1   pound boneless, skinless chicken breasts
1   onion, finely chopped
2   large cloves garlic, minced
1   bag (6 ounces) baby spinach leaves, stems removed
³⁄₄ teaspoon **each** salt and ground black pepper
1   egg beaten with 1 tablespoon water
1   cup (4 ounces) shredded Gruyère cheese

4 to 6   ripe Bartlett pears

Prepare the Pizza Dough. Sprinkle the cornmeal over a large baking sheet.

    Warm 1 tablespoon oil in a medium sauté pan over medium-high heat. Sauté the chicken for 2 minutes on each side, or until browned (it will not be completely cooked). Remove and set aside. Reduce the heat to medium. To the pan, add 1 tablespoon oil and the onion. Cover and cook for 1 to 2 minutes, or until golden. Add the garlic, spinach, salt, and pepper. Cover and cook for 2 minutes. Uncover and cook off any liquid. Remove from the heat.

    Punch down the dough. Transfer to a lightly floured work surface. Divide into 6 equal balls. Cover with plastic wrap and allow to sit for 10 minutes.

    Preheat the oven to 450°F. Cut the chicken into thin slices. With hands or a rolling pin, pat or roll the balls on a floured surface into 8-inch circles. Brush edges with some egg mixture. Place 2 tablespoons of Gruyère on half of each circle. Top with the chicken, the spinach, and the remaining Gruyère. Fold the dough flaps over the filling until the edges almost meet. Pull up the edges of the bottom half of dough to overlap the top half by ¼ inch. Pinch securely to seal. With a floured dough scraper, transfer calzoni to the baking sheet. Brush with the remaining egg mixture.

    Bake for about 16 minutes, or until an instant-reading thermometer inserted in the center of one calzone registers 175°F. Remove to a cooling rack for 5 minutes.

Chill the pears during dinner and serve after the pizza.

SERVES 4 TO 6

A pinch of ground nutmeg may be added to the spinach mixture.

∽

To prepare one large calzone: Roll the dough into a 16 x 12-inch oval. Stuff and seal according to the recipe, then bake in a preheated 450°F oven for about 22 minutes. Remove to a cooling rack for 10 minutes.

Crab is so sweet and succulent but really pricey. When I find pasteurized lump crabmeat on sale, I make these luxurious turnovers. The price per serving is far less than I would pay for a comparable meal at a restaurant.

Crab Calzone ➸ Warm Asparagus Salad with Orange Dressing

Calzone:

	Pizza Dough (page 62)
1	tablespoon cornmeal
1	tablespoon butter
$^1/_2$	cup finely chopped celery heart
$^1/_2$	cup finely chopped red, yellow, or orange bell pepper
$^1/_2$	cup finely chopped onion
1	small serrano chile, minced
2	tablespoons minced fresh flat-leaf parsley
1	pound lump crabmeat
$^1/_4$	cup plain dry bread crumbs
$^1/_2$	teaspoon **each** salt and ground black pepper
3	eggs
1	tablespoon cold water

Salad:

	Juice and 1 teaspoon grated zest from 1 navel orange
$^1/_8$	teaspoon salt
1	pound asparagus, ends trimmed
3	tablespoons olive oil, divided
2	tablespoons water

To prepare the calzone: Prepare the Pizza Dough. Coat a large baking sheet with no-stick spray. Sprinkle with the cornmeal.

In a medium skillet, warm the butter over medium heat. Add the celery, bell pepper, and onion. Stir. Cover and cook, stirring occasionally, for 5 minutes, or until softened. Add the chile and parsley. Set aside to cool slightly.

Punch down the dough. Transfer to a lightly floured work surface. Divide into 6 equal balls. Cover with plastic wrap and allow to sit for 10 minutes.

Preheat the oven to 450°F.

Wine
*Bold **Sauvignon Blanc** from New Zealand— a white wine with herbaceous, citrus, and tropical attributes carried by clean acidity—is delicious with the sweetness of crab, the peppery heat of the filling, and the herbal quality of the asparagus.*

To the skillet, add the crab, bread crumbs, salt, and pepper. Toss. In a small bowl, beat 2 eggs. Add to the skillet; toss. Beat the remaining egg with the cold water. Set aside.

With floured hands or a rolling pin, pat or roll the dough balls on a lightly floured surface into 8-inch circles. Brush the edges with some of the egg mixture. Place equal amounts of the crab mixture over half of each circle. Fold the dough flaps over the remaining filling until the edges almost meet. Pull up the edges of the bottom half of dough to overlap the top half by ¼ inch. Pinch the edges securely to seal. With a floured dough scraper, transfer the calzoni to the baking sheet. Brush with the remaining egg mixture. Bake for about 16 minutes, or until browned. Remove to a cooling rack for 5 minutes.

To prepare the salad: While the calzoni bake, place the orange juice, zest, and salt in a large shallow serving bowl; set aside.

Cut the asparagus on the diagonal into 2-inch-long pieces. Warm 2 tablespoons oil in a large sauté pan. Add the asparagus. Toss and cover. Cook for 1 minute, or until very hot. Stir and add the water. Cover and cook for 2 minutes, or until the asparagus is cooked but still crisp. Turn out into the serving bowl with the orange mixture. Drizzle with the remaining 1 tablespoon oil. Toss.

SERVES 4 TO 6

asparagi

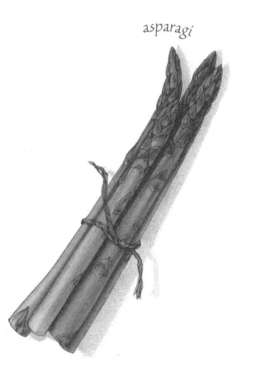

Chilled Crab Calzoni make wonderful picnic fare or dinner appetizers. Cool the calzoni and wrap in aluminum foil. Refrigerate for a few hours or overnight. Cut into 2-inch-wide crosswise slices.

To freeze Crab Calzoni: Bake and cool completely. Wrap in plastic wrap and then in aluminum foil. Store in the freezer for up to 1 month. To serve, remove and unwrap. Place on a rack and cover loosely with foil. Preheat the oven to 325°F. Place the calzoni directly on the oven rack. Bake for about 15 minutes, or until the crust is crisp. Remove to a rack to sit for 5 minutes before cutting into slices.

Pasta Meals

Pasta. The rounded vowels tumble playfully off the tongue.

Just how can a lump of moistened flour become so incredibly sexy? It is sexy because Italians have made it so. Italian cuisine demonstrates that pasta, like love, can satisfy every mood, every budget, every lifestyle.

Look through this chapter and you'll see how pastas range from simple to lush. Spaghetti in Olive Oil and Garlic is about as uncomplicated as a dish can be. Made with dried spaghetti and other pantry staples, it takes all of fifteen minutes to prepare. In contrast, the Fettuccine Bolognese requires that the sauce be gently simmered for nearly three hours before it is united with tender egg noodles. Both are magnificent.

Most of these meal recipes call for dried pasta. It is so convenient, easy to cook, and versatile that you can serve it several times a week and not feel you're eating the same old thing.

In this chapter, you'll also learn about making fresh egg pasta. You may not undertake this task every week, or even every month. To try it even once, however, is to experience the fun that is in the making.

Of course, pasta is only part of the story. Nearly all the sauces in this chapter—whether made with cheeses, sautéed vegetables, seafood, or other accompaniments—are prepared while the pasta cooks.

In "Capturing Summer Flavors for All Meals" (page 232), you will discover garden-fresh pasta accompaniments: Basil Pesto, Plum Tomato Purée with Vodka, Chunky Plum Tomato Sauce, and Roasted Peppers.

Tossing the cooked pasta with its sauce is an instantaneous act that nonetheless resembles the development of a successful marriage. Pasta and sauce must be a couple, not a he and a she. If either dominates, the dish, like the marriage, will be out of whack. Keep the elements in harmony, and the honeymoon lasts forever.

*Only Italians could create such a memorable concoction
as* spaghetti aglio e olio *with so few ingredients.*

Spaghetti in Olive Oil and Garlic
ᔅ Warm Broccoli Salad

Spaghetti:

$1/3$	cup olive oil
2	large cloves garlic, minced
1	tablespoon salt
1	pound dried spaghetti
2	tablespoons minced fresh flat-leaf parsley
	Crushed red pepper

Salad:

1	tablespoon olive oil
1 to $1^{1}/_{2}$	pounds broccoli, stalks peeled and cut into $^{1}/_{4}$-inch-thick rounds, florets separated
1	small red bell pepper, cored, seeded, cut into slivers
	Salt
$^{1}/_{4}$	cup (1 ounce) shredded provolone cheese
1	tablespoon drained capers
1	tablespoon balsamic vinegar

The red bell pepper may be replaced with $^{1}/_{2}$ cup delicatessen roasted peppers; add with the cheese, capers, and vinegar.

To prepare the spaghetti: Set a covered large pot of water over high heat.

Place the oil and garlic in a microwaveable dish. Cover with waxed paper. Microwave on high for about 2 minutes, or until sizzling. Remove and set aside.

When the water boils, add the salt and spaghetti. Stir, cover the pot, and return to the boil. Uncover and boil, stirring occasionally, about 10 minutes, or until al dente. Reserve $^{1}/_{2}$ cup of the cooking water. Drain the spaghetti and return to the pot. Drizzle with the garlic oil. Toss to coat. Add the parsley and some of the cooking water to moisten. Toss. Serve with crushed red pepper.

To prepare the salad: While the spaghetti is cooking, heat the oil in a large sauté pan over high heat. Add the broccoli and bell pepper. Season lightly with salt. Toss. Cover and cook, tossing occasionally, for 2 minutes. Add 1 tablespoon water. Cover and cook, tossing occasionally, about 2 minutes, or until lightly browned. Transfer to a serving bowl. Add the provolone, capers, and vinegar. Toss gently.

SERVES 4 TO 6

This refreshing summer dish of marinated chopped raw tomatoes tossed with hot rotini was a revelation when I first tasted it at Trattoria Benvenuto in Florence, long before pasta salads became trendy.

Rotini in Tomato Basil Sauce ⌒ Fresh Mozzarella

Rotini and Sauce:

4	large or 8 medium very ripe tomatoes, cored and chopped
³/₄ to 1	cup olive oil, divided
¹/₂	cup tightly packed slivered fresh basil leaves
2	cloves garlic, minced
1	teaspoon plus 1 tablespoon salt
1	pound dried rotini

Mozzarella:

12 to 16	ounces fresh mozzarella cheese in whey
	Ground black pepper

To prepare the rotini and sauce: In a large bowl, combine the tomatoes, ³/₄ cup oil, basil, garlic, and 1 teaspoon salt. Stir to mix. Set aside for 30 to 40 minutes at room temperature, or cover and refrigerate for up to 24 hours.

Set a covered large pot of water over high heat. When the water boils, add 1 tablespoon of salt and the rotini. Stir. Cover and return to the boil. Uncover and boil, stirring occasionally, about 10 minutes, or until al dente.

Drain the rotini and return to the pot. Add the tomato sauce. Toss to mix. Allow to sit for 5 minutes. Taste and add up to ¹/₄ cup oil, if needed for flavor.

To prepare the mozzarella: Remove the mozzarella from the whey; pat dry. Cut into ¹/₄-inch-thick slices. Place several slices on each plate and serve the rotini alongside the mozzarella. Season generously with pepper.

SERVES 4 TO 6

This dish must be made with very ripe tomatoes, preferably locally grown. For variety, try adding drained capers, slivered ripe olives, or cooked shrimp or scallops to the sauce.
⌒
Many supermarkets now carry fresh mozzarella in whey; check for the freshest available.

aglio

❧

Wine
Soave Classico from Veneto, composed mostly of the garganega grape, is minerally fine and lemony, with delicate hints of almond. This white wine finishes bone dry on the palate, a truly "anything with tomato" wine.

❧

The vegetables are glorious sizzling from the grill, but you may also cook them in advance and refrigerate them in an airtight container. Microwave the vegetables briefly on medium-high before tossing with the rigatoni.

Rigatoni with Grilled Summer Vegetables

1   small yellow summer squash
1   small yellow or red bell pepper
4   fresh plum tomatoes
1   bunch scallions, white and light green parts
1   tablespoon olive oil
1   tablespoon plus $^1/_4$ teaspoon salt
1   pound dried rigatoni
2   teaspoons grated lemon zest
1   cup (4 ounces) shredded provolone cheese

Prepare a charcoal or gas grill for indirect cooking, firing the briquettes or lighting the gas on one side of the grid only.

Cut the squash crosswise into 4 sections, then into quarters lengthwise. Cut the pepper into $^1/_2$-inch chunks. Cut the tomatoes into quarters lengthwise. Cut the scallions into 3-inch lengths. Place the vegetables in a bowl with the oil. Toss to coat.

Place a portable grill rack on the side of the cooking rack away from the direct heat source. Scatter the vegetables on top, placing the tomatoes farthest from the heat source. Cover and grill about 20 minutes, or until the squash is tender. Using flameproof mitts, slide the portable rack directly over the heat source. Grill, uncovered, about 10 minutes, turning frequently, until the vegetables are nicely browned. (The tomatoes may be removed before the other vegetables.) Remove the vegetables to a tray.

Meanwhile, set a covered large pot of water over high heat until boiling. Add 1 tablespoon salt and the rigatoni. Stir. Cover and return to the boil. Uncover and boil, stirring occasionally, about 10 minutes, or until al dente. Reserve $^1/_2$ cup of the cooking water.

Drain the rigatoni and return to the pot. Add the vegetables, lemon zest, and $^1/_4$ teaspoon salt; toss. Sprinkle on the provolone and toss. Add just enough of the reserved water to help melt the cheese and coat the rigatoni.

SERVES 4 TO 6

Farfalle with Broccoli, Raisins, and Pine Nuts

4	tablespoons olive oil, divided
1	pound broccoli, stalks peeled and cut into ¼-inch-thick rounds, florets separated
3	large cloves garlic, minced, divided
1	tablespoon water
2	cans (14½ ounces each) diced tomatoes, with juice
1	tablespoon plus ¼ teaspoon salt
1	pound dried farfalle
¼	teaspoon ground black pepper
¼	cup raisins
¼	cup pine nuts, toasted
¼	cup (1 ounce) grated Parmesan cheese

Set a covered large pot of water over high heat.

In a large sauté pan, warm 2 tablespoons oil over medium-high heat. Add the broccoli and half of the garlic. Stir to coat with oil. Cover and cook for 2 minutes. Add the water. Cover and cook about 2 minutes, or until the broccoli is bright green. Remove to a plate; set aside.

Place the tomatoes, 2 tablespoons oil, the remaining garlic, and ¼ teaspoon salt in the pan. Stir. Cover and bring to a boil over medium-high heat. Uncover and reduce heat to medium-low. Cook, stirring occasionally, about 5 minutes, or until the tomatoes are softened. Crush some of the tomato chunks with the back of a large spoon.

When the water boils, add 1 tablespoon salt and the farfalle. Stir. Cover to return to the boil. Uncover and boil, stirring occasionally, about 10 minutes, or until al dente. Reserve ½ cup of the cooking water. Drain the farfalle and add to the sauté pan. Add the broccoli and raisins. Toss, adding just enough reserved water to loosen the sauce, if needed. Sprinkle each serving with pine nuts and Parmesan.

SERVES 4 TO 6

Cooking and Saucing Dried Pasta

Commercial dried pasta is one of the great convenience foods. Pasta stored at room temperature stays fresh for a long, long time, so you can have it in your pantry always.

Dried pasta maintains its shape and texture in boiling water because it is made of semolina flour, ground from durum, a high-protein wheat. Whether you are buying American- or Italian-made pasta, the key words to look for on the package label are "100 percent durum" or "100 percent semolina" or some combination of these.

Semolina flour and water make a paste so stiff that it must be processed in factories, where the dough is extruded through metal dies—large disks stenciled with the holes that produce the many shapes of Italian pasta. These hundreds of shapes, in addition to being visually amusing, can actually change the taste and mouth feel of pasta.

Matching a pasta shape with an appropriate sauce requires only common sense and a mental picture of an Italian cook tossing a batch of drained cooked pasta with the sauce, the better to coat each strand. A thick smooth sauce calls for long pastas: *fettuccine*, *linguine*, *fusilli*, and the like. A chunky sauce nestles in the nooks of *rotini*, *penne*, *conchiglie*, and their siblings. Tiny shapes—*orzo*, *ditalini*, *stelline*, and others—shine in a soup or side dish.

Al Dente

Cooking time differs for different shapes, and even for the same shapes from different manufacturers. Fine, thin vermicelli cook in less time than thicker linguine; plump conchiglie take longer than tiny pastina. Follow the cooking time on the package label, but also trust your own taste.

Much has been written about cooking pasta until *al dente* (pronounced ahl DEN-tay), which translates as "to the tooth." Some of this advice complicates a simple concept. When pasta is chewy but not brittle, when it appears springy but not limp—that is pasta al dente.

For a visual test, cut an undercooked piece of pasta in half. You'll see a white dot or line in the center of the noodle. Pasta is cooked al dente at the second that speck disappears.

Alas, few of us are so "one with the noodle" that we intuit the nanosecond of doneness. So testing is the best tactic. After you have practiced cooking it long enough, you can almost feel degrees of doneness when you're stirring pasta in the pot. Start testing a few minutes before the indicated cooking time is over, and your pasta will be fine.

Pasta Waits for No One

Even before you boil the water, look over these tips.

Use a large pot, as full of water as possible. To cook 1 pound of dried pasta, a 6-quart pot or Dutch oven filled with water is adequate. Allow the water to come to a full rolling boil, then add 1 tablespoon of salt. Salt enhances the wheaty flavor, and many cooks believe it helps keep the pasta firm.

Add the pasta gradually to the boiling water while stirring with a wooden spoon or fork. (Why wood? It's less likely than metal to damage the pasta.) Cover the pot and allow the water to return to a rolling boil. Remove the lid, stir, and start timing. Keep the burner temperature high enough to maintain a full boil, but not so high that the water boils over.

As the pasta cooks, find a large colander and place it in the sink so you're not scrambling for it when the pasta is done. Stir the pasta occasionally as it cooks, to prevent clumping and uneven

cooking. Test for doneness a few minutes before the allotted time. When the pasta is cooked al dente, skim off 1 cup of the cooking water and set it aside.

Drain the pasta, shaking the colander a little, but do not rinse. For everyday meals, return the pasta to the cooking pot, which is conveniently hot. Add the sauce and toss immediately, then allow the pasta to sit for a few minutes to absorb the flavors of the sauce. If necessary, add a few tablespoonfuls of the reserved cooking water to loosen the sauce.

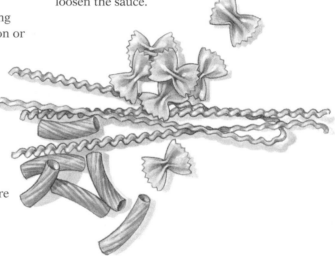

Ziti with Cauliflower, Ripe Olives, and Toasted Bread Crumbs ∽ Cantaloupe Wedges

4	tablespoons olive oil, divided
1	medium head cauliflower, cored, cut into small florets
2	tablespoons water
2	cloves garlic, minced
2	tablespoons plain dry bread crumbs
$1/4$	teaspoon plus 1 tablespoon salt
1	pound dried ziti
2	tablespoons ($1/2$ ounce) grated Pecorino Romano cheese
$1/3$	cup dry-cured ripe olives, pitted and cut into slivers Ground black pepper
1	medium ripe cantaloupe, cut into wedges

To brown the cauliflower, a heavy 12-inch sauté pan with 3-inch-high sides works best. A wok also is large enough to brown the cauliflower without steaming it. If you use a smaller pan, brown the cauliflower in two batches.

Set a covered large pot of water over high heat.

In a large sauté pan, heat 3 tablespoons oil over medium-high heat. Add the cauliflower. Cover and cook, stirring occasionally, for 3 minutes. Turn the florets. Reduce the heat to medium. Add the water. Cover and cook, turning occasionally, about 5 minutes, or until well-browned. Add the garlic, bread crumbs, and $1/4$ teaspoon salt. Toss to combine and cook about 2 minutes, or until the crumbs are golden. Remove from the heat. Transfer the florets to a plate, leaving loose crumbs and garlic in the pan.

When the water boils, add 1 tablespoon salt and the ziti. Stir. Cover and return to the boil. Uncover and boil, stirring occasionally, about 10 minutes, or until al dente. Reserve $1/4$ cup of the cooking water. Drain the ziti and transfer to the sauté pan. Add the Romano, 1 tablespoon oil, and 1 to 2 tablespoons of the cooking water. Toss. Add 1 or 2 tablespoons more of the cooking water, if needed. Add the reserved cauliflower and the olives. Toss to coat. Season with pepper at the table.

Chill the cantaloupe during dinner and serve after the ziti.

SERVES 4 TO 6

Radiatori with Chick-peas, Kale, and Herbs

2	tablespoons olive oil
1	medium-large red onion, chopped
8	ounces kale, stems removed, leaves cut into slivers
1	teaspoon dried thyme
1	teaspoon dried sage
2	large cloves garlic, minced
1	can (14$^{1}/_{2}$ ounces) chick-peas (garbanzo beans), rinsed and drained
1	can (14$^{1}/_{2}$ ounces) chicken broth
$^{1}/_{4}$	teaspoon plus 1 tablespoon salt
1	pound dried radiatori
2	tablespoons ($^{1}/_{2}$ ounce) grated Pecorino Romano cheese

Set a covered large pot of water over high heat.

In a large sauté pan, warm the oil over medium heat. Add the onion and stir. Cover and cook about 5 minutes, or until softened. Add the kale leaves, thyme, sage, and garlic. Toss. Cover and cook about 2 to 3 minutes, or until the kale is wilted.

Add the chick-peas, broth, and $^{1}/_{4}$ teaspoon salt or to taste. Stir and reduce the heat to low.

When the water boils, add the 1 tablespoon salt and the radiatori. Stir. Cover and return to the boil. Uncover and boil, stirring occasionally, about 8 minutes, or until al dente. Drain and add to the sauté pan. Toss over medium-low heat about 3 minutes, or until the radiatori have soaked up most of the broth but are still very moist. Remove from the heat. Add the Romano. Toss.

SERVES 4 TO 6

To cut the kale efficiently, place a bunch of leaves on a cutting board. With one hand, hold the leaves in a tight bundle. With a sharp knife in the other hand, slice the leaf bundle at $^{1}/_{2}$-inch intervals.

A sauté pan that is large enough to hold the cooked vegetables and the radiatori works best for this recipe. A Dutch oven or 6-quart pot may replace the sauté pan.

Penne, rotini, farfalle, or rigatoni may replace the radiatori.

Conchiglie with Tuna, Peas, and Lemon ⌣ Honeydew Melon Wedges

4	tablespoons olive oil, divided
1	medium onion, chopped
1½	cups frozen baby peas
¼	teaspoon plus 1 tablespoon salt
1	pound dried conchiglie
2	cans (6 ounces each) water-packed tuna, drained
1	teaspoon ground black pepper
1	teaspoon grated lemon zest
1	medium honeydew melon, cut into wedges

*Chilled
pineapple
packed in juice
may replace the
melon.*

Set a covered large pot of water over high heat.

Warm 2 tablespoons oil over medium heat in a medium sauté pan. Add the onion. Stir. Cover and cook about 5 minutes, or until softened. Add the peas and ¼ teaspoon salt. Stir. Cover and cook about 3 minutes, or until the peas are thawed. Remove from the heat and set aside.

When the water boils, add 1 tablespoon salt and the conchiglie. Stir. Cover and return to the boil. Uncover and boil, stirring occasionally, about 12 minutes, or until al dente. Reserve ½ cup of the cooking water. Drain the conchiglie and return to the pot. Add the tuna, onion and peas, pepper, lemon zest, and 2 tablespoons oil. Toss. Add just enough reserved water to moisten.

Chill the honeydew during dinner and serve after the conchiglie.

SERVES 4 TO 6

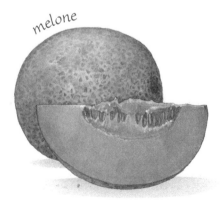

melone

*Long corkscrew strands of pasta pair with
pretty seafood shells in this visual treat.*

Fusilli with Spicy Clams ∽ Chilled White Grapes

3	tablespoons olive oil
1	small onion, minced
1	teaspoon crushed fennel seeds
	Pinch of saffron threads
³/₄	cup dry white wine
1	can (14¹/₂ ounces) diced tomatoes, with juice
¹/₈	teaspoon plus 1 tablespoon salt
1	pound dried long fusilli
36	littleneck clams, scrubbed and rinsed
2	serrano chiles, seeded and minced, divided
1	bunch white grapes

*Spaghetti may
replace the fusilli.
If fresh clams
are not available,
replace them with
1 can (10 ounces)
baby clams,
drained and
rinsed. When the
fusilli is cooked,
add the clams
and the chile to
the tomato sauce.
Toss over low
heat to warm the
clams.*

Set a covered large pot of water over high heat.

In a large sauté pan, warm the oil over low heat. Add the onion, fennel, and saffron. Cover and cook, stirring frequently, about 3 to 4 minutes, or until the onion is translucent. Add the wine. Increase the heat to high and boil about 4 minutes, or until the mixture no longer smells of alcohol. Add the tomatoes and ¹/₈ teaspoon salt. Decrease the heat to medium. Cover and cook, stirring, about 5 minutes, or until the tomatoes are softened.

When the water boils, add 1 tablespoon salt and the fusilli. Stir. Cover and return to the boil. Uncover and boil, stirring occasionally, about 10 minutes, or until al dente. Reserve ¹/₂ cup of the cooking water. Drain the fusilli and return to the pot.

Meanwhile, add the clams and 1 chile to the sauté pan. Cover and turn the heat to high. Cook about 8 minutes, or until the clams open. Discard any unopened clams. Add the clam sauce to the fusilli. Toss, adding small amounts of the reserved cooking water, if needed, to loosen the sauce and coat the fusilli. Pass the remaining chile at the table.

Chill the grapes during dinner and serve after the fusilli.

SERVES 4 TO 6

∽
Wine
*Arneis, a white
wine from
Piedmont,
possesses full
mouth feel with
nutty scents and
round, fresh
fruitiness
carried by crisp
acidity.*

∽

This rich sauce is based on Italian fonduta, *"fondue," from the Alpine region of Piedmont. Those who like a slightly spicier dish may season the penne with ground black pepper.*

Penne with Fondue Sauce, Broccoli, and Ham

2   tablespoons flour

$^1/_8$ teaspoon ground nutmeg

2   tablespoons cold water

2   cups milk

$^3/_4$ cup (3 ounces) shredded Gruyère cheese

$^1/_4$ cup (1 ounce) grated Parmesan cheese

1   tablespoon salt

1   pound broccoli, stalks peeled and cut into $^1/_4$-inch-thick rounds, florets separated

1   pound dried penne

4   ounces thick-cut cooked ham, diced

This dish is usually a big hit with children and can be varied depending on what vegetables they like. Green beans or cut asparagus stalks are very good with the cheese. For garlic lovers, some sautéed minced cloves make a welcome addition.

Depending upon the season, pass a bowl of baby carrots or ripe sweet cherry tomatoes to accompany the penne.

Set a covered large pot of water over high heat.

In a medium saucepan, whisk the flour, nutmeg, and water until smooth. Gradually add the milk, whisking to combine. Cook over medium-high heat, stirring constantly, about 8 minutes, or until the mixture boils. Remove from the heat. Stir in the Gruyère and Parmesan until they melt. Set aside.

When the water boils, add the salt and broccoli. Cover and return to the boil. Uncover and boil about 5 minutes, or until tender. With a slotted spoon, remove the broccoli to a colander set in the sink.

Add the penne to the pot. Stir. Cover and return to the boil. Uncover and boil, stirring occasionally, about 10 minutes, or until al dente. Pour into the colander over the broccoli. Drain and return to the pot. Add the ham and toss. Add the sauce and toss to coat.

Serves 4 to 6

broccoli

Up in Smoke

Smoke got in my eyes . . . but, at last, I could see clearly.

In a remote valley in the Italian Alps, brisk mountain winds swept away all the foolish constraints I had heaped upon *la cucina Italiana*.

For more than two decades, I had doggedly pursued the holy grail of "authentic" Italian cooking. My quest began when I returned to the States after living in Italy during the mid-1970s. I longed to recapture the magic of eating in Florence, especially those long lunches with wine. So I started cooking Italian. At the same time, as an aspiring food writer, I yearned to enter the inner circle of "foodies" who knew authentic Italian food. I felt it was necessary to follow the rules, to cook with only the right ingredients, using only the correct methods.

This was not easy. For example, I craved *spaghetti alla carbonara*, a luxurious dish of hot pasta tossed with sautéed *pancetta*, grated cheeses, and beaten eggs. As these ingredients blend, the pasta's heat coddles the eggs into a silky custard sauce. I consulted the authoritative Italian cookbooks and learned that "true" carbonara can be made only with pancetta—cured and spiced pork belly. Never make carbonara with American smoked bacon, the books scolded. The smoke flavor will overpower this subtle dish.

What to do? Pancetta was not available in supermarkets. When I did find it in Italian food stores, it was always expensive though not always fresh.

At last my craving for carbonara prevailed over my self-imposed limitations. I made the dish with smoked bacon—and loved it.

Still, a nagging embarrassment lingered. I would never admit to a fellow foodie that I made carbonara with smoked bacon. My internal conflict about "authenticity" raged unabated until a few years ago, when I visited Ponte di Legno, a lively ski town in northern Lombardy, just a cowbell's clang from Switzerland.

Ponte di Legno was like nothing I had experienced anywhere else in Italy. People lived and worked in wooden chalets, service was efficient, and sauerkraut was on every restaurant's menu.

Still, it felt like Italy. The patrons at the Bar di Roma seemed in no rush to finish their mid-morning beverages. Every evening the streets came alive for the *passeggiata*, the daily "promenade." Ponte di Legno was a delightful Swiss-Italian hybrid. If Heidi and Pinocchio got married, this is where they'd live.

When I visited, it was June. Days were warm and sunny, ideal T-shirt weather. Yet even on the cusp of summer, the local trattorias offered meals that would have sustained a lumberjack in January. Everywhere I saw menus featuring chestnuts, buckwheat pasta, barley, venison. One first course—gnocchi, potatoes, and sautéed onions buried under an avalanche of melted local cheese—nearly suffocated me.

So much for the light Mediterranean diet. This was the polar opposite of the vegetable-based cuisine of Campania, Sicily, and other semitropical regions far to the south. Yet this, too, was Italy.

Smelling the Bacon

I was at a food shop in Ponte di Legno when I experienced my epiphany. Among the cured meats was a sign offering *pancetta affumicata*, "smoked pancetta." There it was, in black and white. Smoked bacon is Italian, I silently rejoiced. No doubt the counterman chalked up my uncommon interest in the pancetta to the peculiarity of foreigners, and I suppose he was right.

Then and there I understood that my stubborn insistence on "authentic" ingredients was the culinary equivalent of knowing the words but not the music. I understood that slavishly imitating some ideal Italian cuisine is like damming a river to capture its wild beauty. Where and when do you stop this river? Do you stop it before Columbus brought tomatoes, peppers, potatoes, and chocolate from the New World to Europe? Very well. Strike *sugo di pomodoro*, *peperonata*, *gnocchi di patate*, and *torta alla cioccolata* from the canon of la cucina Italiana.

With relief, I realized that Italian foodstuffs aren't identical from one part of Italy to another, nor from one era to another. And I lightened up. I now cook Italian according to the spirit, rather than the letter, of the recipe. My kitchen is always stocked with dried pasta, *Parmigiano-Reggiano*, and extra-virgin olive oil. I buy vegetables in season from an organic farm and the farmer's market. I give herbs space to grow and they do the rest themselves. In winter, I buy supermarket produce that travels well: broccoli, cauliflower, fennel, onions, potatoes, citrus. I rely on my home-dried herbs, frozen pesto, good canned tomatoes, and dried or canned beans. As traditional country cooks in Italy would.

If I happen to be in a shop that sells pancetta, I'll buy some. It is unique and wonderful. But if I have a craving for carbonara on a Tuesday night, I'm more likely to pick up good bacon at the supermarket and make spaghetti with bacon and egg sauce, serving it to my family as carbonara alla Ponte.

So, *grazie mille*, Ponte di Legno. You inspired me to burn the rule book and watch happily as it went up in smoke. ↶

Rich and totally satisfying, this dish is in my family's top ten meals.

Spaghetti in Bacon and Egg Sauce ꙮ Stir-Sautéed Spinach

Spaghetti:

- 1/2 pound sliced bacon, cut into 1/2-inch pieces
- 2 large cloves garlic, minced
- 1 pound dried spaghetti
- 1 tablespoon salt
- 4 eggs
- 1/2 cup (2 ounces) grated Parmesan cheese
- 3/4 cup (3 ounces) shredded Gruyère cheese

Spinach:

- 3 tablespoons olive oil
- 2 bags (10 ounces each) spinach, stems removed
- 1/4 teaspoon salt

To prepare the spaghetti: Set a covered large pot of water over high heat. Scatter the bacon in a large cold sauté pan. Cook over medium-high heat, stirring frequently, about 5 minutes, or until crisp. Remove with a slotted spoon to a paper towel–lined plate. Pour out and discard all but 1 tablespoon of the drippings. Reduce the heat to low. Add the garlic; stir to mix. Cook about 1 minute, or until fragrant. Turn off the heat.

When the water boils, add the spaghetti and salt. Stir. Cover and return to the boil. Uncover and boil, stirring occasionally, about 10 minutes, or until al dente.

Meanwhile, with a fork, beat the eggs in a bowl while gradually adding 1 1/2 cups of hot water from the spaghetti pot. Reserve an additional 1 cup of the cooking water.

Drain the spaghetti. Add to the sauté pan. Add the egg mixture. Cook over medium-low heat, tossing constantly, about 2 minutes, or until a creamy sauce forms. Do not boil. Remove from the heat. Add the Parmesan and Gruyère; toss to melt. Add some of the reserved water, if needed, to loosen the sauce. Sprinkle with the bacon.

To prepare the spinach: Heat the oil in a large pot over high heat. Add half the spinach. Cover and cook about 3 minutes, or until it starts to wilt. Add the remaining spinach. Stir. Cover and cook about 2 minutes, or until wilted. Drain and return to the pot. Toss until no liquid remains. Season with the salt.

SERVES 4 TO 6

If you can find pancetta at your supermarket, by all means use it instead of bacon. Pancetta is pork belly—the same cut of meat as bacon—that has been salt-cured and sometimes seasoned with cloves and pepper. It will add a wonderful depth of flavor to this dish. Cook the pancetta slowly until all the fat melts into the pan.
ꙮ
Tuscan Pecorino or Spanish Manchego cheese may replace the Gruyère.
ꙮ
A sprinkling of crushed red pepper makes a good counterpoint to this rich pasta sauce. A squeeze of fresh lemon on the spinach brings out its flavor.

Inspired by pasta all'arrabbiata—*"angry pasta"—this dish takes its fire from dried red peppers. The amount of pepper in this recipe produces a pleasant glow.*

Mostaccioli in Fiery Tomato Sauce
↪ Sweet and Sharp Carrots

Mostaccioli:

1	tablespoon olive oil
4	ounces prosciutto, cut in slivers
1	can (14½ ounces) diced tomatoes, with juice
¾	teaspoon crushed red pepper
1	tablespoon salt
1	pound dried mostaccioli
2	tablespoons minced fresh flat-leaf parsley
¼	cup (1 ounce) grated Parmesan cheese

Carrots:

1	pound baby carrots
½	tablespoon butter
	Pinch of salt
2	teaspoons sugar
2	tablespoons water
2	teaspoons balsamic vinegar

To prepare the mostaccioli: Set a covered large pot of water over high heat.

In a medium sauté pan, warm the oil over medium-low heat. Add the prosciutto. Cook, stirring occasionally, about 6 minutes, or until any fat is melted. Remove with a slotted spoon and set aside. Add the tomatoes and red pepper to the pan. Cover and cook about 5 minutes, or until softened, crushing some of the tomato chunks with the back of a large spoon.

When the water boils, add the salt and mostaccioli. Stir. Cover and return to the boil. Uncover and boil, stirring occasionally, for about 10 minutes, or until al dente. Reserve ½ cup of the cooking water.

Drain the mostaccioli and return to the pot. Add the reserved prosciutto. Toss. Add the tomato sauce and parsley. Toss, adding some of the reserved water to loosen the sauce, if needed. Sprinkle each serving with Parmesan.

To prepare the carrots: Place the carrots, butter, salt, sugar, and water in a saucepan. Bring to the boil. Reduce the heat and simmer about 10 minutes, or until the carrots are tender and the water evaporates. If any water remains, uncover and cook about 2 minutes, or until the carrots are dry. Remove from the heat. Add the vinegar and toss.

SERVES 4 TO 6

carote

If you can find pancetta at your supermarket, by all means use it instead of prosciutto. Pancetta is pork belly—the same cut of meat as bacon—that has been salt-cured and sometimes seasoned with cloves and pepper. It will add a wonderful depth of flavor to this dish. Cook the pancetta slowly in the olive oil until all the fat melts into the pan.

Tortelloni verdi, plump packets of spinach dough encasing a savory meat stuffing, were my introduction to fresh pasta. It didn't take long for me to meet the rest of the family: *tagliatelle*, *tortellini*, *cappelletti*, and many more. Tender and rich, *pasta fresca*, fresh pasta, was a different culinary experience from spunky *pasta asciutta*, drained and sauced dry pasta.

Fresh pasta is usually made of all-purpose flour kneaded with eggs or egg yolks. If cooked immediately after cutting, it will be done in 2 to 3 minutes. The texture will be tender.

My fondness for fresh pasta led me to take classes. I practiced with a hand-cranked pasta machine. And I got a big surprise. I realized I had grown up watching my mother make pasta. Only she called it egg noodles—a legacy from the Pennsylvania German side of her family. Mostly she served the noodles in chicken soup, which was wonderful, though not nearly so seductive as egg pastas tossed with heavy cream and grated Parmesan, or filled with veal and mortadella.

Still, I conjured up my mental image of Mom and made some pretty good fresh pasta. Her method was to dump flour on a work surface, make a well in the center, break eggs into the well, and then beat the eggs with a fork while working in flour. When the lumpy golden paste came together, she would knead it by hand until it was as smooth as modeling compound. She floured it, covered it with a crockery bowl, and let it sit for about an hour.

Then she rolled it out by hand into a huge sheet. She dusted the sheet with flour and covered it with a white cloth to dry for about an hour. To cut the noodles, she coiled the sheet of dough like a jelly roll. This she sliced with a sharp knife, unfurling the resulting noodles to dry on a floured cloth. Sometimes she cooked them right away. Other times, she dried them completely and stored them.

My mother didn't make noodles every day, and I don't either. I make fresh pasta on weekends or stay-at-home days. The total hands-on time isn't much; I just have to be available for the various stages. Is it worth the trouble? Well, when I serve fresh noodles, my daughters practically swoon.

These noodles may be sauced with Bolognese-Style Meat Sauce (page 91) or Mushroom Sauce (page 88). For a simple seasoning, sprinkle rubbed dried sage into some melted butter in a sauté pan. Add the drained noodles and toss. For *paglia e fieno*—"straw and hay"—combine regular noodles with Fresh Spinach Pasta (page 87).

Basic Egg Pasta

MAKES ABOUT 1 POUND

4	eggs
2 to 2½	cups flour

To prepare by hand: With a fork, beat the eggs in a large mixing bowl. Gradually add 2 cups of flour, beating continuously, to make a sticky dough. One tablespoon at a time, gradually add flour from the remaining ½ cup, until the dough pulls away from the sides of the bowl.

Spread the remaining flour on a work surface, pushing most of it to the side. With a plastic pastry scraper, turn the dough onto the work surface. Sprinkle lightly with some of the flour. Start kneading the dough, using the pastry scraper in one hand at the beginning.

Knead, adding scant amounts of flour as needed, about 5 minutes, or until the dough is as smooth as modeling compound but not quite as stiff. All the flour may not be needed. Check the dough for air bubbles, lumps, or streaks of flour by cutting it down the middle. Shape it into a ball, dust lightly with flour, and cover with a bowl for 30 minutes.

To roll and cut by hand: Cut the dough in half. Keep half covered. On a lightly floured surface, working with a large rolling pin, stretch the other half of the dough from the center outward into as thin a sheet as possible. Dust with flour and set on a clean kitchen towel. Repeat with the remaining dough half. Allow the pasta sheets to rest about 1 hour, or until their edges start to dry but are not yet brittle.

Working with one sheet at a time, dust both sides lightly with flour. Lift one end of the sheet and gently roll into a long cylinder. Cut into 1/4-inch-wide strips. Unfurl the noodles and spread on a kitchen towel. Dust lightly with flour. Cover with a kitchen towel. Repeat with the second pasta sheet. Allow the noodles to rest for up to 2 hours.

To prepare the dough in a food processor: In the bowl of a food processor, beat the eggs just until smooth. Add 2 cups of flour, processing until smooth. With the machine running, add 1 tablespoon of flour at a time from the remaining 1/2 cup of flour. Process just until the dough forms a ball. Spread the remaining flour on a work surface, pushing most of it to the side. Turn the dough out onto the work surface.

Knead, adding scant amounts of flour as needed, about 3 minutes, or until the dough is as smooth as modeling compound but not quite as stiff. All the flour may not be needed. Check the dough for air bubbles, lumps, or streaks of flour by cutting it down the middle. Shape it into a ball, dust lightly with flour, and cover with a bowl for 30 minutes.

To roll and cut on a hand-cranked pasta machine: Cut the dough into quarters. Work with one quarter at a time while keeping the others covered. Set the pasta rollers at the widest opening. Press the dough with your palm to flatten. Dust lightly with flour. Run through the rollers. Dust lightly again with flour. Fold one short side of the dough strip two-thirds over. Fold the other short end over the first fold. Feed the narrow end through the widest roller setting. Dust lightly with flour. Continue rolling, closing the rollers one notch at a time and dusting the dough strip with flour as needed. Roll to the second-narrowest setting, until the dough is 1/16 inch thick. Dust the pasta sheet with flour and set it on a clean kitchen towel.

Repeat with the remaining dough. Cover the pasta sheets with a clean kitchen towel. Allow them to rest for about 45 minutes, or until their edges start to dry but are not brittle.

Move the hand crank of the pasta machine to the fettuccine cutting roller. Working with one pasta sheet at a time, run through the roller. Roll the noodles loosely around one hand to make a nest. Lay the nest on the kitchen towel. Repeat with the remaining sheets. Dust lightly with flour and cover with a kitchen towel. Allow to rest for up to 2 hours.

Variation

Fresh Spinach Pasta: Wash 1 bag (6 ounces) baby spinach leaves. Remove and discard any tough stems. Place in a large pot. Cover and cook over high heat for about 3 minutes, or until wilted. Drain and set aside to cool. Squeeze the spinach dry, then chop as finely as possible. Prepare the Basic Egg Pasta recipe, replacing 2 of the eggs with the spinach.

A pasta machine involves others in the action. The steel hand-cranked machines that attach to a countertop with a C-clamp are relatively inexpensive. They are indestructible, so if you buy one, plan on handing it down to the grand-children. Cleanup is easy: Just brush off any flour or bits of dough that stick to the machine. As the flap on my machine's box warns: "Importante! Non lavare mai la macchina." "Important! Never wash the machine."

*I once stayed at La Pozza, a guesthouse in Tuscany. It was
so magical, I felt as if we were in a movie. On the summer solstice,
the guests shared dinner, including this pasta, on the veranda.*

Fettuccine in Mushroom Sauce
∽ Green Bean–Almond Salad

Salad:

1	tablespoon lemon juice
$1/8$	teaspoon salt
2	tablespoons olive oil, divided
1	pound green beans, trimmed and snapped into 2-inch lengths
1	tablespoon water
2	tablespoons slivered almonds, toasted

Fettuccine and Sauce:

2	tablespoons butter
1	small onion, minced
12	ounces white or brown mushrooms, sliced
$1/8$	teaspoon ground nutmeg
	Salt
1	can ($14^1/2$ ounces) chicken broth
1	carton (8 ounces) whipping cream
1	pound fresh egg fettuccine
$1/2$	cup (2 ounces) grated Parmesan cheese
2	tablespoons minced fresh flat-leaf parsley
$1/8$	teaspoon ground black pepper

To prepare the salad: Combine the lemon juice and salt in a serving bowl. Set aside. Warm 1 tablespoon oil in a medium sauté pan over medium-high heat. Add the beans; toss. Cover and cook 3 minutes. Add the water. Cover and cook about 3 minutes, or until tender. Remove to the serving bowl. Drizzle with 1 tablespoon oil. Toss just before serving, sprinkling each portion with almonds.

To prepare the fettuccine and sauce: Set a covered large pot of water over high heat.

Warm the butter in a large sauté pan over medium-low heat. Add the onion. Cook about 2 minutes, or until golden. Add the mushrooms and nutmeg, sprinkling with $1/2$ teaspoon salt. Stir. Increase the heat to medium-high.

Cover and cook about 3 minutes, or until the mushrooms start to give off liquid. Remove cover. Cook, stirring, about 2 minutes, or until golden. Add 1½ cups of broth, the whipping cream, and an additional ½ teaspoon salt, if needed. Reduce the heat to medium-low.

When the water boils, add 1 tablespoon salt and the fettuccine. Stir. Cover and return to a boil. Uncover and boil, stirring occasionally, about 3 minutes, or until the fettuccine is tender. Drain and add to the mushroom pan. Toss over medium heat about 3 minutes, or until the sauce thickens slightly and coats the fettuccine. Add a little of the remaining chicken broth, if needed, to loosen the sauce. Remove from the heat. Add the Parmesan, parsley, and pepper. Toss to coat.

SERVES 4 TO 6

This pasta dinner calls for a long-simmered Bolognese-style meat sauce, which may be made in advance.

Fettuccine Bolognese
✎ Greens and Mushroom Salad

Fettuccine:

1	pound fresh egg fettuccine
1	tablespoon salt
1	tablespoon butter
4	cups Bolognese-Style Meat Sauce, heated (page 91)
¼	cup (1 ounce) grated Parmesan cheese

Salad:

4	tablespoons olive oil
1	tablespoon red or white wine vinegar
⅛	teaspoon **each** salt and ground black pepper
8	ounces leaf lettuce, torn into pieces
4	ounces white or brown mushrooms, sliced
4	scallions, white and light green parts, thinly sliced

✎

Wine
*Rosso di
Montalcino
from Tuscany
is hearty and
robust, with
nuances of
cherry and
tobacco. It lends
a balanced
acidity that
travels through
the richness of
this meal.*

✎

To prepare the fettuccine: Set a covered large pot of water over high heat until boiling. Add the fettuccine and salt. Stir. Cover and return to the boil. Uncover and boil, stirring occasionally, about 3 minutes, or until tender. Reserve ¼ cup of the cooking water. Drain the fettuccine and return to the pot.

. Add the butter. Toss to coat. Add the meat sauce. Toss over low heat until the sauce coats the fettuccine strands. Add 1 to 2 tablespoons of the reserved water, if needed, to loosen the sauce. Sprinkle each serving with Parmesan.

To prepare the salad: In a serving bowl, whisk the oil, vinegar, salt, and pepper. Add the lettuce, mushrooms, and scallions. Toss.

SERVES 4 TO 6

This rich, mellow sauce is based on a traditional recipe from the city of Bologna. One batch gives you enough for two dinners. The flavor of the sauce improves with refrigeration or freezing.

Bolognese-Style Meat Sauce

- 3   tablespoons butter
- 1   cup finely chopped carrot
- 2   cups finely chopped celery heart
- 2   cups finely chopped onion
- 1   pound ground pork
- 1   pound lean ground beef
- 1   cup dry white Italian wine
- 1   can (14½ ounces) chicken broth
- 1   can (15 ounces) unseasoned tomato purée
- 2   dried bay leaves
- ½   cup whole milk or half-and-half
- ¼   cup minced fresh flat-leaf parsley
- ¾   teaspoon **each** salt and ground black pepper

In a Dutch oven, warm the butter over medium-high heat. Add the carrot, celery, and onion. Stir to coat with butter. Cover and cook, stirring occasionally, about 10 minutes, or until softened. Reduce the heat if the vegetables start to brown. Remove the vegetables to a bowl; set aside.

Crumble the pork into the pot. Cook over medium-high heat, stirring occasionally, about 4 minutes, or until no longer pink. Remove with a slotted spoon to the vegetable bowl. Pour off and discard the fat. Crumble the beef into the pot. Cook, stirring occasionally, about 4 minutes, or until no longer pink. Tip the pot slightly and scrape the beef to the higher side. Skim off and discard any fat. Add the wine. Cook over high heat about 5 minutes, or until the mixture no longer smells of alcohol. Add the broth, tomato purée, bay leaves, and the reserved pork and vegetables. Heat to almost boiling but do not allow to boil.

Reduce the heat to low or medium-low so the sauce bubbles slightly in the center. Cook for 1 hour, stirring occasionally. Stir in the milk or half-and-half and parsley. Cook about 1½ hours, stirring occasionally, or until the mixture is thickened. Stir in the salt and pepper. Remove and discard the bay leaves.

MAKES 8 CUPS

To refrigerate the sauce: Cool to room temperature. Spoon into an airtight container and cover. Refrigerate for up to 4 days. Reheat in a saucepan or in the microwave oven.

To freeze the sauce, cool to room temperature. Cover and refrigerate for several hours. Spoon into plastic freezer containers. Store in the freezer for up to 3 months. To use, thaw for a day in the refrigerator. Reheat in a saucepan or in the microwave oven.

This sauce is wonderful served over Soft Polenta with Fontina (page 98).

Vegetable, Bean, and Grain Meals

Recipes

Stories and Basics

Italians treasure the gifts of the garden and grove. So much so, that certain vegetables and fruits are indelibly associated with their place of origin: the radicchio of Treviso, tomatoes from San Marzano, blood oranges out of Sicily. Vegetables and fruits perform the coloratura role in the Italian kitchen, soaring above the bass notes of pasta, bread, and meat.

Vegetables provide the color and crispness, sweetness and bitterness, in appetizers, soups, and side dishes. From delicate stuffed zucchini blossoms to robust braised cabbage, the range of flavors, textures, and possibilities is remarkable.

Tomatoes—synonymous with Italian cooking—can be a surprise when you're on Italian soil. An Italian salad tomato is ripe, firm, and pleasantly tart. It may even be stippled with green at the blossom end. The deep-red ones, *pelati*, are reserved for fresh tomato sauces. When pelati are ripe, they almost melt as they hit the olive oil in the skillet.

The Italians exhibit an all-consuming passion for beans. In springtime, fresh fava beans are enjoyed with young pecorino, sheep's milk cheese, as an antipasto. Green beans add vegetal sweetness to summer meals. As autumn shivers into winter, dried lentils, chick-peas (garbanzo beans), and cannellini are simmered into soul-sustaining soups, stews, and side dishes.

Corn is rarely eaten as a fresh vegetable in Italy; instead it is dried and ground into cornmeal that will become polenta, cornmeal mush. When it is cooked in water, broth, or milk, polenta may be served soft, as a first course with a ragù or other sauce, or as an accompaniment to roasts or stews. When polenta has cooled, it firms up enough to be sliced, then grilled or sautéed.

Rice and barley, though not vegetables, seem at home in this chapter of mostly meatless dishes. These are northern grains. Rice is extremely popular in Lombardy and the Veneto. For risottos, *superfino* rices such as arborio and carnaroli are best. These stout grains plump up as they absorb broth, but maintain their shape and texture. Shorter types of rice are used in rice salads, fritters, tortas, and other dishes.

Barley, called orzo in Italian (not to be confused with the dried pasta shape of the same name), is rounded and sturdy. It makes an excellent stand-in for superfino rice in risotto-style dishes. ✒

In Tuscany, fresh porcini mushrooms are often grilled like a beefsteak—with olive oil, garlic, and rosemary—as a main dish. Cultivated portobellos stand in for porcini in this dish.

Grilled Portobellos and Onions
❧ Parmesan Crostini ❧ Romaine Salad

Mushrooms, Onions, and Crostini:

8 to 12   portobello mushroom caps

2   large sweet onions, cut into $1/2$-inch-thick slices

$1/3$ cup olive oil (approximately)

1   tablespoon minced fresh rosemary

2   cloves garlic, minced

  Salt

8 to 12   slices ($1/2$ inch thick) rustic bread

$1/2$ cup (2 ounces) grated Parmesan cheese

Salad:

2   tablespoons olive oil

3   tablespoons balsamic vinegar

  Salt

1   medium head romaine, large ribs removed, leaves torn

8   ounces small cherry tomatoes

Two teaspoons crumbled dried rosemary may replace the fresh rosemary.

❧

A liberal grinding of black pepper sharpens the flavors of this meal.

To prepare the mushrooms, onions, and crostini: Prepare a charcoal or gas grill for indirect cooking, firing briquettes or lighting the gas on one side of the grid only.

Place the mushrooms and onions on a large tray. In a glass measuring cup, mix the oil, rosemary, and garlic. Press the garlic with the back of a spoon to extract juice. Drizzle over the mushrooms and onions; rub to coat evenly. Season lightly with salt. Set aside.

Place the onions directly over the heat source. Cook for 2 minutes each side, turning carefully, or until golden. Move the onions to the side away from the heat.

Place the mushrooms, underside facing up, directly over the heat source. Cook for 1 minute each side. Stack over the onions, underside facing up. Lay the bread slices on the tray. Rub both sides with any remaining oil. Place the slices directly over the heat source. Cook for 30 to 40 seconds each side, or just until golden. Remove to the tray and sprinkle evenly with the Parmesan. Set aside.

Cover the grill and cook for 10 to 12 minutes, or until juices start to pool in the mushrooms. Remove the mushrooms and onions to a serving platter. Place the bread slices, cheese side up, on the side of the cooking rack away from the direct heat source. Cover and grill for 5 minutes, or until hot.

To prepare the salad: While the mushrooms are grilling, whisk the oil, vinegar, and a pinch of salt in a large bowl. Add the romaine and tomatoes. Toss.

SERVES 4 TO 6

Wine
Dolcetto d'Alba from Piedmont, with its low tannin and natural fruitiness finishing dry and earthy, works "delicate on delicate" here. This red wine is sometimes referred to as the Beaujolais of Italy.

funghi porcini: freschi e secchi

Supermarkets are increasingly featuring locally grown tomatoes in season, which makes it convenient to buy real tomatoes with your other groceries. Of course, if you grow your own tomatoes, nothing could be finer.

Tomatoes Stuffed with Ditalini Salad

1	pound dried ditalini
	Salt
1	carton (15 ounces) ricotta cheese
1	cup (4 ounces) shredded provolone cheese
½ to ⅔	cup orange juice
¼	cup minced fresh tarragon
1	large clove garlic, minced
	Ground black pepper
4 to 6	medium-large tomatoes (about 8 ounces each)

Bring a large covered saucepan of water to a boil over high heat. Add the ditalini and 1 tablespoon salt. Return to the boil, stirring occasionally, for 8 minutes, or until al dente. Drain and rinse with cold water. Allow to cool.

Meanwhile, in a mixing bowl, combine the ricotta, provolone, ½ cup orange juice, tarragon, garlic, and ¼ teaspoon salt. Beat with a fork. Add the ditalini. Toss to combine. Season with pepper, salt, and more orange juice, to taste.

Core the number of tomatoes needed. Slice downward from the stem end in several places, being careful not to cut all the way through to the bottom, so that the tomato sections can be gently separated to resemble flower petals. Place on serving dishes. Spoon the salad into the center and spilling over the tomato "petals."

SERVES 4 TO 6

Ditalini, which means "little toes," is a short, tube-shaped macaroni. Elbow macaroni may be substituted. For a touch of heat in the salad, add ½ to 1 teaspoon of minced hot chile.

Tuscan Pecorino may replace the provolone.

Fresh flat-leaf parsley may replace the tarragon.

This late-summer dish is a fine choice for a brunch or light dinner. The flavor will actually improve if it sits for up to an hour after baking.

Zucchini-Crust Tomato Basil Tart ↬ Rustic Bread

2 pounds zucchini, shredded

1 bunch scallions, white and light green parts, thinly sliced

¼ cup plus 2 tablespoons plain dry bread crumbs

Salt and ground black pepper

1 egg, beaten

2 cups (8 ounces) shredded Fontina cheese, divided

1 medium-large tomato, quartered, thinly sliced

¼ cup loosely packed slivered fresh basil leaves

Rustic Bread

Place the zucchini and scallions in a cold large sauté pan. Cook over high heat, tossing frequently, until the zucchini shrinks, about 6 minutes. Drain in a colander. Press out excess water with a large spoon. Return the zucchini and scallions to the pan. Off the heat, add ¼ cup bread crumbs and ½ teaspoon each salt and pepper. Allow to cool for 5 minutes, tossing frequently. Add the egg; toss.

Preheat the oven to 400°F. Coat a 9-inch pie pan with no-stick spray. Press the zucchini mixture into the bottom and up the sides, but not over the lip, of the pan. This "crust" is very thick.

Bake for 15 to 18 minutes, until golden. Remove and sprinkle with ½ cup Fontina. Top with the tomato slices, overlapping slightly if needed. Season lightly with salt and pepper. Cover with 2 tablespoons bread crumbs, the basil, and the remaining 1½ cups of Fontina.

Reduce the oven temperature to 350°F. Bake for 30 minutes, or until the cheese is well browned. Allow to sit for at least 10 minutes before cutting.

Serve the bread on the side.

SERVES 4 TO 6

A wok also is large enough to cook the zucchini and scallions. If you use a smaller pan, cook the vegetables in two batches.

↬

This tart may be chilled and thinly sliced, like a vegetable paté, as part of an antipasto buffet.

*Red wine helps to make this sauce as rich as meat gravy.
Another secret is the browning of each vegetable, separately,
in olive oil to caramelize the natural sugars.*

Braised Winter Vegetables
∽ Soft Polenta with Fontina

Vegetables:

1	small butternut squash
2	medium-large onions
1	pound broccoli
12	ounces small brown mushrooms
6	tablespoons olive oil, divided
2	teaspoons minced fresh rosemary
$^1/_2$	cup dry red wine
1	can (14$^1/_2$ ounces) vegetable broth
	Salt
1	teaspoon ground black pepper
2	tablespoons flour whisked with 2 tablespoons cold water

One teaspoon of crumbled dried rosemary may replace the fresh rosemary.

∽

One can (14$^1/_2$ ounces) chicken broth or 2 cups water may replace the vegetable broth.

Soft Polenta:

$^3/_4$	cup cornmeal
3	cups milk
$^1/_8$	teaspoon salt
$^3/_4$	cup (3 ounces) shredded Fontina cheese

To prepare the vegetables: Pierce the squash in several spots with a sharp knife. Microwave on high for 5 to 7 minutes, turning occasionally, or until it yields slightly when pressed. Remove and set aside to cool. Meanwhile, cut each onion in half through the middle. Cut each onion half into 8 wedges. Peel the broccoli stalk. Cut the stalk into $^3/_4$-inch chunks. Separate the florets into similar-sized chunks. Cut the mushrooms, if needed, in halves or quarters so they are all about the size of the broccoli chunks. Peel the squash. Cut in half lengthwise. Scoop out and discard the seeds and pulp. Cut the flesh into 1-inch chunks.

Warm 2 tablespoons oil in a large sauté pan over medium-high heat. Add the broccoli and stir. Cover and cook for about 3 minutes, or until bright green. Remove the broccoli; spread it out on a tray.

Add 2 tablespoons oil to the pan. Reduce the heat to medium. Add the onion wedges and the rosemary. Stir. Cover and cook, stirring occasionally, for about 5 minutes, or until well browned. Remove to the platter, apart from the broccoli.

Add 2 tablespoons oil to the pan. Add the mushrooms and stir. Cover and cook for about 5 minutes, or until browned. Add the wine. Simmer for about 5 minutes, or until syrupy.

Add the squash, onions, broth, ½ teaspoon salt, and the pepper. Reduce the heat to medium-low. Cover and cook, stirring occasionally, for 10 minutes.

Add the broccoli. Stir. Cover and cook for 10 to 12 minutes, or until the broccoli is tender. Ladle about ½ cup of the cooking liquid into the flour mixture. Whisk. Add the flour mixture to the pan, stirring constantly, until the sauce is thickened. Taste and adjust the seasoning.

To prepare the polenta: Whisk the cornmeal, milk, and salt in a saucepan. Cook, whisking constantly, over medium-high heat, for about 5 minutes, or until thickened. Reduce the heat to low. Simmer, stirring occasionally, for about 2 minutes. Remove from the heat. Stir in the Fontina until melted.

Spoon the polenta onto plates. Top with the vegetables and sauce.

SERVES 4 TO 6

Wine
Cabernet Franc from California is one of the five Bordeaux blending grapes. It has luscious dark fruit and a "down home" herbaceous appeal. This red wine is great with vegetables.

vino rosso

Returning from a festival in Volterra one night, my husband and I liberated some corn from a field. We got our comeuppance, however. We had picked field corn—not the sweet corn of our summer memories.

Vegetable-Ricotta Gratin ∽ Corn on the Cob with Garlic Butter ∽ Rustic Bread

Vegetables:

1	tablespoon olive oil
2	red or yellow bell peppers, quartered and sliced
1	large sweet onion, quartered and sliced
2	teaspoons crushed fennel seeds
½	teaspoon salt
2	tablespoons cornmeal
1	carton (15 ounces) ricotta cheese
2	eggs
½	cup (2 ounces) packed grated Parmesan cheese

Corn:

3	tablespoons butter
2	cloves garlic, minced
6	ears of corn, husked and cut in half crosswise
	Salt and ground black pepper
	Rustic Bread

To prepare the vegetables: Preheat the oven to 350°F. Coat a 12 x 8-inch baking dish with no-stick spray.

Heat the oil in a large sauté pan. Add the peppers, onion, fennel, and salt. Cook over medium-high heat, tossing occasionally, for 8 to 10 minutes, or until the onion is softened. Sprinkle with the cornmeal. Spoon into the prepared baking dish; set aside.

In a bowl, beat the ricotta, eggs, and Parmesan with a fork until smooth. Spread over the vegetables. Set aside.

To prepare the corn: Place the butter in a 13 x 9-inch glass or ceramic baking dish. Bake for 2 to 3 minutes to melt the butter. Remove the pan from the oven. Add the garlic and the corn. Turn the ears to coat with the butter mixture. Cover the pan tightly with aluminum foil.

To bake the vegetables and corn: Bake for 25 to 30 minutes, turning the corn once, until the vegetable topping is set and the corn is hot. Season the corn with salt and pepper to taste.

Serve the bread on the side.

SERVES 4 TO 6

cipolle

Scatter some minced fresh flat-leaf parsley, if you have it, over the plate.

Cooking and Keeping Dried Beans

Beans, much like Italians, seem capable of making the most of any situation. Beans take to lusty seasonings such as garlic, sage, and rosemary, and they fit right in with tomatoes, tuna, pork, pasta, polenta, bread, and other robust foods.

Whether it's a winter supper of steaming beans in tomato-garlic sauce or a refreshing summer salad of cooked beans lightly dressed in olive oil and lemon juice, I can make a meal of beans and leave the table happy.

Canned Beans

The recipes in this book call for canned beans, which are inexpensive, convenient, and fully cooked. To use them, drain the beans, rinse them with cold tap water, and add them to the dish as the recipe indicates.

You might like to try different brands to determine which have the texture you like best. I like a well-cooked bean that holds its shape. Some brands may be mushy, so it pays to do some comparisons.

Great Northern beans and chick-peas (also called garbanzo beans) are packed in cans weighing 15 to 16 ounces, which yield about 1½ cups of drained beans. Cannellini are most often packed in 19-ounce cans, which yield 2 cups of drained beans.

Dried Beans

For even greater economy and to better control the texture of the beans, you may cook dried beans and freeze them in recipe-ready portions. One pound of dried beans (about 2½ cups) will yield 6 to 7 cups of cooked beans.

Cooking dried beans is literally as simple as boiling water. On an at-home day, the beans cook themselves while you are otherwise engaged. Some tips for best results:

- Before cooking, rinse the beans well in a large colander set under cold running water. Pick out and discard any pebbles or broken beans.

- Cook the beans in water that's fit to drink. If your tap water tastes bad, cook beans with filtered or bottled water. For really delicious beans, use chicken or vegetable broth as the cooking medium. Adding aromatic vegetables and herbs will result in more complex flavor.

- Be flexible about cooking time. Depending upon how long the dried beans have been stored, they may take from 1 to 3 hours to become tender. After 1 hour of cooking, start testing the beans by tasting one. To get the freshest dried beans, shop at a food store where the turnover for such shelf-stable products is fast.

- Beans may be cooked without soaking beforehand. They will take only about 20 minutes longer to cook than beans that have been soaked overnight.

- Conventional wisdom dictates that if beans are salted during cooking, they won't soften.

After reading Mark Bittman's opinion to the contrary in *How to Cook Everything*, however, I decided to try it for myself. I divided a 1-pound bag of Great Northern beans and cooked half in plain water, half in salted water. Both cooked to the same consistency, but I preferred the salted batch. The beans had more flavor.

Great Northern Beans

MAKES 7 CUPS

1	pound dried Great Northern Beans, sorted and washed
12	cups water or broth (approximately)
1	carrot, cut into 2-inch chunks
2	ribs celery heart, cut into 2-inch chunks
1	small onion, cut in half
1	dried bay leaf
	Several fresh flat-leaf parsley stems
1 to 2	teaspoons salt

Place the beans in a large pot with water or broth to cover by 2 inches. Add the carrot, celery, onion, bay leaf, and parsley. Cover and bring almost to a boil. Remove the cover and reduce the heat so the liquid simmers. Skim any foam and discard.

Partially cover the pot. Adjust the heat so the liquid simmers but does not boil. Cook for 1 hour. Add 1 teaspoon salt. Add slightly more liquid if needed to keep beans covered. Stir gently. Cook for 1 to 2 more hours, adding more liquid as needed, or until beans are tender but still hold their shape. Taste. Add up to 1 teaspoon salt.

Remove from the heat to cool. Remove and discard the carrot, celery, onion, bay leaf, and parsley stems. Place the beans in a covered container and refrigerate for up to 3 weeks. Or freeze the beans with the cooking liquid in 2-cup batches in freezer-proof containers for up to 3 months.

For a subtle spice note, add 4 whole cloves to the beans with the vegetables and herbs. Remove and discard after cooking.

Dried cannellini beans or dried chick-peas (garbanzo beans) may replace the Great Northern beans.

Other Italians tease Tuscans as mangiafagioli, *"bean eaters," because they are so crazy for legumes. This hearty Tuscan-inspired salad is simple to put together from pantry staples and delicatessen ingredients.*

Cannellini Bean Salad ~ Rustic Bread

Roasted bell pepper from the delicatessen may be used. Or, roast and peel one red bell pepper following the directions on page 235.

If you grow summer savory, known as the "bean herb," use it instead of the parsley.

Two sliced hard-cooked eggs or 1 can (6 ounces) of drained and flaked water-packed tuna may be added to the salad.

$^1/_2$ cup olive oil

$^1/_4$ cup red or white wine vinegar

$^1/_4$ teaspoon salt

  3   cans (19 ounces each) cannellini beans, rinsed and drained

  1   cup roasted red bell pepper, cut into slivers

  3   ribs celery heart, sliced

$^1/_2$ small red onion, chopped

  1   tablespoon minced fresh flat-leaf parsley

$^1/_4$ teaspoon dried oregano

     Lettuce leaves

     Peperoncini

     Rustic Bread

In a large bowl, whisk the oil, vinegar, and salt. Add the beans, pepper, celery, onion, parsley, and oregano. Taste and adjust the seasoning. Toss gently. Serve on lettuce leaves. Garnish with the peperoncini.

Serve the bread with the salad.

Serves 4 to 6

peperoni

*Lentils, once considered peasant food, have gained
newfound status for their earthy flavor and healthful profile.*

Lentils with Macaroni
↬ Curly Endive and Sun-Dried Tomato Salad

Lentils:

$^1/_4$	cup olive oil
1	small onion, minced
1	small carrot, minced
1	rib celery heart, minced
2	cloves garlic, minced
2	dried bay leaves
$1^1/_4$	cups (8 ounces) green or brown lentils
$^1/_8$	teaspoon **each** salt and ground black pepper
1	can ($14^1/_2$ ounces) vegetable broth
3	cups water, divided
1	cup dried elbow macaroni
3	tablespoons minced fresh flat-leaf parsley, divided

*One can
($14^1/_2$ ounces)
chicken broth
or 2 cups water
may replace the
vegetable broth.*

Salad:

1	tablespoon red or white wine vinegar
$^1/_8$	teaspoon **each** salt and ground black pepper
3	tablespoons olive oil
8	cups (8 ounces) torn curly endive
$^1/_3$	cup minced recipe-ready sun-dried tomatoes

To prepare the lentils: Warm the oil in a Dutch oven over medium-low heat. Add
the onion, carrot, celery, garlic, and bay leaves. Stir. Cover and cook, stirring
occasionally, for 10 minutes, or until golden. Add the lentils, salt, and pepper. Stir.
Add the broth and $2^1/_2$ cups water. Bring to a boil, then reduce the heat to medium-
low. Cover and cook for 20 minutes. Add the macaroni and 2 tablespoons parsley.
Partially cover and cook for about 6 minutes, or until the macaroni is almost
al dente. If the mixture is dry, add just enough of the remaining $^1/_2$ cup water to
moisten. Remove to sit for 5 minutes. Remove and discard the bay leaves. Sprinkle
with parsley.

To prepare the salad: While the lentils cook, whisk the vinegar, salt, and pepper
in a bowl. Add the oil and whisk. Add the endive and tomatoes. Toss.

SERVES 4 TO 6

Ceci, pronounced CHAY-chee, are chick-peas. They are beloved throughout Italy, used in antipasti, soups, stews, and side dishes.

Chick-pea, Pork, and Spinach Sauté
∽ Scallion Rice

Chick-peas:

1	pound pork tenderloin
	Salt and ground black pepper
3	large cloves garlic, minced
¼	cup cornmeal
4	tablespoons olive oil, divided
2	cans (15½ ounces each) chick-peas (garbanzo beans), rinsed and drained
½ to ¾	teaspoon crushed red pepper
1	can (16 ounces) tomato purée
1	bag (10 ounces) baby spinach leaves, stems removed
4 to 6	lemon wedges

Rice:

1	tablespoon butter
¾	cup long-grain rice
½	bunch scallions, white and light green parts, sliced
	Salt
1	can (14½ ounces) chicken broth

spinaci

To prepare the chick-peas: Cut the tenderloin in half lengthwise, then cut each half into 2 lengthwise strips. Flatten each strip and cut into 1-inch chunks. Season with salt and pepper. Toss with ⅓ of the garlic. Sprinkle with the cornmeal. Toss to coat, then shake off excess cornmeal.

Heat 2 tablespoons of oil in a large sauté pan over medium-high heat. Add the pork. Cook for about 6 minutes, turning as needed, until browned on all sides. Remove the pork to a tray in a single layer. Add 2 tablespoons oil and the remaining garlic to the pan. Cook for 30 seconds, or until sizzling. Add the chick-peas, ½ teaspoon red pepper, and ¼ teaspoon salt. Stir. Turn the heat to high and cook for 3 minutes.

Add the tomato purée. Reduce the heat to medium-low. Cover and cook, stirring occasionally, for 10 minutes. Add the pork and any accumulated juices from the tray. Cover and cook, stirring occasionally, for 5 minutes. Add the spinach and stir. Cover and cook, stirring occasionally, for about 5 minutes, or until the spinach wilts.

To prepare the rice: Meanwhile, melt the butter in a saucepan. Add the rice. Cook for about 2 minutes, or until coated with butter. Add the scallions, a pinch of salt, and broth. Bring to a boil. Reduce the heat to a simmer. Cover and cook for 10 minutes. Remove from the heat to sit for 5 minutes, or until all the broth is absorbed.

Serve with the chick-peas. Garnish each serving with a lemon wedge.

SERVES 4 TO 6

I recommend using canned reduced-sodium broth or salt-free Basic Broth (page 38) to cook the rice. If you use regular canned broth, you may want to omit the salt.

This summer classic is a fine company dish. The recipe makes a generous amount and it may be prepared in advance. I serve it as a main dish for a luncheon or as a side dish with grilled meats, poultry, or seafood.

Summer Rice Salad

2	cups medium- or long-grain rice
2	cups water
1	can (14½ ounces) chicken broth
	Salt
1	medium-large sweet or red onion, chopped
5	to 6 tablespoons red or white wine vinegar, divided
⅓ to ½	cup olive oil
3	ribs celery heart, chopped
1½	cups frozen baby peas, rinsed
2	cups (8 ounces) shredded provolone cheese
1	roasted red or yellow bell pepper, chopped
3	tablespoons drained capers
	Ground black pepper

In a large pot, combine the rice, water, broth, and a pinch of salt. Cover and bring to a boil over high heat. Reduce the heat to medium-low so rice simmers. Cook for 15 minutes. Remove from the heat and set aside, covered, for 5 minutes.

Coat a large tray with no-stick spray. With a fork spread the rice on the tray. Stir occasionally to speed cooling.

In a small bowl, combine the onion, 2 tablespoons vinegar, and enough cold water to cover. Cover with plastic wrap and refrigerate.

In a large bowl, whisk ⅓ cup oil, 3 tablespoons vinegar, and 1 teaspoon salt. Add the celery, peas, provolone, roasted pepper, capers, and rice. Toss to mix. Cover with plastic wrap. Refrigerate for at least 1 hour to chill.

To serve, drain and rinse the onions. Add to the salad. Season with black pepper to taste. Toss the salad. Taste and adjust the seasoning. Toss.

SERVES 8 TO 10

Cooking rice in broth adds flavor, but canned broth can be high in sodium. I recommend using canned reduced-sodium broth or salt-free Chicken Broth (page 39). If you use regular canned broth, you may want to reduce the salt.

Roasted bell peppers from the delicatessen may be used. To roast peppers, see page 235.

Drained tuna, cooked shrimp, or sliced cooked Italian sausage may be added to make a more substantial salad.

Swiss Gruyère, Parmesan, or Tuscan Pecorino cheese may replace the provolone.

Slivered ripe or green olives may replace the capers.

What I Learned About Life from the Risotto King of Milan

The 1980s, an era that made princes of junk-bond traders, also made media stars of many chefs who, a few years earlier, might have toiled in obscurity. Celebrity cooks vied to outdo each other. Exotic ingredients, laborious preparations, and fussy plates were the currency of culinary fame.

As a food reporter at a Chicago newspaper at the time, I was dazzled by the show. Yet I found that translating these chefs' recipes for our readers to cook at home was not always an enviable task—nor a successful one. To tell the truth, if I had known then what I know now, I would have advised readers, "Don't try this at home."

I learned this lesson from the risotto king of Milan, and it resonates more with each passing year.

It was 1987 and I was on assignment in Lombardy, researching the foods of the region. In Milan I visited Il Ristorante Gran San Bernardo, which was known to locals simply as Alfredo's. The owner and chef, "risotto king" Alfredo Valli, agreed to show me how to make the fashionable city's trademark *risotto alla Milanese*.

Valli, a compact, vigorous man in his sixth decade, invited me into his kitchen. There he selected a veal shank bone and melted its marrow. To this he added butter and some minced onion. When the onion was sautéed, he poured in raw arborio rice and sprinkled it with saffron threads, stirring until each grain was burnished gold before splashing some white wine into the pan. He let the rice absorb the wine. He added a ladleful of beef broth. The rice simmered briskly. "The risotto must never sleep in the pot," he advised as he vigilantly stirred and added more broth, a ladleful at a time.

Valli was so mindful of his task, one would think he was perfecting a brand-new recipe, not a dish he had mastered decades ago. After 16 minutes of stirring, and several tastes to assess doneness, he removed the pot from the heat. In went more butter—this time, a lump the size of a small fist—followed by a mound of grated *Parmigiano-Reggiano*. "To make a good risotto, you must wet it with butter and dry it with cheese," Valli said, smiling and stirring.

At last he proudly served up a sample in a pasta bowl. It was good, yet it seemed plain after the baroque risottos I had sampled in Italian restaurants back home.

"Do you ever add fresh herbs like parsley or basil?" I asked.

"No," replied Valli.

"How about sun-dried tomatoes?" I ventured.

"No," replied Valli, looking slightly puzzled.

"What about shrimp or sausage?"

"No," Valli responded with as much grace as he could muster. "This is risotto alla Milanese. Butter, onion, rice, saffron, wine, broth, and Parmigiano-Reggiano. That is all."

I looked into Valli's bright eyes and saw amusement. He was a direct man who came from a farm family. He had learned to cook in his grandmother's kitchen. Now I felt a bit foolish.

I tasted the risotto again. This time I felt the distinct round grains of tender rice on my tongue. The velvet sauce of melted Parmesan, butter, and broth was rescued from complete decadence by the slight astringency of the saffron and the acidity of the wine. It was superb. In fact, it could not be improved upon.

As time passed, I began to understand that risotto alla Milanese was wonderful *because* of its simplicity. I had expected Valli to paint earrings on the

Mona Lisa, but he knew better. It taught me that a good cook knows when to stop—when to add fewer ingredients, not more.

I started to simplify other recipes, paring them down to the smallest number of ingredients necessary to create the best flavor. I've tried to apply this principle to my life, as well, eliminating the excess to better savor the really important things.

Risotto alla Milanese

SERVES 6 TO 8 AS A SIDE DISH

4$\frac{1}{2}$	cups broth (see note)
2	tablespoons butter, divided
1	small onion, finely chopped
1$\frac{1}{4}$	cups superfino rice
$\frac{1}{4}$	teaspoon saffron threads, crumbled
$\frac{1}{4}$	teaspoon salt
$\frac{1}{3}$	cup dry white wine
1	cup (4 ounces) grated Parmesan cheese

I recommend salt-free Basic Broth or Chicken Broth (pages 38 and 39). If you use reduced-sodium canned broth, you may want to reduce the salt.

Choose arborio, carnaroli, or other rice labeled "superfino." A Dutch oven made from enameled cast iron, anodized aluminum, or stainless steel-clad aluminum will allow the rice to cook evenly.

Heat the broth to a boil in a saucepan. Reduce the heat to low.

In a Dutch oven, melt 1 tablespoon butter over medium-low heat. Add the onion and cook, stirring occasionally, for 10 minutes, or until soft. Add the rice, saffron, and salt. Stir to color the rice evenly. Add the wine. Increase the heat to medium-high. Cook for about 4 minutes, or until the wine is absorbed.

Reduce the heat to medium-low. Add $\frac{1}{2}$ cup of the broth. Start timing the cooking.

Simmer the rice, stirring constantly, until the broth is absorbed. Continue adding broth, $\frac{1}{2}$ cup at a time, and stirring frequently. After 18 minutes of cooking, start testing the rice. The rice should be tender but still hold its shape. When it is cooked, remove from the heat. (All of the broth mixture may not be needed.) Add the remaining 1 tablespoon of butter. Stir. Add the cheese and stir.

The first asparagus of the season is showcased in markets in Italy. It is often served as a separate course garnished with olive oil and lemon, or sprinkled with Parmesan cheese.

Risotto with Asparagus and Shrimp

1	can (14½ ounces) chicken broth
2½	cups water
2½	tablespoons butter, divided
1	small onion, minced
1¼	cups superfino rice
½	teaspoon salt, divided
½	cup dry white wine
1	pound thin asparagus, trimmed and cut into 2-inch pieces
1	pound medium shrimp, peeled
½	cup (2 ounces) grated Parmesan cheese

Wine
Sauvignon Blanc from Santa Barbara, California, or New Zealand, has a mineral and herbaceous character— carried by a citrusy palate and grassiness— that works well with seafood, asparagus, and the richness of risotto.

Heat the broth and water in a saucepan. Reduce the heat to low.

In a Dutch oven set over medium heat, melt 1 tablespoon butter. Add the onion. Cook, stirring, for 3 minutes, or until golden. Add the rice and ¼ teaspoon salt. Cook for 2 minutes, stirring, until coated with butter. Add the wine. Increase the heat to medium-high. Cook for 5 minutes, or until the wine is absorbed. Reduce the heat to medium-low. Add ½ cup of the broth mixture. Start timing the cooking. Cook, stirring frequently, until the broth is absorbed. Continue adding the broth, ½ cup at a time, and stirring frequently.

Meanwhile, in a large sauté pan, warm 1 tablespoon butter and 2 tablespoons of the broth. Add the asparagus and the remaining ¼ teaspoon salt. Cover and cook, tossing occasionally, for about 4 minutes, or until bright green. Add the shrimp. Cook, stirring frequently, for about 2 minutes, or until the shrimp are opaque. Remove from the heat.

After 18 minutes of cooking, start testing the rice. The rice should be tender but hold its shape. When it is cooked, remove from the heat. (All of the broth mixture may not be needed.) Add the shrimp, asparagus, and any pan juices. Add the Parmesan and the remaining ½ tablespoon butter. Stir.

SERVES 4 TO 6

This rice dish needs far less hands-on attention than risotto. The liquid is added all at once so there's no need for continual stirring. It may be prepared with long-grain or medium-grain rice.

Rice with Pea Pods and Mussels

$1/4$	cup olive oil
3	large cloves garlic, minced
$1^1/2$	cups long-grain rice
	Salt
$1/2$	cup dry white wine
1	can ($14^1/2$ ounces) diced tomatoes, drained
2	cans ($14^1/2$ ounces each) chicken broth
$1/4$	teaspoon crushed red pepper
1	pound mussels, scrubbed
8	ounces pea pods, trimmed

I recommend using canned reduced-sodium broth or salt-free Chicken Broth (page 39). If you use regular canned broth, you may want to omit the salt.

Warm the oil and garlic over medium heat in a large sauté pan for about 2 minutes, or until the garlic is golden. Add the rice and $1/4$ teaspoon salt. Increase the heat to high. Stir for about 2 minutes to coat with oil.

Add the wine. Reduce the heat to medium-high. Cook for about 5 minutes, or until the wine evaporates.

Add the tomatoes, broth, and red pepper. Bring to a boil. Reduce the heat until mixture simmers gently. Cover and cook for 8 minutes.

Stir in the mussels. Increase the heat to medium-high. Cover and cook for 4 minutes.

Stir in the pea pods. Cover and cook for about 3 minutes, or until the mussels open and the rice is tender. Remove from the heat to sit for about 3 minutes. Discard any mussels that do not open. Taste and adjust the seasoning.

SERVES 4 TO 6

From pantry ingredients, this satisfying winter meal comes together in minutes.

Polenta-Pesto Casserole
∽ Braised Green Beans and Leeks

Polenta:

1¼	cups cornmeal
4	cups milk
¼	teaspoon salt
⅓	cup basil pesto
1	can (14½ ounces) diced tomatoes, drained
1	cup (4 ounces) shredded provolone cheese

Beans:

1	small leek
12	ounces green beans, snapped into 2-inch pieces
¼	cup water
1	tablespoon olive oil
⅛	teaspoon salt
4 to 6	lemon wedges
	Ground black pepper

To prepare the polenta: Preheat the oven to 375°F. Coat a 13 x 9-inch baking dish with no-stick spray.

Whisk the cornmeal, milk, and salt in a saucepan. Cook, whisking constantly, over medium-high heat, for about 5 minutes, or until thickened. Spread in the prepared dish. Spoon on the pesto, spreading and pressing it into the polenta with the back of a spoon. Sprinkle with the tomatoes, then the provolone.

Bake for about 25 minutes, or until the cheese is browned. Remove and allow to sit for 5 minutes.

To prepare the beans: While the polenta is baking, trim the leek and slice it in quarters lengthwise. Cut the quarters into 1½-inch lengths. Cut the white and light green parts into thin strips.

In a medium sauté pan, combine the leek, beans, water, oil, and salt. Cover and cook over medium heat for about 6 minutes, or until the beans are tender.

Remove the lid and cook over high heat for 1 to 2 minutes, if needed, to cook off any remaining liquid. Serve with the lemon wedges and pepper.

SERVES 4 TO 6

Fresh portobellos are meaty and full-flavored,
making them an ideal partner for the hearty barley.

Barley with Mushrooms Risotto-Style
∽ Red Cabbage and Clementine Salad

Barley:

1	bunch scallions, all parts, sliced
8	ounces portobello mushroom caps
2½	tablespoons butter, divided
1	box (11 ounces) quick-cooking barley
2	cans (14½ ounces each) chicken broth or vegetable broth
	Salt
¼	teaspoon ground black pepper
½	cup (2 ounces) grated Parmesan cheese

Salad:

1½	tablespoons red or white wine vinegar
⅛	teaspoon **each** salt and ground black pepper
3	tablespoons olive oil
½	small head red cabbage, cored
3	clementines, separated into sections

To prepare the barley: Mince 2 tablespoons of the scallion greens; set aside. Cut the mushrooms into ¼-inch-wide slices, then crosswise into ¼-inch chunks.

Warm 2 tablespoons butter in a Dutch oven over medium heat. Add the mushrooms. Stir and cover. Cook, stirring occasionally, for about 3 minutes, or until the mushrooms give off liquid. Uncover and cook for about 4 minutes, or until browned.

Add the barley and scallions. Stir to combine. Add the broth, a pinch of salt, and the pepper. Bring almost to a boil. Cover and reduce the heat so the mixture just simmers. Cook for 10 to 12 minutes, or until almost all of the liquid is absorbed. Remove from the heat. Stir in almost all of the Parmesan and the remaining ½ tablespoon of butter. Taste and adjust the seasoning. Sprinkle each serving with scallion greens and some of the remaining Parmesan.

To prepare the salad: In a large bowl, whisk the vinegar, salt, and pepper. Add the oil and whisk. Slice the cabbage as thinly as possible to make 4 cups. Add the cabbage and the clementines to the bowl. Toss.

SERVES 4 TO 6

I recommend using canned reduced-sodium broth or salt-free Basic Broth (page 38). If you use regular canned broth, you may want to omit the salt.

∽

Regular pearl barley may replace the quick-cooking barley. Sauté the mushrooms in 1 tablespoon of butter. Remove and set aside. Sauté 1½ cups pearl barley in 1 tablespoon of butter. Add the broth. Cover and simmer for 30 minutes. Add the reserved mushrooms and the scallions. Cover and cook for about 15 minutes, or until tender.

Fish and Shellfish Meals

Recipes

Stories and Basics

The elegant Italian boot steps thigh-high into the salt water of the Mediterranean, Ligurian, Tyrrhenian, and Adriatic Seas. Even a freshwater northern coast is created by the mighty Po River and the grand mountain lakes of Garda, Maggiore, Como, and Iseo.

Whether it's trout in Turin, swordfish in Palermo, or rock lobster on the island of Elba, Italian cooks exhibit a deft touch with fish and shellfish. Fishing is popular sport throughout the country. Even in cosmopolitan Florence, fishermen stake out spots on the banks of the Arno River, in the shadow of the Ponte Vecchio, to cast their lines.

The freshly caught fish may be grilled, baked, pan-fried, poached, or braised. Olive oil, lemon, garlic, and fresh herbs are common seasonings, and preparations are generally simple.

Two dishes, however, deserve special notice because of their complexity. *Fritto misto di mare*, "mixed seafood fry," and *zuppa di pesce*, "fish soup," appear on tables all around Italy.

Fritto misto di mare, with only a splash of sunny lemon, is best sampled on Italian soil at a good *ristorante sul mare*. When it is executed well, a mixed seafood fry is as light as the finest tempura. Anything that swims is fair game: various white-fleshed fish cut into chunks, peeled shrimp, shelled mussels or clams, tender rings of calamari. The seafood pieces are encased in a light batter— often flour, olive oil, water, and beaten egg white—then flash-fried in canola or sunflower oil. The intense heat seals the batter and captures the sweetness of the seafood as effectively as Vesuvian lava trapped the artifacts of Pompeii.

Zuppa di pesce, a generic name for seafood soup, surfaces in different regions as *brodetto*, *ciuppin*, and *cacciucco*. As Marcella Hazan explains in her *Essentials of Classic Italian Cooking*: ". . . there are not enough names around to attach to every variation of the dish. Each town makes it in its distinctive style, of which each family in the town usually has its own version." In truth, this dish— brimming with succulent morsels—is more a stew than a soup. ໆ

Sea Bass on Fried Polenta with Mushroom Sauce ∽ Capered Peppers

Bass and Polenta:

³/₄	cup cornmeal
3	cups chicken broth, divided
	Salt
3	tablespoons butter, divided
1	small onion, minced
12	ounces brown button mushrooms, sliced
1	teaspoon minced fresh rosemary
2 to 2¹/₂	pounds sea bass fillets
1	tablespoon flour whisked with 1 tablespoon cold water

Peppers:

2	tablespoons olive oil
3	red or orange bell peppers, cut into thick slices
1	small hot chile, minced
¹/₄	teaspoon salt
1	tablespoon drained capers

To prepare the bass and polenta: Turn a 9-inch cake pan upside down. Coat the bottom with no-stick spray.

Whisk the cornmeal, 2 cups of broth, and salt to taste in a saucepan. Cook, whisking constantly, over medium heat for about 3 minutes, or until thick. Spread on the prepared pan. Set in the refrigerator for at least 15 minutes, or as long as several hours.

Meanwhile, warm 2 tablespoons butter in a large sauté pan over medium-low heat. Add the onion. Cook for 2 minutes, or until golden. Add the mushrooms, rosemary, and ¹/₄ to ¹/₂ teaspoon salt. Stir. Increase the heat to medium-high. Cover and cook for 2 to 3 minutes, or until the mushrooms start to give off liquid.

Remove the cover. Cook, stirring, for 1 to 2 minutes, or until golden. Add the remaining 1 cup broth and bring to a boil. Add the bass fillets. Spoon some of the mushrooms and liquid over the fish. Reduce the heat so the broth simmers but does not boil.

Cover and cook for about 10 minutes, or until the bass is opaque in the center. Remove the fillets to a platter. Cover loosely with aluminum foil. Add the flour mixture to the pan and cook, whisking constantly, until the sauce thickens. Keep the sauce warm over low heat.

While the bass is cooking, warm the remaining 1 tablespoon butter in a medium frying pan over high heat. Run a butter knife between the polenta and the pan bottom to loosen. Slide the polenta into the frying pan. Cook for about 3 minutes, or until browned on the bottom.

Cut the polenta into 6 wedges. One at a time, flip the wedges. Cook for 2 minutes, or until heated through. Place the polenta on dinner plates. Top with the reserved fillets. Spoon on the mushroom sauce.

To prepare the peppers: Wipe the polenta pan with a paper towel. Add the oil and warm over high heat. Add the bell peppers, chile, and salt. Stir and cover. Cook, stirring occasionally, for 5 minutes, or until peppers are tender but still crisp. Add the capers and stir. Spoon onto the side of each plate.

Serves 4 to 6

peperoncini

Chef Paul Bartolotta of Spiaggia restaurant in Chicago taught me how to prepare red snapper in acqua pazza, *"crazy water," so named because of the hot pepper in the broth. This simple meal is based on his fine recipe.*

Red Snapper and Spinach in Spicy Tomato Broth

2	large cloves garlic
8	tablespoons olive oil, divided
1/2	teaspoon crushed red pepper
1	can (14 1/2 ounces) diced tomatoes, with juice
1	cup chicken broth
	Salt
2 to 2 1/2	pounds red snapper fillets
1	bag (10 ounces) baby spinach leaves, stems removed
8 to 12	slices thick-cut rustic bread

Wine
Cirò from Calabria. The gaglioppo grape produces a red wine that marries well with the assertive flavor and acidity of this seafood meal.

Cut 1 garlic clove in half; set aside. Mince the other clove.

In a large sauté pan, cook 4 tablespoons oil, the minced garlic, and red pepper over low heat for 3 minutes, or until the garlic is soft. Add the tomatoes. Increase the heat to medium-high. Cook, stirring, for 5 minutes, or until the tomatoes soften.

Add the broth and 1/4 teaspoon salt. Stir. Bring to just under a boil. Add the red snapper. Spoon the broth mixture over the fillets. Cover partially and lower the heat until the liquid simmers but does not boil. Cook for about 8 minutes, or until the fillets are opaque in the center. Remove the fillets to pasta bowls. Add the spinach to the pan. Cover and increase the heat to high. Stir. Cook for about 3 minutes, or until the spinach is wilted. Taste and adjust the seasoning. Spoon the tomato-spinach mixture around the fillets. Drizzle with 2 tablespoons oil.

Place the bread on a baking sheet in a single layer. Brush or spray the tops with 2 tablespoons oil. Broil 4 inches from the heat source for about 2 minutes, or until golden. Rub with the cut sides of the remaining garlic clove. Cut the slices in half diagonally. Serve with the snapper.

Serves 4 to 6

Tilapia, also known as St. Peter's fish, is a mild, sweet, and versatile white-fleshed fish. It is increasingly available in supermarkets because it is now farm-raised.

Tilapia with Onions, Peppers, and Olives ∽ Mashed Parslied Potatoes

Tilapia:

4	tablespoons olive oil, divided
1	large red onion, halved and sliced
2	large red bell peppers, halved and sliced
2	teaspoons dried thyme
1/2	cup chicken broth
3/4	teaspoon **each** salt and ground black pepper
2 to 2 1/2	pounds tilapia fillets
1/2	cup ripe olives

Potatoes:

2 to 2 1/2	pounds red- or white-skinned potatoes, peeled
1/2	teaspoon salt
1	cup milk
1/4	cup coarsely chopped fresh flat-leaf parsley

To prepare the tilapia: Preheat the oven to 375°F. Coat a 13 x 9-inch baking dish with no-stick spray; set aside.

Warm 2 tablespoons oil in a large sauté pan over medium-low heat. Add the onion, bell peppers, and thyme. Stir. Cover and cook, stirring occasionally, for 10 minutes, or until golden. Add the broth, salt, and pepper. Bring to a boil.

Meanwhile, arrange the tilapia, slightly overlapping, in the prepared baking dish. Cover with the vegetable mixture. Sprinkle with the olives. Drizzle lightly with 2 tablespoons oil. Bake for 20 minutes, or until the fillets are opaque in the center.

To prepare the potatoes: While the tilapia bakes, place the potatoes and salt in a saucepan. Add cold water to cover. Cover and bring to a boil over high heat. Reduce the heat slightly and leave the cover ajar. Cook for 20 minutes, or until tender. In a glass measuring cup, combine the milk and parsley. Heat in a microwave oven for 2 minutes, or until hot. Drain the potatoes and return to the pan. Mash with a potato masher. Add the milk mixture. Whip with the masher. Cover to keep warm.

SERVES 4 TO 6

Baccalà, salted dried cod, is often served with soft polenta in the Veneto region. In this dish the flavors unite, as fresh cod is breaded with cornmeal and fried until crisp.

Polenta-Crusted Cod
↪ Green Beans in Chunky Tomato Sauce

Cod:

2 to 2½	pounds cod fillets
2	cups milk
1	cup flour
2	cups cornmeal
2	eggs
¼	cup water
1½	teaspoons salt
½	teaspoon ground red pepper
	Vegetable oil for frying
4 to 6	lemon wedges

Beans:

3	tablespoons olive oil
1 to 1½	pounds green beans, trimmed
1	large clove garlic, minced
1	teaspoon dried oregano
½	teaspoon salt
1	can (14½ ounces) diced tomatoes, drained

Tilapia, grouper, catfish, or any other mild white-fleshed fish fillets may replace the cod.

To prepare the cod: Cut the cod into equal serving-size pieces. Place in a shallow pan with the milk. Add a bit more milk, if needed, to cover. Cover with plastic wrap and refrigerate for 30 minutes.

Meanwhile, lay 3 large pieces of waxed paper on a work surface near the stove top. Spread the flour on 1 sheet, the cornmeal on the other. In a shallow pan, beat the eggs, water, salt, and pepper. Set between the flour and the cornmeal. Line a large tray with paper towels. Set aside.

Drain the fillets. One at a time, dip each piece in the flour, the egg mixture, and the cornmeal to coat all sides, shaking off excess. Use one hand for wet dipping and one hand for dry dipping so your hands don't become breaded, too. Lay the coated fillets on the empty sheet of waxed paper. Set aside.

To prepare the beans: Warm the oil in a large sauté pan over medium-high heat. Add the beans, garlic, oregano, and salt. Stir. Cover and cook for 3 minutes. Reduce the heat to medium. Add the tomatoes and stir. Cover and cook for about 4 minutes, or until the beans are tender.

To cook the cod: Heat ¼ cup oil in a large skillet until very hot. Add enough fillets to fill the pan. Cook over high heat for 2 minutes on each side, or until the cod is golden outside and opaque in the center. Carefully remove to the paper towel–lined tray. Pour off and discard the oil. Wipe the pan clean with paper towels. Add ¼ cup oil and repeat frying with remaining fillets. Serve with the lemon wedges.

SERVES 4 TO 6

Oven-Baked Polenta-Crusted Cod: Coat a large broiler pan with no-stick spray. Arrange the cornmeal-coated fillets on the pan. Coat both sides of the fillets with olive oil from a mister or olive oil dabbed on with a pastry brush. Bake in a pre-heated 450°F oven for 10 minutes, or until the fish is crisp outside and opaque in the center.

fagiolini

Buying and Cooking Fresh Fish

It's ironic that cooking fish intimidates so many confident cooks. Filleted fish are versatile, require scant preparation, and cook quickly. Also, there's virtually no waste. There are issues to consider with fish, but cooking is the least of them. Knowing which fish to buy, when to buy it, and how to store it can eliminate 99.9 percent of fish phobia.

Fillets in a fish case often look pretty much alike and this can cause confusion. Most of us have no frame of reference for separating tilapia from turbot. Try looking at it this way: When you shop the meat case, you immediately register the differences among beef, pork, and chicken. Fish types fall into three basic categories that can be likened to beef, pork, and chicken.

"Beef" Fish: Shark, swordfish, tuna, mahi-mahi, and halibut have full flavor and firm texture, much like a fine beefsteak. In fact, these fish are usually cut into steaks, which are wonderful grilled over charcoal or pan-seared in a skillet.

"Pork" Fish: Salmon, mackerel, bluefish, and others have distinctive flavors that can handle more assertive seasonings, but their texture is softer than that of the beef fish. Salmon, in particular, is widely available in a good state of freshness, and its versatility—grilled, baked, poached—is appealing.

"Chicken" Fish: Catfish, grouper, tilapia, red snapper, sea bass, flounder, haddock, cod, and many other white-fleshed fish offer mild sweet flavor and delicate flaky texture. The moist-heat methods of poaching and braising work best for these fish, although some can be fried or grilled successfully.

Shop Early, Cook Quickly

Informed by the beef-pork-chicken analogy, you shop for fish on the day the shipment arrives at the supermarket, often a Wednesday or Thursday, well in advance of the weekend shoppers. At the fish counter, you detect not a whiff of "fish" aroma. The fillets are displayed on ice in a case, not packaged in tight shrink wrap.

Recipe in hand, you step closer to examine what's available for Pan-Seared Tuna on Greens with Warm Balsamic-Currant Sauce (page 130). Bad news: The tuna steaks in the case look slightly flabby and sunken. Their flesh is starting to pull apart from itself; they look almost tattered.

But there's good news here, too. The halibut steaks are shiny and their flesh looks solid yet resilient. Confident in the knowledge that both tuna and halibut are in the "beef" fish category, you choose the halibut.

You get it home fast and store it in the coldest part of the refrigerator before cooking it that very evening. You know, after all, that fish is high in protein and moisture and thus can spoil quickly.

At dinnertime, you rinse the halibut steaks under cold water and pat them dry. That's the extent of your preparation. You season the steaks with salt and sear them in olive oil in a hot skillet. It takes about ten minutes to cook them just to the point where the flesh in the center of the steak is opaque.

The secret to perfect fish isn't in the cooking. It's in the choosing and the handling. Do these carefully, and the cooking is simple.

Tarragon and asparagus—early arrivals in the garden—make this meal a salute to la primavera, *"springtime." Serve with steamed new potatoes.*

Salmon in Wine Sauce with Tarragon ⌒ Asparagus Parmesan

Salmon:

2 to 2½	pounds salmon fillets
4	tablespoons fresh tarragon leaves, divided
	Salt and ground black pepper
2	tablespoons butter
1	cup dry white wine

Asparagus:

1	tablespoon butter
1 to 1½	pounds thin asparagus, trimmed
1	tablespoon water
	Salt
½	cup (2 ounces) grated Parmesan cheese

The Zuccotto (page 220) is a charming dessert if you are serving this meal to company.

To prepare the salmon: Preheat the oven to 400°F. Coat a 13 x 9-inch baking dish with no-stick spray.

Season the salmon evenly with 3 tablespoons of tarragon. Sprinkle with salt and pepper. Place in the baking dish. Dot with butter. Pour the wine into the dish, being careful not to pour it directly on the salmon. Cover with aluminum foil.

Bake for 25 to 30 minutes, or until the salmon is opaque in the center. Remove the fillets to a platter. Pour the pan juices through a fine sieve into a saucepan. Boil for about 5 minutes, or until reduced by at least half. Season with ⅛ teaspoon salt. Pour over the fillets. Sprinkle with the remaining tarragon.

To prepare the asparagus: While the salmon is baking, place the butter in a 13 x 9-inch baking dish. Place in the 400°F preheated oven for 2 minutes, or until the butter melts. Add the asparagus and water. Season with salt. Cover tightly with aluminum foil. Bake for 15 minutes, or until the asparagus is tender when pierced with a knife.

Remove the foil and discard. Sprinkle with the Parmesan. Return to the oven for about 5 minutes, or until the cheese melts.

SERVES 4 TO 6

*A surprisingly sophisticated dish comes together
from a mere handful of ingredients.*

Orange-Glazed Roasted Salmon and Fennel ∽ Spinach Linguine

Salmon:

2 to 3	navel oranges
2	tablespoons olive oil
1½	teaspoons salt
2	large bulbs fennel
1	large salmon fillet (2 to 2½ pounds)

Linguine:

6	ounces fresh spinach linguine
2	teaspoons salt

To prepare the salmon: Preheat the oven to 400°F. Coat a 16 x 10-inch baking pan with no-stick spray.

Grate 1 tablespoon orange zest. Squeeze the oranges to get ½ cup juice. In a small bowl whisk the zest, juice, oil, and salt.

Trim the fennel. Mince about 2 tablespoons of the feathery leaves; set aside. (The remaining leaves may be reserved for salads or other recipes.) Cut the bulbs lengthwise in quarters. Cut out and discard the cores. Cut the fennel into thick slices.

Place the fennel in the baking pan. Drizzle with half of the juice mixture. Toss to coat. Place in the oven for about 20 minutes, stirring occasionally, or until lightly browned.

Remove the pan from the oven. Clear a space in the center and lay the salmon diagonally in the pan, skin side down. Drizzle with the remaining juice mixture. Spread to coat the salmon. Place in the oven and roast for about 15 minutes, or until the salmon is opaque in the center.

To prepare the linguine: While the fennel and salmon are baking, set a covered large pot of water over high heat. When the water boils, add the linguine and salt. Stir. Cover and return to a boil. Uncover and boil, stirring occasionally, for about 2 minutes, or until tender.

Reserve ½ cup of the cooking water. Drain the linguine and return to the pot. Drizzle with just enough of the water to moisten; toss. Place the linguine on dinner plates. Top with the salmon, fennel, and pan juices.

SERVES 4 TO 6

finocchio

Wine
*Oregon **Pinot Noir**, with cherry-black pepper notes and minerally delicacy, goes wonderfully with salmon and orange.*

This entire meal is cooked on the grill, eliminating the frustrating shuffle between the kitchen and the deck.

Grilled Swordfish and Red Potatoes with Rosemary ∽ Braised Swiss Chard

Swordfish and Potatoes:

1	lemon
4	tablespoons olive oil, divided
¼	cup plain dry bread crumbs
¾	teaspoon salt, divided
2	tablespoons minced fresh rosemary
2	pounds swordfish steaks
1¼ to 1½	pounds red-skinned potatoes, cut into 2-inch chunks

Swiss Chard:

1 to 1¼	pounds Swiss chard, stalks and leaves, cut into 1-inch pieces
2	tablespoons olive oil
2	cloves garlic, minced
¼	teaspoon salt

Halibut, blue marlin, yellowfin tuna, or salmon steaks may replace the swordfish.

bietola

To prepare the swordfish and potatoes: Grate the lemon zest into a large glass or ceramic dish. Cut the lemon in half. Set one half aside. Squeeze the juice from the other half. Add the juice, 3 tablespoons oil, bread crumbs, ½ teaspoon salt, and all but 2 teaspoons of the rosemary to the dish. Stir to mix. Add the swordfish, and dip both sides of the steaks in the mixture to coat. Cover tightly with plastic wrap and refrigerate for 1 hour.

Meanwhile, place the potatoes in a single layer in a shallow microwaveable dish. Cover with waxed paper. Microwave for 8 to 10 minutes, or until a knife easily pierces the flesh. Remove and season with ¼ teaspoon salt, 1 tablespoon oil, and 2 teaspoons rosemary. Toss to coat; set aside at room temperature.

To prepare the Swiss chard: Fold a 32-inch-long piece of aluminum foil in half to create a 16 x 12-inch rectangle. Raise the ends slightly. Place the chard, oil, garlic, and salt in the center. Toss to mix. Seal tightly.

To grill the swordfish, potatoes, and chard: Prepare a charcoal or gas grill for indirect cooking, firing briquettes or lighting the gas on one side of the grid only.

Place the foil packet on the cooking rack away from direct heat. Toss the potatoes. Remove the potatoes from the dish and place directly over the heat. Grill, turning every 1 or 2 minutes, until browned all over. Move the potatoes to the side of the rack with the foil packet. Cover and grill for 20 minutes.

With the potatoes and chard still on the grill, place the steaks directly over the heat for 3 to 4 minutes on each side, or until the crumbs are browned and the steak is opaque in the center. Cut the swordfish into serving portions.

Cut the reserved lemon half into wedges to serve with the swordfish and chard.

SERVES 4 TO 6

Season the swordfish, potatoes, and chard with freshly ground black pepper at the table.

One tablespoon crumbled dried rosemary may replace the fresh rosemary.

Pan-Seared Tuna on Greens with Warm Balsamic-Currant Sauce

Shark, swordfish, or other meaty-textured fish may replace the tuna steaks.

Golden or dark raisins may replace the currants.

3	tablespoons olive oil, divided
	Salt and ground black pepper
1	bag (10 ounces) mixed leafy greens
1	carrot, thinly sliced
1½ to 2	pounds tuna steaks
½	cup balsamic vinegar
½	cup water
½	cup dried currants

Place 1 tablespoon oil and a pinch of salt in a large bowl. Add the greens and carrot. Toss the salad. Place the salad on dinner plates. Set aside.

Warm the remaining 2 tablespoons oil in a large skillet over high heat. Season the tuna steaks lightly with salt on both sides. Cut the steaks in half, if needed, to create equal portions. Place in the pan. Cook 2 to 4 minutes on each side over high heat, or until browned and cooked to the desired degree of doneness. Add the vinegar, water, and currants. Season with salt and pepper to taste. Bring to a boil. Swirl or spoon the sauce over the tuna.

Place the tuna over the reserved salads. Spoon the sauce and currants over all.

Serves 4 to 6

Wine
***Rosé* Champagne** or a **Blanc de Noirs** *sparkler, composed mostly of pinot noir or pinot meunier grapes, pairs a deep cherry, plummy palate with delicate bubbles.*

Baked Trout Fillets with Bread Stuffing
ᕽ Sugar Snap Peas with Basil

Trout:

6	trout fillets (about 4 ounces each)
4	tablespoons butter
$^1/_2$	bunch scallions, all parts, sliced
1	carrot, shredded
6	cups cubed lightly toasted rustic bread
$1^1/_2$	cups chicken broth
1	egg, beaten
	Salt
$^1/_2$	teaspoon ground black pepper

Peas:

2	tablespoons olive oil
1 to $1^1/_2$	pounds sugar snap peas
$^1/_4$	teaspoon salt
$^1/_2$	cup slivered fresh basil leaves

This dish may be put together several hours in advance. Allow the stuffing to cool to room temperature before mounding on the fillets. Cover with plastic wrap and refrigerate. The baking time may increase by 5 minutes.

ᕽ

Chinese snow peas may replace the sugar snap peas.

To prepare the trout: Preheat the oven to 400°F. Coat a large baking sheet with no-stick spray. With a tweezer or pin-nosed pliers, remove any tiny bones from the fillets. Lay the fillets, skin side down, on the baking sheet.

In a large sauté pan, melt the butter over medium heat. Pour half into a cup; set aside. Add the scallions and carrot to the pan. Cook for about 3 minutes, or until soft. Add the bread cubes, broth, egg, $^1/_4$ teaspoon salt, and the pepper. Toss to moisten. Spoon oval mounds of the stuffing on the fillets. Press lightly to pack. Drizzle with the reserved butter.

Bake for 18 to 20 minutes, or until the stuffing is golden. With a pancake turner, transfer the stuffed fillets to plates.

To prepare the peas: When the trout is nearly finished baking, warm the oil in a large sauté pan over high heat. Add the peas and salt. Cook, stirring constantly, for 1 to 2 minutes, or until hot. Remove from the heat. Transfer to a serving bowl or plate. Sprinkle with the basil. Spoon onto the side of the reserved plates.

SERVES 4 TO 6

Taking the Plunge

Committing a cherished memory to paper is not without risk. Like pinning the wings of a butterfly, using words to capture a reminiscence can destroy its beauty.

Conjuring *cacciucco* on paper is just such a challenge. If, for me, cacciucco were simply a spicy stew of seafood and tomato broth, a recipe would suffice. My first cacciucco in a Florentine trattoria was much more than dinner. It was an intoxicating fusion of time and place and feeling. It tasted of spontaneity, passion, recklessness—flavors foreign to me at that time.

I was AWOL from the American tour bus on that April evening, sitting in a crowded trattoria with a man I had just met, as waves of sensation swept over me. Even now, everything I recall seems intensified. The conversation in the small bright restaurant reached a dizzying crescendo. Discussions at every table seemed vital. Though I could hardly ignore the charming Casanova at my side, the characters around me were staging a performance worthy of grand opera.

A young Florentine couple—so chic, so sure of themselves—parked their Vespa in view of the door to the street. I suppose they meant to keep watch over their tiny vehicle, though they never took their eyes off each other.

The grizzled expatriate artist from Bucks County, Pennsylvania, whom I had been introduced to moments before, was now sharing his table with a dazzling transvestite from the neighborhood.

Nearby, dining solo, an impeccable elderly gentleman in a suit jacket peeled his after-dinner orange with surgical precision.

As the vivacious proprietor served our courses *primi* through *dolci*, she called me "Wallina," the diminutive of my companion's name. At the time, I thought she was patronizing me. Now I've come to believe she was sending me a woman-to-woman signal. *So many other girls—who can remember names?*

Capture that savory stew? I don't even remember with certainty what was in the bowl. But I'll know it if I taste it. I pull out my trusted Italian cookbooks and spread them on the floor. These experts will know the recipe.

Stewing over Cacciucco

From the books I learn that cacciucco (pronounced ka-CHOO-ko) is much like love: Never twice the same, its outcome depends on who's stirring the pot. Consensus exists only on a few features.

Livorno, the port west of Florence on the Ligurian Sea, gets credit for creating the dish. Variously called "fish soup" or "fish stew," cacciucco is a meal, not a first course like other soups. The substantial character is bolstered by serving it over toasted bread that has been rubbed with oil and garlic.

The general method of making *cacciucco alla Livornese* is to heat olive oil in a pot to sauté onion and garlic, sometimes with sage, rosemary, or parsley, and almost always with the addition of a hot red chile. The pleasant acidity of wine, red or white, or of wine vinegar or lemon, counters the sweetness of the fish. Plum tomatoes in some form are essential.

Mackerel, bluefish, or any other oily, strong-flavored fish are to be avoided. As for what types of seafood are required, possibilities cover the waterfront. In *The Dictionary of Italian Food and Drink*, John Mariani writes that the recipe is traditionally made with "five kinds of seafood like squid, red mullet, cod, shrimp, and scallops to correspond to the five c's in the word."

In *Italian Regional Cooking*, Ada Boni calls for all, or any, of the following: "eel, squid, a delicate crustacean *squilla mantis*, for which shrimps or prawns could well be substituted, gurnard, whiting, hake, red mullet, small octopus, John Dory, cuttlefish, and crayfish."

Nancy Harmon Jenkins in *Flavors of Tuscany* is flexible, stipulating only that shellfish, a finfish, and either squid or octopus are thrown into the pot. Elizabeth David, in her classic *Italian Food*, recommends a variety of bony fish, tiny squid, and small lobsters.

Giuliano Bugialli in *The Fine Art of Italian Cooking* offers substitutes for Mediterranean seafood. "For *palombo*, a full-fleshed fish may be substituted, such as cod, haddock, or striped bass. Smelts may be substituted for *triglie*, and crabs, preferably soft-shelled, for the sweet flavor of the *cicale*. Seafood used in Italy and found [in North America] are calamari (squid) and shrimp (used raw, in their shells), and while clams and mussels are also used, some people may prefer to avoid them."

Some recipes are decidedly more complex than others. The recipe in *Flavors of Tuscany* runs for more than two pages and contains two subrecipes—for fish broth and tomato sauce—before cooking the cacciucco. In contrast, the recipe in *Italian Food* consists entirely of two elegant paragraphs.

Pino Luongo's recipe in *A Tuscan in the Kitchen* is straightforward, too, but I like it more for the emotions it evokes. Luongo recalls that as a young man, he often visited an old fisherman who lived on the beach and cooked cacciucco in an iron pot over a wood fire. He served his customers at a few tables beneath the shady overhang of his bungalow roof. "You didn't mind waiting because the beach was right there and you could just lie down on the sand with a glass of the local wine. Between the sun and the wine you usually fell asleep, but you knew when your cacciucco was ready because the smell woke you up," Luongo writes.

Committing a precious memory to paper is not without risk, but when it succeeds, it can be as thrilling as that first cacciucco. ✑

Try this streamlined version of cacciucco *(page 132)—then take the plunge and create your own variation. Include a variety of fish and seafood to create layers of flavor.*

Tuscan Seafood Stew ∽ Chilled White Grapes

¾	cup olive oil
1	large red onion, coarsely chopped
4	large cloves garlic, minced
1½	teaspoons crushed red pepper
1	cup dry red wine
1	can (28 ounces) crushed plum tomatoes
½	cup minced fresh flat-leaf parsley, divided
1½	teaspoons salt
24	littleneck clams
24	medium or large unpeeled shrimp
2 to 2½	pounds mild white-fleshed fish fillets, cut into 2-inch chunks
3	cups cold water
6 to 8	thick slices rustic bread, toasted
	White Grapes

Choose the freshest fish available. Use one type or as many as three or four, as long as the total is 2 pounds. Sea bass, monkfish, cod, halibut, swordfish, shark, tilapia, turbot, catfish, and red snapper are good choices.

In late spring or early summer, 6 to 8 fresh soft-shell crabs may replace the shrimp.

Heat the oil in a 6-quart Dutch oven over medium heat. Add the onion, garlic, and red pepper. Cook, stirring occasionally, for 10 minutes, or until soft. Add the wine. Increase the heat to medium-high. Cook at a brisk simmer for 5 minutes, or until the wine no longer smells of alcohol. Add the tomatoes, all but 2 tablespoons of the parsley, and the salt. Bring to a boil, then reduce the heat until the sauce simmers gently. Cover and cook for 10 minutes, stirring occasionally, for the flavors to blend.

Add the clams and shrimp; stir. Add the fish and stir gently. Increase the heat to high. Cook for 2 minutes, or until the liquid starts to bubble. Add the water. Cover and reduce the heat so the mixture simmers but does not boil. Cook for 10 minutes, or until the clams open and the other seafood is opaque in the center. Discard any clams that do not open. Set the bread in pasta plates or large shallow bowls and spoon the stew over it. Sprinkle with the remaining parsley.

Chill the grapes during dinner and serve after the stew.

SERVES 6 TO 8

pomodori pelati

The shrimp shells add flavor to the stew. Before cooking, snip the back of the shell with scissors for easier peeling at the table. Of course, if you prefer, you may use peeled shrimp.

⌒

In season, 4 cups of peeled, chopped plum tomatoes may replace the canned crushed tomatoes.

⌒

The tomato base may be cooled, covered, and refrigerated for up to 2 days before completing the fish stew.

⌒

Wine
Chianti Classico *from Tuscany. Berry and tobacco earthiness and the acidity of the sangiovese grape nicely complement this tomato-based stew.*

⌒

These kebabs are fun to include in a buffet accompanied
by Summer Rice Salad (page 108) and cut fresh fruit.

Scallop-Tomato-Bacon Kebabs on Romaine with Pesto Dressing

8	ounces thick-sliced bacon
2 to 2½	pounds large sea scallops
1	pint cherry tomatoes
6	tablespoons basil pesto, divided
2	teaspoons white or red wine vinegar
1	large head romaine lettuce

Choose firm large scallops, at least 1½ inches in diameter, for this recipe. To thread them securely on the skewers, envision each scallop as a miniature can of tuna. Push the skewer through the "tuna can label" sides, not through the top and bottom of the "tuna can."

Prepare a charcoal or gas grill.

On a microwaveable grill dish or several layers of paper toweling, microwave the bacon on high for 4 minutes, turning once, or until hot but not crisp. Remove and pat dry. Cut each strip crosswise into 4 pieces.

Fold 1 piece of bacon in half crosswise and then in half again. Thread on a 12-inch skewer. One at a time, alternately thread 3 or 4 scallops and 3 tomatoes with a folded piece of bacon between each. End with another piece of bacon. Repeat with 5 more skewers, starting and ending with the bacon. Lay the kebabs in a 13 x 9-inch pan. Spoon 4 tablespoons of the pesto over the kebabs, turning and coating all surfaces with the back of the spoon.

Coat a portable grill rack with no-stick spray. Place the kebabs on the rack, leaving space between them. Set on the grill. Cook for about 10 minutes, turning once, until browned. Remove from the grill.

Place 2 tablespoons pesto in a bowl with the vinegar. Whisk. Tear the romaine leaves. Add to the bowl and toss. Place the salad on dinner plates. Serve the kebabs over the salad.

SERVES 4 TO 6

The pot of mussels may also be served as an appetizer for a more elaborate meal for 8 to 12, followed by a grilled meat or poultry main dish.

Mussels Oregano ∽ Rustic Bread ∽ Chilled Sliced Peaches

Mussels:

¾	cup olive oil
4	large cloves garlic, minced
4	teaspoons dried oregano
1	bottle (750 milliliters) dry white wine
2	cans (14½ ounces each) diced tomatoes, with juice
1	teaspoon salt
4 to 6	pounds mussels

Rustic Bread

Peaches:

1	bag (20 ounces) frozen loose-pack sliced peaches, thawed
2	tablespoons sugar

To prepare the mussels: Warm the oil, garlic, and oregano in an 8-quart pot over medium-low heat. Cook for about 5 minutes, or until the garlic is soft. Take care not to brown the garlic. Add the wine. Increase the heat to high. Boil for about 7 minutes, or until the wine no longer smells of alcohol.

Add the tomatoes and salt. Decrease the heat to medium. Cover and simmer for 10 minutes.

Add the mussels. Stir. Increase the heat to high. Cover and cook, stirring occasionally, for 3 to 5 minutes, or until the mussels open. Discard any mussels that do not open. Spoon the mussels into large bowls and ladle the broth over them.

Serve the bread on the side.

To prepare the peaches: While the sauce is cooking, in a bowl, mix the peaches and sugar. Stir. Cover and refrigerate for 15 minutes. Serve the peaches after the mussels.

SERVES 4 TO 6

Most farm-raised mussels need only scrubbing with a stiff brush under cold running water. Some mussels may still have their "beards," wiry dark ligaments, attached. If so, cut off the beard and any marine life clinging to it with scissors and discard, then scrub the mussel.

∽

When peaches are in season locally, replace the frozen peaches with 3 to 4 large ripe peaches, chilling before peeling. A splash of dry white wine on the peaches is a refreshing addition.

Chicken and Turkey Meals

Recipes

Stories and Basics

Italians flock to *girarrosti* and *rosticcerie* for succulent chicken, spit-roasted over glowing wood embers. The seasonings are simple: olive oil, a little salt, and that aromatic smoke. Regional variations are many, including the addition of rosemary or sage, lemon juice or wine vinegar, ground black pepper or crushed red pepper.

Roast chicken on a spit—a legacy of the Italian farmhouse hearth—exerts a powerful pull on the Italian psyche, as author Elizabeth Romer wryly observes in *The Tuscan Year: Life and Food in an Italian Valley.*

"Silvana is preparing an excellent lunch for the official [an inspector who will set the price for the tobacco harvest] knowing quite well that these city men often have a sentimental nostalgia for country life and a good lunch would be likely to put him into a mellow mood. . . . One of her enormous Tuscan chickens would seem to be the answer, well cooked over the open fire."

Here, Balsamic Grilled Chicken gives a modern twist to this ancient method of cooking chicken. A broiler-fryer is split and flattened for faster cooking, then seasoned with balsamic vinegar and sage, and roasted in a covered grill.

Turkey also has a presence in the Italian kitchen, but as an exotic import from the New World, it has always enjoyed a special status. Turkey stuffed with fruits, nuts, minced veal, salt pork, herbs, and brandy is a classic Christmas dish in Lombardy; in Bologna, turkey breast is blanketed with ham and grated Parmesan before baking.

Chicken and turkey are mild and neutral in flavor, which makes them wonderfully versatile. And boneless cuts cook in a wink—whether over charcoal, in a stove-top grill pan, or in a skillet—ready to be served with a squeeze of lemon or garnished with a savory condiment. Turn to "Capturing Summer Flavors for All Meals" (page 232), for accompaniments that are handy to have in the freezer: Caponata, Basil Pesto, Chunky Plum Tomato Sauce, Roasted Peppers, and Sweet and Sharp Onions with Raisins. ↜

Soon after we met, my future husband cooked a romantic lunch just for me. He seemed genuinely convinced that he had invented this classic dish and, naturally, I played along.

Marsala Chicken Breasts Bolognese
↜ Broccoli with Orange ↜ Rustic Bread

Chicken:

2½ to 3	pounds skinless, boneless chicken breast halves
	Salt and ground nutmeg
½	cup flour
2	tablespoons butter
6 to 8	thin slices (4 to 5 ounces) cooked ham
6 to 8	thin slices (4 to 5 ounces) Gruyère cheese
1	cup Marsala wine

Broccoli:

2	tablespoons olive oil
1 to 1½	pounds broccoli, stalk peeled and cut into ¼-inch-thick rounds, florets separated
¼	teaspoon salt
2	tablespoons water
1	navel orange, cut into wedges

Rustic Bread

Prosciutto may replace the cooked ham.

To prepare the chicken: Lay the chicken breasts, smooth side down, on a work surface. Loosen the tenderloins and open them like a book. With a scaloppine pounder or heavy skillet, flatten the breasts to ¾-inch thickness. Season both sides with salt and a dusting of nutmeg.

Place the flour on a large sheet of waxed paper. Lay an empty sheet of waxed paper beside it. Dip the chicken in the flour to coat both sides. Shake off excess and place the chicken on the empty sheet.

Heat the butter in a large sauté pan over medium-high heat until the foam subsides. Add the chicken in a single layer. Cook for about 4 minutes on each side, or until well browned. Top each chicken breast with a slice of ham and a slice of Gruyère. Add the Marsala to the pan. Bring to a brisk simmer. Cook, swirling occasionally, for about 5 minutes, or until it no longer smells of alcohol.

Reduce the heat to low. Cover and cook for 5 to 7 minutes, or until the chicken is no longer pink in the center. With a spatula, place the chicken breasts on dinner plates. Drizzle with the wine sauce.

To prepare the broccoli: Heat the oil in a Dutch oven. Add the broccoli and salt; stir. Cover and cook for 2 minutes. Add the water. Cover and cook for 2 to 3 minutes, or until lightly browned. Spoon onto the side of the reserved plates. Serve each portion with an orange wedge for garnishing at the table.

Serve the bread on the side.

SERVES 4 TO 6

Wine
Aromatic Alsatian *Gewürztraminer,* *with its spice and floral lychee nut flavors, plays well with the richness and sweetness of the cheese and Marsala wine.*

arancia

*This meal appeals to grown-ups as much as it does to children.
For a larger group, it's easy to prepare two pans of the chicken and
potatoes. The baking time may be slightly longer.*

Baked Oregano Chicken and Potatoes
ᔯ Mixed Greens Salad

Chicken and Potatoes:

¹/₂	cup (2 ounces) grated Parmesan cheese
¹/₄	cup plain dry bread crumbs
³/₄	teaspoon dried oregano
2	cloves garlic, minced
¹/₂	teaspoon **each** salt and ground black pepper
2¹/₂ to 3	pounds skinless, boneless chicken breast halves
6	medium-large red- or white-skinned potatoes (about 2 pounds), cut into ¹/₂-inch-thick slices
1	can (14¹/₂ ounces) diced tomatoes, drained
¹/₂	cup olive oil

Salad:

¹/₄	cup olive oil
1	tablespoon lemon juice or white wine vinegar
¹/₈	teaspoon **each** salt and ground black pepper
1	bag (10 to 12 ounces) mixed greens

To prepare the chicken and potatoes: Preheat the oven to 375°F. Coat a 16 x 10-inch baking pan with no-stick spray.

In a shallow bowl, mix the Parmesan, bread crumbs, oregano, garlic, salt, and pepper. Dip both sides of the chicken and potato slices into the mixture. Shake off any excess. Arrange the chicken and potatoes in slightly overlapping rows in the pan. Sprinkle with the tomatoes and the remaining crumb mixture. Drizzle with the oil.

Bake for about 45 minutes, or until the potatoes are tender when pierced with a knife.

To prepare the salad: In a bowl, whisk the oil, lemon juice or vinegar, salt, and pepper. Add the greens. Set aside. Toss just before serving.

SERVES 4 TO 6

My Dinner with Luciano

I once had dinner with Luciano Pavarotti.

So what if dozens of others shared in our meal? I had eyes only for the great tenor. The occasion was Pavarotti's twenty-fifth anniversary on the world's stage, and the Lyric Opera of Chicago was throwing a really nice party to honor him. And I—*che buona fortuna!*—was assigned to write a story about it.

We dined on dishes from Luciano's hometown of Modena in Emilia-Romagna, the heart of the Italian pork and cream belt. How we feasted that evening . . . from *tortellacci alla panna* (stuffed pasta in cream sauce) through *torta di riso* (sweet rice tart kissed with lemon).

In my souvenir photograph, Luciano's right arm is draped warmly over my shoulder. We're both showing plenty of teeth. And next to my postpartum padding, he looks quite trim.

Luciano and I were brought together by our shared passion for *la cucina Italiana*—a passion that, for me, has served as a passport to many other adventures.

A lunch in the country outside Fiesole led me to Giancarlo Giannini, *il bell'uomo* of the Italian cinema in the 1970s. Under Lina Wertmuller's direction, he steamed up the screen in such films as *Swept Away* . . . and *Seven Beauties*.

It was the day after my wedding that Giancarlo and I met. (Too bad for him—missed by only twenty-four hours.) We were sitting on a shady veranda, waiting to be seated. We chatted . . . talked of this and that . . . and then he was gone, abruptly called with his friends to a table indoors. Strangely, Giancarlo has never contacted me to this day. Probably he sensed it would be futile even to try.

Please don't think I've limited my food adventures to the arts. I've broken bread in Italian government circles as well, from high to low. Once I dined with the Italian ambassador to the United States and his wife in the formal dining room of the gracious embassy in Washington, D.C. So what if a dozen other food writers shared in the meal? I had eyes only for the white-gloved waiters who served us *timballo del Gattopardo* (sauced pasta baked in a pastry drum), *involtini di spada* (swordfish bundles), and other Sicilian delicacies.

At the other end of the international-relations spectrum, I've broken bread at the home of a friend who is a retired *statale*, a foot soldier of the state. On a patio off a tree-lined cul de sac perched above Florence, we ate *pasta con tonno e caperi* (tuna and caper pasta) and *vitello arrosto* (pan-roasted veal).

In Turin, at the rococo Ristorante Del Cambio, I sat on a red velvet banquette among glittering mirrors and crystal chandeliers. I felt as if I were inside Caterina de Medici's jewel box as I indulged in stylish carpaccio and panna cotta.

At a converted monastery in Tuscany—in a vast and still room of dark wood, glazed terra cotta floor tiles, and white light muted through frosted glass—I savored an earthy *tagliatelle alla lepre* (egg noodles tossed in rabbit ragú).

With the Cordero family, of Piedmont's renowned Monfalletto vineyard, I lunched upon *bresato* (beef braised with vegetables) and sipped Barolo wine, one of Italy's superb big reds.

With Guido and Mary Corsi, who live in the slate belt of eastern Pennsylvania, I sipped slightly *frizzante* basement white wine and nibbled figs that, in defiance of the climate, the Corsis grow in their backyard.

At Peck, the Tiffany of food shops in downtown Milan, I believe I drooled openly while wandering a boutique-like cluster of food shops and restaurants. Peck offers stuffed fresh pastas, spit-roasted suckling pig with rosemary, mascarpone-pesto torte, prosciutti, salame, and much much much much more.

Along Harlem Avenue, on Chicago's far west side, I have shopped for imported Parmesan, *superfino* rice, and dried porcini in little family-owned storefronts. Cruising the aisles, inhaling the evocative aromas, I have fantasized being back in Italy.

Whenever la cucina Italiana calls, wherever it takes me, *sono sempre pronta*. I am always ready for the feast.

So, Luciano, if you're reading this . . . let's have dinner again sometime. ↫

A paillard, a French term that is often seen on Italian restaurant menus, is a thinly pounded piece of meat or chicken. It cooks fast and is usually highly seasoned due to the larger surface area.

Chicken Paillard Salad with Tomatoes and Basil

2½ to 3	pounds skinless, boneless chicken breast halves
	Salt and ground black pepper
¼	cup (1 ounce) grated Parmesan cheese
¼	cup plain dry bread crumbs
	Olive oil
2	tablespoons lemon juice
1	bag (10 ounces) mixed greens
2	medium-large fresh tomatoes, cut in wedges
1	bunch scallions, all parts, sliced
1	cup slivered fresh basil leaves

Lay the chicken breasts on a work surface. With a scaloppine pounder or heavy skillet, flatten to ½-inch thickness. Season with salt and pepper. Sprinkle with the Parmesan and bread crumbs on both sides, pressing to adhere.

Glaze a large sauté pan, stove-top griddle, or grill pan with oil. Set over high heat. Sear the breasts for about 4 minutes on each side in 2 batches if necessary, or until well browned and no longer pink in the middle. Press down occasionally with a pancake turner. Remove to a tray. Allow to rest for 5 minutes. Cut into thick diagonal slices.

In a large bowl, combine ¼ cup oil, the lemon juice, and ½ teaspoon salt. Whisk. Add the greens, tomatoes, scallions, basil, and chicken. Toss gently.

SERVES 4 TO 6

The scallions may be replaced with ½ cup of minced fresh chives.

~

To prepare the salad when tomatoes are not in season, replace the basil with 2 teaspoons rubbed dried sage, sprinkling it over the chicken breasts after the salt and pepper. Replace the tomatoes with ½ cup recipe-ready, sun-dried tomatoes. Add 2 peeled and sliced navel oranges.

~

Wine
Soave Classico, a white wine from Veneto, works with the acidity levels and citrus flavors in this meal. It is full of fruit on the palate but finishes bone dry.

~

Gorgonzola delivers a thrill of opposites: the pungency of the blue-green veining encased in the sweet creaminess of cow's milk cheese. Produced in Lombardy and Piedmont, it is one of the world's fine cheeses.

Gorgonzola Chicken Thighs ∽ Braised Red Cabbage

Chicken:

$^1\!/_3$	cup (2$^1\!/_2$ ounces) Gorgonzola cheese
6	tablespoons plain dry bread crumbs, divided
1	teaspoon ground black pepper
2 to 2$^1\!/_2$	pounds skinless, boneless chicken thighs
	Olive oil
$^1\!/_4$	teaspoon salt

Cabbage:

2	tablespoons olive oil
1	red onion, halved, cut into thick slices
1	small head red cabbage, cored and cut into thick slices
$^1\!/_2$	cup dry red wine
2	tablespoons red or white wine vinegar
1	tablespoon sugar
1	teaspoon salt

To transform this dish into a summer meal, bake the thighs and cool to room temperature. Cut into slices and serve on a bed of thinly sliced red cabbage and sliced scallions dressed with olive oil, lemon juice, salt, and pepper.

∽

The cooled and sliced chicken thighs make a tasty party appetizer.

To prepare the chicken: Preheat the oven to 400°F. In a small bowl, mix the Gorgonzola, 2 tablespoons bread crumbs, and pepper with a fork. Lay the thighs, smooth side down, on a work surface. Crumble on the cheese mixture; press to flatten. Roll up the chicken thighs and secure with sturdy pointed toothpicks.

Spray all sides of the chicken bundles with olive oil from a mister or dab with a pastry brush dipped in oil. Spread 4 tablespoons bread crumbs and the salt on a sheet of waxed paper. Dip the thighs into the crumbs to lightly coat all sides. Shake off excess. Set on a large baking sheet. Mist all sides with oil.

Bake for 18 to 20 minutes, or until golden.

To prepare the cabbage: While the chicken is baking, heat the oil in a Dutch oven over medium-high heat. Add the onion. Stir. Cover and cook for 5 minutes, or until soft. Add the cabbage, wine, vinegar, sugar, and salt. Bring to a boil. Reduce the heat so the mixture simmers. Cook, stirring occasionally, for 8 to 10 minutes, or until the cabbage is crisp-cooked and glazed.

SERVES 4 TO 6

Roast Lemon-Parsley Chicken Drums and Carrots with Fettuccine

	Olive oil
3½ to 4	pounds chicken drumsticks
3	teaspoons salt, divided
1	pound baby carrots
2	bunches scallions, all parts, cut into 2-inch-long pieces
¼	cup minced fresh flat-leaf parsley
	Grated zest of 1 lemon
8 to 10	ounces fresh fettuccine

Preheat the oven to 425°F. Using a mister or pastry brush dipped in oil, coat a 17 x 12-inch metal baking sheet with sides (or two smaller pans with sides). Place the drumsticks on the pan. Season on all sides with ¼ teaspoon salt. Bake for 20 minutes.

Remove the pan from the oven. Add the carrots, scallions, parsley, lemon zest, ¾ teaspoon salt, and 2 tablespoons oil. With a pancake turner, toss thoroughly to combine the vegetables and seasonings. Spread in a single layer.

Bake for about 25 minutes, turning occasionally, or until no pink remains at the chicken bone and the carrots are tender.

Meanwhile, place a covered large pot of water over high heat. When the water boils, add 2 teaspoons salt and the fettuccine. Stir. Cover and return to a boil. Uncover and boil, stirring occasionally, for about 3 minutes, or until tender. Drain and return to the pot.

If the chicken skin is not well browned, heat the oven broiler. Broil the chicken 6 inches from the heat source for about 3 minutes, or until browned. Remove the drumsticks to a platter. Add the carrots, scallions, and pan juices to the fettuccine. Toss to combine.

SERVES 4 TO 6

The cooled and refrigerated drumsticks (meat taken off the bones) and carrots may be used for chicken salad. Bring the leftovers to room temperature. Place on a bed of torn lettuce and drizzle with red or white wine vinegar. Season with ground black pepper.

Preparing Poultry

Crackling golden skin and tender, juicy flesh: This is poultry cooked to perfection. Chicken and turkey are lean, with little of the interior fat marbling that is characteristic of pork and beef. It's all too easy to dry out poultry with overcooking.

One of the simplest ways to ensure moist cooked poultry is to flatten the meat to a uniform thickness before cooking, so it cooks more evenly and quickly. Anything from boneless chicken breasts to a whole broiler-fryer can benefit from this technique.

Flattening Boneless Poultry Parts

To flatten boneless chicken breasts or thighs, turkey scaloppine, and other cuts with minimal effort, I use an Italian-made scaloppine pounder. It's heavy, nearly a pound and a half, so it really does the work. It consists of a metal disk, about 3 inches in diameter, perpendicular to a handle that is rubberized and ridged for a comfortable grip. The disk itself is smooth; this is important to avoid tearing the delicate flesh. In a pinch, a small cast iron skillet can double for a scaloppine pounder.

To pound boneless whole chicken breasts, place them with the smooth side down (this is the side where the skin was attached), allowing enough space for expansion between the cutlets. Find the transparent membrane that holds the long narrow tenderloin portion to the breast. Break through it with a finger and open the tenderloin as you would open a book. Bring the scaloppine pounder down sharply on the center of each breast, pushing toward the edges with a smooth motion. Continue until the desired thickness is reached.

A skinless boneless turkey breast may be treated in the same way before seasoning it with minced herbs and garlic, or topping it with spinach stuffing (page 160). The breast is then rolled, tied, and roasted. When it's cut, each slice reveals a pretty spiral.

Because a turkey breast is so much thicker than a chicken breast, it needs to be butterflied (cut almost in half through the middle) before it can be flattened. To butterfly, lay the turkey breast, smooth side down, on a cutting board. Loosen the membrane that attaches the tenderloin to the breast; fold the tenderloin down to the side of the breast. Holding a sharp knife parallel to the cutting board, cut through the thickest part of the breast (this will be opposite the tenderloin) almost, but not quite, through to the other side. Open this slice like a book. The turkey breast will be twice as wide. With a scaloppine pounder or heavy skillet, flatten to 1-inch thickness.

Splitting and Flattening Small Whole Birds

A popular dish in Tuscany is *pollo al mattone*, "chicken cooked under a brick." A young chicken, usually weighing no more than a pound and a half, is seasoned, split down the back, opened, flattened, then cooked on a sizzling stove-top griddle or pan while weighted under a brick. The brick holds the chicken in contact with the hot surface, so it cooks quickly and evenly.

Even if you don't keep a brick in your pantry, you can adopt the technique of splitting young birds before cooking. You'll need sturdy kitchen scissors, a cleaver, or a chef's knife, any of which will cut handily through the backbone. When you've done that, open the chicken, skin side up, on a work surface. Cut off the last section of the wing tips; discard. Remove and discard any big clumps of fat in the cavity. With an open palm, smack the breast sharply to flatten.

Now you can loosen the skin. With the fingers of one hand, reach into the neck opening under the skin. Pull gently to separate the transparent membrane that loosely attaches the skin to the flesh. Take care not to tear the skin. Reach all the way down to the tips of the drumsticks.

The chicken may be grilled at once with just a sprinkling of salt under the skin. Or it may be marinated in a mixture such as the balsamic vinegar and sage marinade (page 150). Either way, first secure the drumsticks by cutting a slit in the skin at the base of each breast. Tuck the tip of each drumstick into a slit to secure it during cooking.

Allowing marinade to reach the flesh of the chicken, rather than sitting on its skin, results in better penetration and a more juicy, flavorful bird. Vinegar and other acidic ingredients help to dissolve the fat under the chicken skin, crisping the skin as it roasts or grills. And because the split chicken is flat, not rounded like a whole chicken, the marinade is able to penetrate its surface more evenly.

Rock Cornish game hens are ideal for splitting, flattening, and grilling. Season 2 or 3 hens under the skin with lemon juice, olive oil, salt, and some crushed garlic. Starting skin side up, grill the birds over hot briquettes, turning every 10 minutes, for a total cooking time of about 40 minutes.

One final tool takes the guesswork out of cooking poultry thoroughly without overcooking. An instant-reading digital thermometer will let you know immediately whether the interior has reached the recommended safety temperature. To use the thermometer, insert its tip into the center of a cutlet or, for a whole chicken, into the thickest part of the thigh not touching a bone. Recommended doneness temperatures are included in the recipes.

Flatten, marinate, cook. The result? Crackling golden skin and tender, juicy flesh.

The time-honored Italian technique of splitting and flattening the chickens produces succulent flesh with crackling skin.

Balsamic Grilled Chicken with Tomatoes ↬ Cheese Orzo

Chicken and Tomatoes:

2	small broiler-fryer chickens (about 3 pounds each)
¹⁄₂	cup balsamic vinegar
2	teaspoons salt, divided
1¹⁄₂	tablespoons rubbed dried sage
8 to 12	fresh plum tomatoes, halved lengthwise
¹⁄₄	cup olive oil
¹⁄₄	cup plain dry bread crumbs
1	large clove garlic, minced

Provolone or Spanish Manchego cheese may replace the Tuscan Pecorino.

↬

Any leftover chicken is delicious cut off the bone and served cold in sandwiches or salads.

Orzo:

1	pound dried orzo
1	tablespoon salt
1	tablespoon flour
2	tablespoons cold water
1	cup milk
¹⁄₂	cup (2 ounces) shredded Tuscan Pecorino cheese

To prepare the chicken and tomatoes: Split the chickens, loosen the skin from the flesh, and press down hard to flatten (page 148). Place the chickens, skin side up, in a large tray with sides or in two 13 x 9-inch pans.

In a glass measuring cup, whisk the vinegar and 1¹⁄₂ teaspoons salt to dissolve. Stir in the sage. One at a time, lift the chickens and pour the mixture under the skin. Rub under the skin to distribute the marinade down to the drumsticks. With a paring knife, make a small slit at the base of each breast. Tuck a drumstick tip into each slit to secure. Grill right away or refrigerate, skin side down, for several hours.

Prepare a charcoal or gas grill for indirect cooking, firing briquettes or lighting the gas on one side of the grid only.

Place a 13 x 9-inch drip pan on the center of the lower grate. Add 1 cup of hot water. Position the cooking rack. Place the chickens, skin side up, in the center. Cover and grill, adding additional hot water to the drip pan if needed, for about 1 hour and 15 minutes, or until an instant-reading thermometer inserted in the thickest part of the thigh, not touching a bone, registers 175°F. Remove the chicken to a platter to sit for 10 minutes, or until the thermometer rises to 180°F. Pour the pan juices into a microwaveable measuring cup. Skim and discard any fat. Add ¼ teaspoon salt. Microwave for 1 minute to heat before drizzling over the chicken.

While the chicken is cooking, cut a shallow cross in the cut side of each tomato half. Arrange on a baking sheet, cut side up. In a bowl, combine the oil, bread crumbs, garlic, and the remaining ¼ teaspoon salt. With the back of a spoon, spread the crumbs over the cut side of the tomato halves, pressing lightly; set aside.

Just before serving, preheat the oven broiler. Broil the tomatoes 6 inches from the heat source for about 5 minutes, or until golden.

To prepare the orzo: Shortly before the chicken is done cooking, bring a covered large pot of water to a boil. Add the orzo and salt. Stir, cover, and return to a boil. Uncover and cook, stirring occasionally, for about 6 minutes, or until al dente. Drain and rinse lightly.

Add the flour and water to the pot. Whisk until smooth. Add the milk and whisk. Cook over medium-high heat, whisking constantly, for 4 minutes, or until thickened. Remove from the heat. Stir in the Pecorino to melt. Add the orzo. Stir to coat.

SERVES 4 TO 6

pomodori pelati

To roast the chickens in the oven: Preheat the oven to 375°F. Place the chickens in a shallow roasting pan. Roast for about 60 minutes, or until an instant-reading thermometer inserted in the thickest part of the thigh, not touching a bone, registers 175°F. Remove to a platter to sit for 10 minutes, or until the thermometer rises to 180°F.

Egg-Lemon Chicken and Winter Vegetables

3½ to 4   pounds chicken parts

1 to 1½   pounds red- or white-skinned potatoes, cut into 2-inch chunks

4   ribs celery heart, cut into 2-inch lengths

4   carrots, cut into 2-inch lengths

1   onion, cut into 8 wedges

2   teaspoons dried thyme leaves

  Salt

1¼   teaspoons ground black pepper

3   cups chicken broth

2   tablespoons cornstarch

¼   cup lemon juice

2   eggs

2   tablespoons minced fresh flat-leaf parsley

Choose fleshy chicken parts of equal size such as drumsticks and thighs. If using chicken breasts, leave on the bone and use kitchen shears to cut into two equal chunks.

I recommend using canned reduced-sodium broth or salt-free Chicken Broth (page 39). If you use regular canned broth, you may want to reduce the amount of salt.

Preheat the oven to 375°F.

Remove the skin and any clumps of fat from the chicken; discard. Place in a Dutch oven. Add the potatoes, celery, carrots, onion, thyme, ¾ to 1¼ teaspoons salt, and the pepper. Toss with your hands to coat the chicken and vegetables evenly with the seasonings. Add the broth. Cover tightly with a double layer of aluminum foil and the pan lid.

Bake for 1 hour. Remove from the oven. Uncover the pan and carefully peel back the foil, starting from the far side of the pan. With a sharp knife, test if vegetables are tender and no pink remains at the chicken bone. If more cooking is needed, re-cover and bake for 10 to 15 minutes.

Meanwhile, set a fine sieve over a medium saucepan. In a large bowl, whisk the cornstarch and lemon juice until smooth. Add the eggs and beat until smooth.

With a slotted spoon, remove the chicken and vegetables to a platter. Pour the broth through the sieve. Gradually ladle the broth into the egg mixture, whisking constantly. Pour into the saucepan. Cook over medium heat, whisking constantly, for about 3 minutes, or until thickened. Pour over the chicken and vegetables. Sprinkle with the parsley.

SERVES 4 TO 6

Turkey and Ham Loaf ∽ Pesto Potato Salad

Turkey:

	Olive oil
6	tablespoons plain dry bread crumbs, divided
1	egg
1/2	teaspoon salt
1/2	teaspoon ground red pepper
2	pounds ground turkey breast
8	ounces thick-cut cooked ham, coarsely ground
1	small onion, minced
1/2	cup (2 ounces) shredded provolone cheese

Salad:

6 to 8	medium red-skinned potatoes, cut into 2-inch chunks
1/4	cup basil pesto
1/4	cup mayonnaise
1/4	teaspoon salt
1	bunch scallions, white and light green parts, sliced

To prepare the turkey: Preheat the oven to 350°F. Coat a 9 x 5-inch loaf pan with oil. Dust the bottom and sides with 3 tablespoons bread crumbs. Spray the crumbs with oil from a mister or pat with a pastry brush dipped in oil.

In a mixing bowl, beat the egg, salt, and red pepper with a fork. Add the turkey, ham, onion, provolone, and 2 tablespoons crumbs. Mix with your hands just to combine. Do not overmix. Transfer to the pan. Pat gently to mound the top. Coat with oil. Sprinkle with 1 tablespoon crumbs.

Bake for about 1 hour, or until an instant-reading thermometer inserted into the center registers 165°F. Remove from the oven and set aside for 10 minutes. The internal temperature will rise to 170°F. Turn out onto a cutting board. Turn crumb-side up. With a serrated knife, cut into slices.

To prepare the salad: Place the potatoes in a single layer in a microwaveable dish. Cover with waxed paper. Microwave on high for about 10 minutes, rotating occasionally, until tender. Remove and set aside for 10 minutes, or until cool.

Cut potatoes into 1/2-inch chunks. In a bowl, combine the pesto, mayonnaise, salt, scallions, and potatoes; toss.

SERVES 4 TO 6

For everyday meals, I cook thin slices of turkey breast as cooks in Italy would treat veal scaloppine. If the turkey scaloppine are no thicker than 1/8 inch, they'll cook in a flash.

Capered Turkey Scaloppine
∽ Tomato-Cucumber Salad ∽ Rustic Bread

Salad:

3	tablespoons olive oil
2	tablespoons red or white wine vinegar
1/4	teaspoon **each** salt and ground black pepper
2	fresh tomatoes, cut into small wedges
1	English cucumber, halved lengthwise, sliced
1	head Boston lettuce, leaves torn
1	bunch scallions, all parts, sliced

Turkey:

1/2	cup flour
1 1/2 to 2	pounds turkey scaloppine
	Salt
2	tablespoons butter
1/2	cup water
1/4	cup drained capers
	Rustic Bread

pane rustico

To prepare the salad: In a large bowl, whisk the oil, vinegar, salt, and pepper. Add the tomatoes, cucumber, lettuce, and scallions; set aside.

Just before serving, toss to coat all the ingredients with dressing.

To prepare the turkey: Place the flour on a large sheet of waxed paper. Lay an empty sheet of waxed paper beside it. Season the scaloppine on both sides with salt. Dip into the flour to coat both sides. Shake off excess and place the scaloppine on the empty sheet.

Heat the butter in a large sauté pan over medium-high heat until the foam subsides and the pan is very hot. Add the scaloppine in a single layer. Cook for 1 to 2 minutes on each side, or until browned. Remove the scaloppine to plates or a serving platter. Add the water and capers to the pan. Scrape the bottom of the pan to remove any browned bits. Bring to a boil. Pour over the scaloppine.

Serve the bread with the scaloppine and salad.

SERVES 4 TO 6

Variations

Turkey Scaloppine with Marsala: Replace the water with Marsala wine. Omit the capers.

Turkey Scaloppine with Lemon: Reduce the water to $1/3$ cup. Omit the capers. Garnish each serving with a lemon wedge to squeeze over the scaloppine.

Turkey Scaloppine with White Wine: Replace the water with dry white wine. Omit the capers.

An aluminum or cast iron sauté pan, which conducts heat evenly, will allow the turkey to brown beautifully.

Sweet and Sharp Turkey with Zucchini and Apricots ∽ Ditalini Romano

Turkey:

1½	pounds skinless, boneless turkey breast tenders
4	tablespoons olive oil, divided
1	pound zucchini, cut into ½-inch rounds
1	large red onion, coarsely chopped
1	tablespoon minced fresh rosemary
1	can (14½ ounces) chicken broth
2 to 3	tablespoons red or white wine vinegar
	Salt
1	teaspoon ground black pepper
2	tablespoons flour whisked with ¼ cup cold water
1	package (7 ounces) dried apricots

Ditalini:

3	cups dried ditalini
2	teaspoons salt
2	tablespoons (½ ounce) grated Pecorino Romano cheese

I recommend using canned reduced-sodium broth or salt-free Chicken Broth (page 39). If you use regular canned broth, you may want to reduce the salt.

To prepare the turkey: Cut the tenders in half lengthwise. Cut out the white tendons and discard. Cut the strips into 1-inch chunks. Heat 2 tablespoons oil in a large sauté pan over high heat. Add the turkey. Cook for 5 minutes, turning as needed, or until well browned on all sides. Remove to a tray.

Add 2 tablespoons oil to the pan. Add the zucchini. Cook, turning once, for 5 minutes, or until well browned on both sides. Remove to the tray. Reduce the heat to medium. Add the onion and rosemary to the pan. Stir. Cover and cook, stirring occasionally, for 5 minutes, or until the onion is caramelized. Remove to the tray.

Turn off the heat. Add the broth, 2 tablespoons vinegar, ½ to 1 teaspoon salt, and the pepper to the pan. Add the flour water, whisking constantly. Turn on the heat to medium-high. Cook, whisking constantly, for about 2 minutes, or until thickened.

Return the turkey, zucchini, and onion to the pan. Add the apricots. Cover and reduce the heat so the mixture simmers. Cook for 5 minutes, or until the turkey is no longer pink in the center. Taste and add up to 1 tablespoon of the remaining vinegar if needed.

To prepare the ditalini: While you're cooking the turkey and vegetables, set a covered medium pot of water over high heat. When the water boils, add the ditalini and salt. Stir. Cover and return to a boil. Uncover and boil, stirring occasionally, for about 10 minutes, or until al dente.

Reserve ½ cup of the cooking water. Drain the ditalini and return to the pot. Add just enough water to moisten. Sprinkle with the Romano.

SERVES 4 TO 6

olive

The zucchini may be replaced with yellow summer squash; the rosemary with 2 teaspoons of dried rosemary (page 242); the apricots with golden raisins; and the ditalini with elbow macaroni or any other small dried pasta.

Toasted pine nuts may be added for a complementary flavor. Sprinkle the turkey and apricots with the nuts just before serving.

Turkey-Porcini Ragoût ➻ Rotini with Broccoli

Turkey:

$^1/_2$	ounce dried porcini mushrooms
$1^1/_2$	cups dry white wine
4	tablespoons olive oil, divided
$1^1/_4$ to $1^3/_4$	pounds turkey tenders, cut crosswise into $^3/_4$-inch-wide pieces
1	pound brown button mushrooms, halved
3	large cloves garlic, minced
1	can ($14^1/_2$ ounces) diced tomatoes, with juice
1	teaspoon salt
1	teaspoon crushed red pepper

Rotini:

2	teaspoons salt
$3^1/_2$	cups dried rotini
12	ounces broccoli florets, cut into small florets
$^1/_4$	cup (1 ounce) grated Parmesan cheese

If you're cooking for some diners who don't care for heat, you may reserve the red pepper to pass at the table.

To prepare the turkey: Place the porcini and wine in a microwaveable glass measuring cup. Cover with plastic wrap, leaving a vent. Microwave on high for 4 minutes, or until bubbling. Set aside to soften.

Heat 1 tablespoon oil in a large sauté pan over high heat. Add half the turkey. Cook for 5 minutes, turning, until golden on both sides. Remove to a tray. Repeat with 1 tablespoon of oil and the remaining turkey. Remove to the tray.

Add 2 tablespoons oil, the button mushrooms, and the garlic to the pan; stir. Reduce the heat to medium. Cover and cook for 3 minutes, or until the mushrooms give off liquid. Remove the cover and cook for 2 minutes, or until browned.

Meanwhile, line a fine sieve with a coffee filter. Hold over the pan and drain the porcini so the wine goes into the pan. Cook, uncovered, for 4 minutes, or until the sauce no longer smells of alcohol.

Rinse the porcini and cut into slivers. Add to the pan along with the tomatoes, salt, red pepper, and turkey. Stir. Cover and bring the mixture to a simmer.

Reduce the heat so the mixture simmers gently for 10 minutes, or until the turkey is no longer pink in the center. With a slotted spoon, remove the turkey and mushrooms to a platter. Keep the remaining sauce warm over low heat.

To prepare the rotini: Set a covered large pot of water over high heat. When the water boils, add the salt and rotini. Stir. Cover and return to a boil. Uncover and boil, stirring occasionally, for 6 minutes. Add the broccoli. Cover and return to a boil. Cook for 2 minutes, or until the pasta is al dente. Drain the pasta and broccoli and add to the reserved sauce. Toss over medium-high heat for 1 to 2 minutes, or until coated with the sauce. Remove from the heat. Add the Parmesan and toss.

S*ERVES* 4 *TO* 6

⤸

Wine
*A lighter-styled **Gattinara** from the nebbiolo grape. With a warm, herbal, rose petal nuance and flavors of truffles and earth, this red wine from Piedmont is delightful with mushroom dishes.*

⤸

broccoli

Stuffing a plain turkey breast not only makes it look prettier, but moistens and flavors the meat as well.

Turkey Breast Stuffed with Spinach ∽ Tomato-Scallion Risotto

Turkey:

1	skinless, boneless turkey breast half (about 3 pounds)
	Olive oil
2	large cloves garlic, minced
1	bag (6 ounces) baby spinach leaves, stems removed
	Salt
$^1/_2$	teaspoon ground black pepper
$^1/_2$	cup (2 ounces) grated Parmesan cheese

Risotto:

1	can (14$^1/_2$ ounces) chicken broth
2 to 2$^1/_2$	cups water
1	tablespoon olive oil
1 to 1$^1/_4$	cups superfino rice
	Salt
$^1/_2$	cup canned diced tomatoes, with juice
1	bunch scallions, all parts, sliced
1	teaspoon grated lemon zest

Choose arborio, carnaroli, or other rice labeled "superfino" for this dish. A Dutch oven made from enameled cast iron, anodized aluminum, or stainless steel–clad aluminum will cook the rice evenly and gently.

∽

I recommend using canned reduced-sodium broth or salt-free Chicken Broth (page 39). If you use regular canned broth, you may want to reduce the amount of salt or omit it.

aglio

To prepare the turkey: On a work surface, butterfly the turkey breast (page 148). With a scaloppine pounder or heavy skillet, flatten it to 1-inch thickness.

Preheat the oven to 375°F. Coat a 13 x 9-inch baking pan with oil.

In a medium sauté pan, cook 2 tablespoons oil and garlic for 2 minutes over low heat, or until the garlic is fragrant. Add the spinach. Toss. Cover and increase the heat to medium-high. Cook for 2 minutes, or until wilted. Drain any liquid.

Scatter the spinach over the turkey. Season with salt to taste. Sprinkle with the pepper and Parmesan. Press lightly. Starting at one short end, roll into a cylinder. Tie with kitchen string at 3-inch intervals. Season all over with salt and coat well with oil. Place on a diagonal in the prepared pan.

Roast, adding scant amounts of hot water if the pan juices start to brown too deeply, for about 1 hour, or until an instant-reading thermometer inserted into the center registers 165°F. Remove to a cutting board. Allow to sit for at least 15 minutes, or until the internal temperature rises to 170°F, before removing the string and slicing the turkey.

Pour any pan juices into a microwaveable measuring cup. Skim off the fat. Pour ½ cup hot water into the baking pan, scraping to remove any browned particles. Add to the cup. Microwave for 1 minute to heat before drizzling over the turkey slices.

To prepare the risotto: In a saucepan, heat the broth and water. Keep warm over low heat. Heat the oil in a Dutch oven set over medium heat. Add the rice and ¼ to ½ teaspoon salt. Cook, stirring, for 2 minutes. Reduce the heat to medium-low.

Add the tomatoes and ½ cup of the broth mixture. Start timing the cooking. Cook, stirring frequently, until the broth is absorbed. Continue adding the broth, ½ cup at a time, and stirring frequently. After 18 minutes of cooking, start testing the rice. The rice should be tender but still hold its shape. When it is cooked, remove from the heat. Stir in the scallions and lemon zest. (All of the broth mixture may not be needed.)

SERVES 4 TO 6

The stuffed turkey makes a stunning centerpiece for a winter holiday feast. Add 1 tablespoon rubbed sage to the spinach mixture. Replace the Tomato-Scallion Risotto with Risotto alla Milanese (page 111). Serve Sweet and Sharp Carrots (page 84) as one of the side dishes.

☙

Wine
Nero d'Avola is a varietal gaining recognition on the labels of many newly imported Sicilian wines. This red wine possesses a lively acidity and subtle richness of fruit.

☙

Pork and Beef Meals

Recipes

Stories and Basics

From early summer through late autumn, an aromatic cloud hugs central Italy. The intoxicating aroma of *porchetta*, spit-roasted suckling pig, seems to be everywhere. Porchetta is the centerpiece of many an open-air *festa* in Tuscany, Umbria, Marche, and beyond.

The allure is visceral: Crackling skin yields to sweet roast pork, seasoned liberally with robust garlic, bracing rosemary, fruity olive oil, biting black pepper, and coarse salt.

Porchetta's prime role in celebrational eating is actually representative of Italian meat cooking in general. Traditionally, meat in Italy has been a luxury reserved largely for the wealthy. So, for most Italians, it is the food of special occasions. Meat rarely dominates a meal. Portions are generally moderate and often are enhanced with various vegetable, cheese, or grain stuffings that add tremendous flavor and stretch the servings. Meat usually is *il secondo*, "the second course," brought to the table after *il primo*, "the first plate" of pasta, soup, or rice.

The tender cuts of pork and beef are prepared with little fuss. Grilled pork chops, for instance, are often served with only a wedge of lemon to squeeze over the meat. The citrus dissolves the caramelized crust of the chop, creating a savory pool of natural juices.

It is the preparation of less tender, cheaper cuts of pork and beef that draws out the true talent of Italian home cooks. Uncooked meat often is tenderized by pounding, as in *braciole*, "beef slices," from cuts such as the round, that are pounded thin and then stuffed and rolled to make *involtini*, "little bundles." Or meat may be ground into tenderness, as in *polpettone*, "meat loaf," and *polpette*, "meatballs," the classic forms of ground beef and pork.

Larger or thicker cuts of meat surrender to slow cooking in moist heat. *Stufati*, "stews," and *brasati*, "braises," combine cuts such as beef round or pork shoulder with wine, broth, vegetables, and savory seasonings. Time is the final, crucial ingredient that dissolves tough connective tissue into tender morsels that reward both cook and diners. ᔧ

Ossobuco, veal shanks braised in a rich vegetable wine mixture, inspired this variation prepared with more readily available pork chops.

Pork Chops Ossobuco-Style
↬ Lettuce with Parmesan Dressing
↬ Rustic Bread

Pork:

4 to 6	pork chops on the bone (1 inch thick)
	Olive oil
1	large carrot, chopped
3	ribs celery heart, chopped
1	medium-large onion, chopped
3	large cloves garlic, minced
1	cup dry white wine
1	can (14$\frac{1}{2}$ ounces) diced tomatoes, with juice
$\frac{3}{4}$	teaspoon **each** salt and ground black pepper
2	tablespoons minced fresh flat-leaf parsley

Salad:

$\frac{1}{3}$	cup olive oil
$\frac{1}{4}$	cup (1 ounce) grated Parmesan cheese
2	tablespoons lemon juice
	Salt and ground black pepper
2	heads Boston lettuce, torn
	Rustic Bread

To prepare the pork: Pat the chops dry with a paper towel. In a large sauté pan, heat 1 tablespoon oil over high heat. Add the chops and cook, turning once, for about 5 minutes, or until well browned on both sides. Remove to a platter.

Reduce the heat to medium. Add the carrot, celery, onion, and garlic to the pan. Stir. Cover and cook, stirring occasionally, for about 5 minutes, or until browned. Add the wine. Increase the heat to high. Cook for 3 minutes, or until the mixture no longer smells of alcohol. Add the tomatoes, salt, pepper, and parsley; stir. Bring to a boil. Cover and reduce the heat to medium-low. Cook for 10 minutes to blend the flavors.

Return the chops and any accumulated juices to the pan, spooning some of the sauce over them. Cover and reduce the heat until the mixture just simmers. Cook for about 10 minutes, or until an instant-reading thermometer registers 155°F when inserted into the center of one chop.

Remove the chops to a clean platter. Transfer slightly more than half of the vegetable mixture to a blender or food processor. Blend or process until smooth. Return to the pan. Stir. Add up to ½ cup of hot water, if needed, to loosen the sauce. Spoon the sauce over the chops.

To prepare the salad: While the chops are cooking, whisk the oil, Parmesan, and lemon juice in a bowl. Add a pinch each of salt and pepper. Add the lettuce. Set aside. Toss just before serving.

Serve the bread on the side.

SERVES 4 TO 6

sedano

For a special dinner, replace the bread with Risotto alla Milanese (page 111), which is the classic accompaniment to ossobuco.

There are probably as many bean recipes in Italy as there are cooks. This simple home-style dish marries the mellowness of pork with buttery beans and sweet-tart tomatoes.

Pork with White Beans and Tomatoes ꙮ Penne with Parmesan

Pork:

1	tablespoon olive oil
1 to 1½	pounds boneless pork sirloin chops
¾	teaspoon salt, divided
1	tablespoon minced fresh rosemary, divided
3	cans (14½ ounces each) Great Northern beans, rinsed and drained
2	cans (14½ ounces each) diced tomatoes, with juice
3	large cloves garlic, minced
¼	cup minced fresh flat-leaf parsley

Penne:

1	pound dried penne
1	tablespoon salt
1	tablespoon olive oil
¼	cup (1 ounce) grated Parmesan cheese

Two teaspoons of crumbled dried rosemary may replace the fresh rosemary.

To prepare the pork: Heat the oil in a large sauté pan over high heat. Season the chops with ¼ teaspoon salt and half of the rosemary. Cook the chops for about 3 minutes on each side, or until well browned. Remove to a platter.

To the pan, add the beans, tomatoes, garlic, ½ teaspoon salt, and the remaining rosemary. Bring to a boil. Reduce to a simmer. Cover and cook for 10 minutes. With the back of a large spoon, crush some of the beans and tomatoes. Return the chops to the pan, spooning the beans over them. Cover and simmer for about 15 minutes, or until the pork is no longer pink in the center. Stir in the parsley.

To prepare the penne: Set a covered large pot of water over high heat. When the water boils, add the penne and the salt. Stir. Cover and return to a boil. Uncover and boil, stirring occasionally, for about 10 minutes, or until al dente. Reserve ½ cup of the cooking water.

Drain the penne and return to the pot. Add the oil; toss. Add a few tablespoons of reserved water if needed to moisten. Pass the Parmesan at the table.

Serves 4 to 6

Grilled Sausage-Stuffed Zucchini
↬ Carrot-Raisin Salad with Mint

Zucchini:

4	medium zucchini
	Olive oil
1½	pounds uncooked mild or hot Italian sausage with fennel
4	fresh plum tomatoes, peeled and chopped
¼	cup plain dry bread crumbs
2	cloves garlic, minced
1½	cups (6 ounces) shredded provolone cheese, divided

Salad:

¼	cup olive oil
2	tablespoons red or white wine vinegar
2	teaspoons minced fresh mint
¼	teaspoon salt
4 to 6	medium carrots, shredded
2	tablespoons raisins, minced

To prepare the zucchini: Prepare a charcoal or gas grill for indirect cooking, firing briquettes or lighting the gas on one side of the grid only.

Cut the zucchini in half lengthwise. With a spoon, scoop out the seeds and discard. Rub zucchini lightly with olive oil. Place on a tray.

Cut the casing from the sausage and put the meat in a large bowl. Add the tomatoes, bread crumbs, garlic, and ½ cup provolone. Stir with a fork or your hands to mix. Spoon the sausage mixture into the zucchini shells, patting down the mixture evenly to the ends. Sprinkle with the remaining provolone. Pat gently.

Place the zucchini directly on the cooking rack, on the side away from the hot briquettes or burner. Cover and grill for about 30 minutes, or until nicely browned. Remove from the grill and allow to sit for 10 minutes.

To prepare the salad: While the zucchini is grilling, whisk the oil, vinegar, mint, and salt. Add the carrots and raisins; toss. Allow to sit for 30 minutes. Toss.

SERVES 4 TO 6

Fresh flat-leaf parsley or basil may replace the mint.

↬

To bake the Sausage-Stuffed Zucchini in the oven: Preheat the oven to 400°F. Coat a large baking pan with no-stick spray. Arrange the zucchini on the pan. Cover and bake for about 30 minutes, or until nicely browned. Remove from the oven and allow to sit for 10 minutes.

↬

Wine
Primitivo from Puglia, the same grape as American zinfandel, is softer in its Italian incarnation. It is lively and delicious with this meal.

↬

The More Things Change . . .

Supermarkets happen—even in Italy.

Outsiders like me, who are obsessed with *la cucina Italiana*, cherish the illusion that Italians shop daily for the freshest ingredients in lively open-air markets. These days, however, millions of Italians buy their food, at least some of the time, in supermarkets. This doesn't necessarily mean Italians care less passionately about food—I don't think they are capable of eating poorly—but supermarkets do displace the idealized image we foreigners have nurtured.

In the Italy of myth, happy peasants pluck homegrown plum tomatoes under the Mediterranean sun as mandolins vibrate with the strains of "O Sole Mio." In the Italy of the second millennium, consumers stock up on canned tomatoes under fluorescent lights and Muzak. Which is the real Italy? I'm not sure.

I do know that on a recent visit to Tuscany, as I shopped in a small supermarket in the Florentine suburb of Le Sieci, I noticed a display of apples that had come all the way from Chile. Yes, the Chile in South America—half a world away from Italy.

Twenty-five years ago, in the springtime, I would not have seen apples from Chile in that market. I would not have seen apples at all. Why? Because apples aren't harvested in spring. One of the bedrock tenets of Italian cooking has always been that fruits and vegetables are grown locally and savored in season.

Things change, not always for the better.

A Florentine friend, a talented businesswoman, half jokingly suggests that I write a book of fast recipes because she could really make use of it. She doesn't have time to cook; and besides, she's looking for different sorts of dishes, not the same old thing.

Can I be hearing this in Italy?

Another Tuscan friend, a talented cook who worked for many years, confides that her married son often cajoles her into preparing his favorite dishes. "They come here when they want to eat well," she says.

"What do he and his wife eat every day?" I ask.

"Mostly frozen foods." She sighs. "They both work. They have no time."

Am I really in Italy?

My husband reports that he'll have dinner, not lunch as he had hoped, with his buddies from the Leather School. The shop, and the church of Santa Croce in which it is housed, no longer closes for two hours at midday. Both the secular and the divine now operate from morning until night to accommodate the crush of tourists. This onslaught of pilgrims thirsty for the elixir of Italian life may be drying up the fountain they seek.

Will these changes be the downfall of Italian culture? Probably not. Italians have survived mad Roman emperors, corrupt Popes, and invading hordes—Goths, Normans, Saracens, Hapsburgs, American tourists, and others too numerous to mention. More recently, they have contended with the Mafia, the Red Brigade, some of the tackiest television programs on the planet, and their own post–World War II governments, which tumble into disarray with the predictability of dominoes.

Surely, resilient Italians will survive supermarkets.

There are reasons to hope that the culture will adapt, yet endure, in a distinctly Italian fashion. I was reassured of this on my most recent visit to Italy. My husband, daughters, and I landed in Milan on a Saturday. We climbed right into our rented green Alfa Romeo sedan and set out for northeastern Lombardy, almost to the Swiss border.

We took the scenic route recommended by the rental staff. It curved from picture-postcard Lecco at the eastern base of Lake Como, then climbed dizzyingly into the Alps as we left the town of Sondrio. The *autostrada* to Bergamo would have been quicker, but not as beautiful. We reached our rental apartment at dusk and dined in the restaurant on the property before tumbling, exhausted, into bed.

Sunday morning dawned and we were ravenous. My husband and I tiptoed out to shop for groceries. We would be back with fruit, milk, and cereal for our daughters before the girls awakened. In nearby Ponte di Legno, we easily located the *Supermercato Spesa Mia*, "My Shopping Supermarket," but it had a *chiuso la domenica* sign in the window. "Closed on Sunday." Well, of course, we told ourselves, this is a small town. The market would be closed on Sunday. We'll just drive down the valley to a bigger town with an open supermarket.

We cruised to the town of Edola and beyond, driving for miles and miles, only to see chiuso chiuso chiuso—in every market, *alimentari*, and green-grocer's window.

Finally we looked at each other and laughed. Were we groggy with jet lag? What were we thinking? Shop for groceries on Sunday? We really were in Italy, the Italy where the ideal and the real duke it out every day. It was wonderful to revisit the utter frustration of traditional Italian culture defying modern convenience.

A while later, back in a caffè in Ponte di Legno with the girls, we enjoyed a very late breakfast of sandwiches, strawberries, and chocolate croissants. As we ate and laughed, we reflected that some things don't change . . . and that is for the better. ✍

The vegetable for this meal was inspired by the Brussels sprouts at Trattoria Benvenuto in Florence. Lots of garlic and tomato tamed any harshness in the sprouts.

Sage Pork Tenderloin ❧ Brussels Sprouts in Tomato Sauce ❧ Cheese Polenta

Pork:

2 to 2½   pounds pork tenderloins
       2   tablespoons olive oil
       2   tablespoons rubbed dried sage
       ½   teaspoon salt

Brussels Sprouts:

       2   tablespoons olive oil
    1¼   pounds Brussels sprouts, quartered
       1   can (8 ounces) tomato purée
       2   cloves garlic, minced
       ½   teaspoon salt

Polenta:

       1   cup cornmeal
       2   cans (14½ ounces each) chicken broth
       ½   cup (2 ounces) shredded Tuscan Pecorino cheese
           Salt

olive

To prepare the pork: Preheat the oven broiler.

Pat the pork dry and place on a large baking sheet with sides. Pierce at 2-inch intervals with a small sharp knife. In a small bowl, mix the oil, sage, and salt. Rub evenly over the tenderloin, pushing some of the paste into the holes.

Broil 6 inches from the heat source, turning occasionally, for about 10 minutes, or until well browned and an instant-reading thermometer registers 155°F when inserted into the center of the tenderloin. Remove from the oven and allow to sit for 5 minutes, or until the internal temperature is 160°F.

To prepare the Brussels sprouts: While the pork is cooking, in a large sauté pan, heat the oil. Add the Brussels sprouts. Cover and cook for about 3 minutes, turning occasionally, or until they start to brown. Add the tomato purée, garlic, and salt. Stir. Cover and reduce the heat to low. Cook for about 8 minutes, or until the Brussels sprouts are tender.

To prepare the polenta: Meanwhile, whisk the cornmeal and broth in a saucepan. Cook, whisking constantly, over medium-high heat, for about 3 minutes, or until boiling. Reduce the heat to low. Cook, whisking frequently, for 2 to 3 minutes, or until very thick. Remove from the heat and stir in the Pecorino. Season with salt to taste. Set aside, covered, to keep warm if necessary.

Cut the pork into thin slices. Place on dinner plates. Spoon the Brussels sprouts and the polenta on the side. Drizzle any pan juices from the pork over the pork and polenta.

SERVES 4 TO 6

A sprinkling of crushed red pepper adds zest to the Brussels sprouts.

Spanish Manchego or provolone cheese may replace the Tuscan Pecorino.

To grill the roast:
Prepare a charcoal
or gas grill for
indirect cooking,
firing briquettes or
lighting the gas on
the sides of the
grid only. Set a
drip pan in the
center of the lower
grid. Add 1 cup
of hot water.
Place the roast on
the center of the
cooking rack over
the drip pan.
Cover and cook
for about 1 hour
and 15 minutes,
or until an
instant-reading
thermometer
registers 155°F
when inserted into
the center. Remove
and allow the pork
to sit for at least
10 minutes, or
until the
temperature rises
to 160°F. Remove
the drip pan and
skim off any fat.
Add ¹/₂ cup of hot
water. Scrape to
remove any
browned particles.
Pour into a glass
measuring cup.
Microwave for
1 minute. Season
with salt.

In Tuscany, this roast is called arista. *It is the home cook's more manageable version of suckling roast pig, a savory centerpiece for a summer outdoors gathering.*

Roast Pork with Rosemary and Garlic ⤳ Stir-Sautéed Spinach ⤳ Rustic Bread

Pork:

3¹/₂ to 4	pounds boneless pork roast (page 173)
	Salt and ground black pepper
	Olive oil
4	cloves garlic, coarsely chopped
2	tablespoons minced fresh rosemary
¹/₂	cup hot water

Spinach:

¹/₄	cup olive oil
1	large clove garlic, minced
2	bags (10 ounces each) spinach, stems removed, leaves torn into pieces
1	tablespoon red or white wine vinegar
¹/₄	teaspoon **each** salt and ground black pepper

Rustic Bread

To prepare the pork: Preheat the oven to 375°F.

On a work surface, open the roast with the boned side facing up. Cut a slit the length of the roast. Season generously with salt and pepper. Drizzle with oil. Spread about two-thirds of the garlic and rosemary evenly over the surface. Roll the pork and tie at intervals with kitchen string.

With a thin knife, make about 8 slits in the outside of the roast. Insert some garlic and rosemary into each slit. Season the outside with salt and drizzle with olive oil.

Place the roast on a roasting rack set in a roasting pan. Roast for about 1 hour and 15 minutes, or until an instant-reading thermometer registers 155°F when inserted into the center. Remove from the oven and allow the roast to sit for at least 10 minutes, or until the temperature rises to 160°F.

Pour off any fat in the roasting pan. Add the hot water to the pan. Scrape the bottom of the pan to remove any browned particles. Pour into a glass measuring cup. Microwave for 1 minute. Season with salt to taste.

To prepare the spinach: Place the oil and garlic in a large sauté pan or Dutch oven. Cover and cook over low heat for 5 minutes, or until the garlic is fragrant. Don't allow the garlic to brown.

Add the spinach and toss to coat with the garlic oil. Cover and cook over high heat for 2 to 3 minutes, or until the spinach is wilted. Uncover and toss until no liquid remains. Add the vinegar, salt, and pepper. Toss.

Cut the pork into thin slices. Place on dinner plates. Drizzle with the reserved pan juices. Spoon the spinach on the side.

Slice the bread and place it on a baking sheet. Warm in the oven for 10 minutes. Serve with the pork and spinach.

SERVES 6 TO 8

Select a boneless double top loin roast, a boneless center loin roast, or a boneless sirloin roast.

If you grow rosemary or have access to an inexpensive source, several branches make a pretty addition to the roast. Twine 3 long sprigs under the string on the outside of the roast. Rub with olive oil. Remove and discard before slicing.

Wine
Pinot Noir from Santa Barbara, California, is a fruit-forward red wine dancing with cherry and black pepper nuances.

Sometimes I season pork tenderloin with rosemary and garlic and broil it according to the method on page 171 just so I can use it for this salad.

Pork Roast Salad with Crunchy Vegetables and Green Olives

Extras from the Roast Pork with Rosemary and Garlic (page 172) are ideal for this salad.

Italian pork roast, "porchetta," is sold in the prepared-foods department of some supermarkets.

For a kick, look for Sicilian olives packed with crushed red pepper. Or, use plain green Sicilian olives and add ¼ teaspoon crushed red pepper.

Slivers of roasted peppers may be added.

Radicchio may replace some of the lettuce.

1 to 1½	pounds cooked Italian pork roast, cut into ½-inch-thick slices
½	cup olive oil
3	tablespoons red or white wine vinegar
½	teaspoon dried oregano
½	teaspoon salt
3	carrots, thinly sliced
4	ribs celery heart, thinly sliced
1	cup (5 ounces) pitted and slivered Sicilian green olives
10	ounces leaf lettuce, torn

Cut the pork slices into ½-inch cubes; set aside.

In a large bowl, whisk the oil, vinegar, oregano, and salt. Add the carrots, celery, olives, lettuce, and pork. Toss to coat with the dressing.

Serves 4 to 6

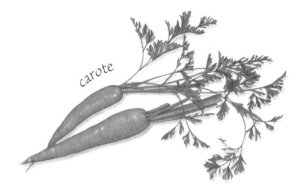

carote

Angelino and the Secret of Tuscan Grilling

My husband's mastery of the grill is firmly established at our house. Perhaps he learned a thing or two from all his outings to Angelino's. Here's how he tells it.

Man, oh, man—talk about testosterone.

My first trip abroad, to study art history in 1971, stretched out to a five-year stay. I just couldn't get my fill of Florence. I liked the food, the wine, the women, and my friends.

To pay the rent, I got work designing and selling leather goods at La Scuola del Cuoio—the Leather School—in the monastery of Santa Croce in Florence.

There were ten salesmen. I was the only American; all the others were Italian. We were in our twenties, and a couple of the lads were married, but all of us enjoyed the ebb and flow of human traffic into our display rooms.

We competed at everything. Who sold the most. Who had the best dates. Who won at backgammon during the slow days in February. After lunch we competed at soccer in the private parking lot behind the church. Marcello Gori, who directed the school, fostered the competition. It was good for business.

This atmosphere created a great deal of camaraderie, and during our busiest months in May, June, and July, we would often break away from a tough day of selling and head out to the countryside to Angelino's.

It was always a group thing, always in summer. At least three or four of us, sometimes with dates, sometimes without, would make that beautiful early evening drive from Florence out to Angelino's for dinner. It didn't take long to escape the heat, congestion, and noise of tourist-choked Florence as we roared and soared through the Tuscan hills.

Angelino's was about an hour's drive from Florence. On the way to San Casciano? Greve? I don't remember exactly where—but I do remember the way.

We would weave our way out of the *centro* and climb into the cool hills. Those country roads begged for fearless driving, and we conquered every bend with skill and power. *"Fai la linea!"* was the call from the back seat. "Make the line" is the crude translation, but it meant taking the shortest distance through curves—bisecting them with a straight line.

Then, all of a sudden, past one of those curves, we would be there. A small one-room building, it looked like a large shed you would see behind a Tuscan country home. There were no signs, no electricity, just lanterns outside and in. And, of course, Angelino, an apron over his sport shirt, working the meat on a large, open, wood-burning grill.

You could eat in or out and we always ate outside at rough-hewn tables with benches. Angelino's wife was inside making salads and side dishes and managing the bread and wine. The wine was always red. So was the meat.

It was automatic. There were no menus, only Angelino coming by the table, gripping with three gnarled fingers a bottle of mineral water and a bottle of the local red wine by their respective necks. His other hand held a basket of rugged Tuscan bread and a plate of sliced salami and prosciutto.

He would unload both handfuls on our table. Then the one-word question: *"Carne?"*

Why even ask? We didn't come to Angelino's for pork or lamb. We came for *la bistecca alla fiorentina*, Florentine beefsteak.

With each order, another single word: *"Come?"* How do you want it prepared? And we'd tell him. Then off he would go, no nonsense or small talk, and grill the steaks to perfection. He would drop off the meat for everyone at the very instant his wife brought salads and whatever vegetable she had prepared that night.

We would eat and drink. Laugh and lie. My friend Massimo would bellow: "Angelino, my beefsteak is tough tonight. Are you sure there are no horses missing in the *zona*?" And Angelino would scowl, grab a cleaver and cock it at Massimo. And so it went into the night.

The grilled meals at Angelino's were superb. But why? Now, after all this time, I think I know.

It had nothing to do with the wonderful beef. I have no idea what blend of woods he used on his open grill to complement that beef. It wasn't special wine or masterful appetizers.

It was the cooling grace of a summer night in Tuscany. It was the piney smell of dew-dropped *rosmarino* growing in hedges near the grill. It was the fading profiles of cypresses on the hill that disappeared in the dusk and didn't come into view again until the moon found them, and us, by now into our third bottle of *rosso*.

It was friends laughing. It was crickets singing. It was frogs croaking in Italian.

It was the assumptive power of youth, taking for granted something so miraculous and wonderful, knowing that you could come back the next night, the next week, the next summer, to Angelino's, and have it all again.

—*Walter Sanders*

The best carpaccio I ever ate was at a restaurant near Pisa. The thinly sliced beef was served with rucola (rocket), extra-virgin olive oil, and slivers of Parmesan. This dish pairs the accompaniments with charred flank steak.

Flank Steak Carpaccio-Style with Spinach and Shaved Parmesan ⌇ Rustic Bread

1½ to 2 pounds flank steak

½ cup balsamic vinegar

1 bag (10 ounces) spinach, stems removed, leaves sliced into strips

   Salt and ground black pepper

4 to 6 tablespoons olive oil

1 chunk (1½ ounces) Parmesan cheese

Rustic Bread

Place the steak and vinegar in a 13 x 9-inch glass or ceramic pan. Turn to coat evenly. Cover with plastic wrap and refrigerate, turning occasionally, for at least 1 hour.

Prepare a charcoal or gas grill. Remove the steak from the marinade. Pour the marinade into a glass measuring cup; set aside.

Grill the steak directly over the heat source for about 8 minutes per side, or until the internal temperature registers 145°F on an instant-reading thermometer. Remove and set aside on a cutting board with a well to catch the juices. Allow to rest for 5 minutes.

Meanwhile, place the spinach on dinner plates or a large platter. Microwave the reserved marinade for 2 minutes, or until boiling. Remove and allow to cool.

Cut the steak into thin diagonal slices. Arrange over the spinach. Drizzle with the collected meat juices. Season to taste with salt and pepper. Drizzle with the oil. Cut shavings from the Parmesan cheese and scatter over the top. Pass the reserved marinade at the table.

Serve the bread on the side.

SERVES 4 TO 6

The flank steak may be broiled on a pan set 6 inches below the heat source for about 8 minutes on each side.

A *classic* bistecca alla fiorentina, *Florentine steak, is big enough to make even a Texan blush. Cut from prized young Chianina cattle, the steak is the identical cut to an American T-bone.*

T-Bone Florentine ↭ Green Beans and Plum Tomatoes ↭ Rosemary Potatoes

Potatoes:

¼	cup olive oil
6	medium-large red- or white-skinned potatoes, unpeeled, cut into ½-inch chunks, patted dry
2	teaspoons minced fresh rosemary
¼	teaspoon salt

Beans:

3	tablespoons olive oil
1	pound green beans
1	pound fresh plum tomatoes, peeled and quartered
2	large cloves garlic, minced
½	teaspoon salt

Steak:

2 to 3	T-bone steaks (1 pound each), cut 1 inch thick
	Olive oil
¼	teaspoon salt
	Ground black pepper

↭
Wine
A "Super-Tuscan" Red, a full-flavored blend of sangiovese (the principal Chianti grape) and cabernet sauvignon, is very well structured, with well-balanced fruit, acidity, and tannins.
↭

To prepare the potatoes: In a large skillet, heat the oil over medium-high heat. Add the potatoes and stir to coat with oil. Cook, without stirring, for 5 minutes, or until browned on the bottom. Reduce the heat to medium. Sprinkle the potatoes with the rosemary. Cook, stirring occasionally, for about 12 minutes, or until well browned. Remove to a platter. Season with the salt.

To prepare the beans: Meanwhile, heat the oil in a large sauté pan over high heat. Add the beans and stir. Cover and cook for about 3 minutes, or until the beans start to brown.

Add the tomatoes, garlic, and salt. Reduce the heat to medium. Cover and cook for about 5 minutes, or until the beans are tender.

To prepare the steak: Prepare a gas or charcoal grill.

Season both sides of the steaks with the oil and salt. Place on the cooking rack directly over the heat source for about 3 minutes per side, or until an instant-reading thermometer registers 145°F for medium-rare doneness. Cook from 30 to 90 seconds longer for medium or well doneness.

Remove to a platter. Set aside for 5 minutes. Carve each steak into two portions. Season with pepper at the table.

SERVES 4 TO 6

vino rosso

For a true taste of Florence, purchase a small bottle of the best estate-bottled extra-virgin Tuscan olive oil. Pass it at the table to drizzle lightly over the steak and beans.

My husband and I were once invited to dinner by an elderly Florentine acquaintance. His wife was a sweet woman, but after eating her leaden polpette—meatballs—we gained insight into our host's chronic crankiness.

Meatballs in Tomato Onion Sauce ❧ Cauliflower Salad ❧ Rustic Bread

Meatballs:

1½   cups ¼-inch cubes of day-old Italian bread
¼   cup milk
1½   pounds ground beef
¼   cup (1 ounce) grated Pecorino Romano cheese
2   large cloves garlic, minced
1   egg, beaten
1   teaspoon salt, divided
½   teaspoon ground black pepper
2   tablespoons olive oil
1   medium-large onion, coarsely chopped
2   cans (14½ ounces each) diced tomatoes, with juice
¼   cup minced fresh flat-leaf parsley

Salad:

1   cup water
1   medium head cauliflower, cored, separated into florets
¼   cup olive oil
1   tablespoon red or white wine vinegar
⅛   teaspoon salt
¼   teaspoon crushed red pepper
3   tablespoons drained capers

Rustic Bread

To prepare the meatballs: Place the bread and milk in a mixing bowl. Toss until the milk soaks into the bread. Add the beef, Romano, and garlic. In a small bowl, beat the egg, ½ teaspoon salt, and pepper. Add to the beef mixture. Combine the mixture with your hands. Shape into 12 meatballs; set aside.

Preheat the oven to 350°F. Heat the oil in a large skillet over high heat. Fry the meatballs for 5 minutes, turning frequently, until browned on all sides. Remove to a large baking sheet with sides. Bake for about 15 minutes, or until an instant-reading thermometer registers 160°F in the center of a meatball.

Meanwhile, pour off and discard any fat in the skillet. Add the onion. Cook over medium heat for about 5 minutes, or until well browned. Add the tomatoes. Bring to a boil. Reduce the heat to low. Cover and simmer for about 8 minutes, or until softened. Add ½ teaspoon salt and the parsley.

Place the meatballs in the skillet, spooning some sauce over them. Simmer for about 3 minutes to marry the flavors.

To prepare the salad: Bring the water to a boil in a covered saucepan. Add the cauliflower. Cover and cook for 5 minutes, or until a knife can be inserted into the cauliflower. Drain and rinse with cold water. Cut the florets into thick slices.

In a serving bowl, whisk the oil, vinegar, salt, and red pepper. Add the capers and cauliflower. Toss.

Serve the bread on the side.

SERVES 4 TO 6

cipolle

During testing, I kept putting this beef recipe aside because the preparation seemed like a hassle. But the taste kept drawing me back—like the boyfriend you can't stay away from but who's nothing but trouble.

Beef Bundles with Peppers and Provolone ⮑ Artichoke and Red Onion Rice

Beef:

18	thin slices (2 pounds) beef top or bottom round
	Salt
2	roasted red peppers, cut into 18 strips
6	ounces provolone cheese, cut into ¼-inch-thick sticks
1	tablespoon olive oil
1	cup dry red wine

Rice:

2	tablespoons olive oil
1	medium red onion, chopped
3	large cloves garlic, minced
1	cup medium- or long-grain rice
2	packages (10 ounces each) frozen artichoke hearts, thawed
1	can (14½ ounces) chicken broth
	Salt

To prepare the beef: Lay the beef slices on a large work surface. With a smooth scaloppine pounder, flatten each beef slice into a 6 x 4-inch rectangle. Season with salt. Curl a pepper strip in the center of each slice; crumble a stick of provolone to fit in the center of the curl. Fold the narrow ends of the beef slightly over the pepper and cheese. Fold the long ends over each other to create a tight bundle. Close with sturdy pointed toothpicks. Continue stuffing the remaining slices.

Heat the oil in a large sauté pan over high heat. Add the beef bundles, seam side down. Cook for about 6 minutes, turning once, until well browned. Reduce the heat to low. Partially cover the pan and cook for 5 minutes.

Place the beef bundles on a tray; set aside. Add the wine to the sauté pan. Increase the heat to medium-high. Boil for about 5 minutes, or until the wine is reduced slightly and no longer smells of alcohol. Place the beef bundles, and any

The artichokes do not need to be completely thawed. Separate the partially thawed chokes and place in a large colander. Rinse thoroughly with cold water. Do not thaw the chokes in the microwave, which would toughen them.

⮑

Thin "braccciole"-style slices of beef are sold in many supermarkets. Or, look for thin slices labeled "eye steak" or "sandwich steak." If not available, ask the meat cutter to slice ¼-inch-thick slices from the top or bottom round.

⮑

The beef bundles can be stuffed, covered, and refrigerated for up to 2 hours before cooking.

juices accumulated in the tray, in the sauté pan. Swirl the pan to coat the bundles with wine. Remove from the heat and allow to sit for 5 minutes. Remove and discard the toothpicks before serving.

To prepare the rice: While the beef is cooking, in a Dutch oven, heat the oil over medium heat. Add the onion and garlic. Cook for 5 minutes, stirring occasionally, or until golden. Add the rice and stir to coat. Add the artichokes, broth, and ¼ teaspoon salt. Bring to a boil. Reduce the heat so the mixture simmers. Cover and cook for 10 minutes. Remove from the heat and set aside, covered, for 5 minutes. Taste and adjust the seasoning.

SERVES 4 TO 6

A scaloppine pounder is a 3-inch-wide metal disk attached to a perpendicular rubberized handle. It is heavy and smooth so it doesn't tear thin slices of meat.

peperoni

〜

Wine
Chianti Classico Riserva *is more refined, elegant, and mellow than Chianti Classico because of longer barrel time. It complements peppers, garlic, and beef.*

〜

This stew offers exceptional flavor for minimal work. Simply combine all the ingredients in a heavy ovenproof pot (I favor an enameled cast iron Dutch oven) and bake for several hours.

Chianti Beef Stew ∽ Herbed Gemelli Pasta

Stew:

3	pounds trimmed lean top round, cut into 1½-inch cubes
¾	cup flour
8	ounces brown or white mushrooms, sliced
4	carrots, sliced
2	onions, sliced
4	ounces thick-cut ham, finely diced
1	large clove garlic, minced
¼	cup minced fresh flat-leaf parsley
1	tablespoon chopped fresh rosemary
½	teaspoon **each** salt and ground black pepper
1	can (14½ ounces) diced tomatoes, with juice
1	can (14½ ounces) beef broth
1½	cups Chianti wine
2	tablespoons balsamic vinegar

Gemelli:

1	pound dried gemelli
1	tablespoon salt
1	tablespoon butter
½	cup minced fresh flat-leaf parsley
1	tablespoon dried thyme or rubbed dried sage

Two teaspoons crumbled dried rosemary may replace the fresh rosemary.

∽

Standing time improves the flavor of this stew with its robust wine base. Cook it several days before serving, cool, cover, and refrigerate. Reheat the stew gently on the stove top. If the gravy is too thick, stir in a little beef broth or water. The stew also freezes beautifully for several weeks.

To prepare the stew: Preheat the oven to 350°F.

In a large bowl, combine the beef and the flour. Toss with hands to evenly coat. Lift the cubes out, sifting through your fingers to shake off most, but not all, of the excess flour. Place in a 6-quart ovenproof Dutch oven. Add the mushrooms, carrots, onions, ham, garlic, parsley, rosemary, salt, and pepper. Toss with your hands to incorporate the vegetables with the meat and flour. Add the tomatoes, broth, wine, and vinegar. Cover tightly with aluminum foil, then with the pan lid.

Bake for 2½ to 3 hours, or until the beef is fork tender. Remove from the oven and allow to sit for 30 minutes.

To prepare the gemelli: Meanwhile, set a covered large pot of water over high heat. When the water boils, add the gemelli and salt. Stir. Cover and return to a boil. Uncover and boil, stirring occasionally, for about 10 minutes, or until al dente.

Reserve ½ cup of the cooking water. Drain the gemelli and return to the pot. Add the butter; toss to coat. Add the parsley and thyme or sage. Add a bit of the reserved water to loosen the herb coating.

SERVES 6 TO 8

funghi porcini: freschi e secchi

For a thicker gravy, whisk 2 tablespoons of flour with 4 tablespoons cold water in a bowl. Gradually add the flour mixture into the hot stew. Cook over medium heat, stirring constantly, until thickened.

Any shape of small pasta— farfalle, rotini, penne—may replace the gemelli.

Appetizers and Desserts for Special Meals

Appetizer Recipes

Dessert Recipes

(continued)

Stories and Basics

In today's Italy *la tredicesima*, "the thirteenth," is good luck indeed. It's the extra month's salary given to workers each December.

This chapter is also a tredicesima: something special, something extra. Appetizers and desserts are additions to the core meals of earlier chapters, building each into a little feast for a special time—be it Saturday night, your best friend's birthday, or the first day of spring.

A classic meal in Italy is composed of small courses, one after the other, to prolong the pleasure. To plan a dinner party like this, first select the *secondo e contorno*, "main dish and side," from among the vegetable, meat, poultry, and fish recipes in this book.

Here's how it works. Marsala Chicken Breasts Bolognese and Broccoli with Orange (page 140), for instance, will serve eight to ten instead of four to six, once you have added more courses. Select a light antipasto, Porcini-Stuffed Baby Bello Mushrooms (page 194) and a *primo*, or "first plate," that contrasts with the main dish ingredients. Try Fusilli with Spicy Clams (page 79). This pasta recipe will also serve eight to ten when it's part of a more elaborate meal. For the *dolce*, "dessert," present a stunning *Zuccotto* (page 220). This Florentine ice cream bombe is a show-stopper, yet may be prepared completely in advance.

When your "occasion" is a more relaxed Sunday supper, start by setting out some cut raw vegetables and a dip, such as the crostini pesto spread (page 203) or white bean–sage spread (page 205). Serve a main dish of Chianti Beef Stew (page 184), accompanied by warm Crescentine (page 207) in place of the Herbed Gemelli Pasta in the original recipe, followed by a simple green salad. The moist Almond Cake with Caramelized Orange Slices (page 222) is a comforting way to close the evening.

A delightful idea to serve a larger gathering—whether for the winter holidays or for a summer patio party—is to present appetizers and desserts as the meal. Purchase antipasti such as salami, olives, and cheeses. Add a variety of *crostini*, some frittate, and loaves of bread. Select contrasting desserts that hold up well: Roman Cheesecake (page 230) and Chocolate Torte (page 228) anytime; Fresh Strawberry Tart with Rum Pastry Cream (page 215) for summer, Fig-Walnut Tart with Lemon Glaze (page 231) for winter. ✑

Three-Melon Salad with Prosciutto

¹/₂ honeydew melon
¹/₂ cantaloupe
 3   thick slices watermelon
 2   tablespoons sugar
 2   tablespoons lemon juice
 1   serrano chile, seeded and minced
 8   ounces thinly sliced prosciutto
¹/₄ cup slivered fresh basil leaves

Scoop out the honeydew, cantaloupe, and watermelon in balls, or cut into cubes, removing and discarding the rinds. There should be about 6 cups of cut melon.

In a bowl, combine the sugar, lemon juice, and 1 teaspoon chile. Reserve any additional chile in a small dish. Cover the chile with plastic wrap and refrigerate. Add the melons to the bowl and toss to combine. Cover with plastic wrap and refrigerate, stirring occasionally, for about 2 hours.

Drape the prosciutto on individual appetizer plates. Spoon a serving of melon salad on the side. Sprinkle with the basil. Pass the additional minced chile at the table.

MAKES 8 SERVINGS

Variation

Melon and Prosciutto Bocconcini: To prepare 48 individual "small mouthfuls," tear 1 pound of thinly sliced prosciutto lengthwise into 1-inch-wide strips. Stir the melon salad. Wrap a prosciutto strip around each piece of melon, making sure some pepper is included. Secure with a toothpick. Place on a serving dish. Sprinkle with the basil.

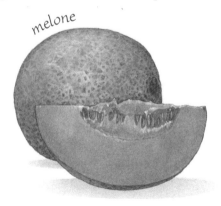

melone

This seafood salad travels beautifully.

Shrimp and Tomato Salad with Basil-Vodka Dressing

1	pint fresh grape or cherry tomatoes
¼	cup tightly packed fresh basil leaves
⅓	cup olive oil
2	tablespoons vodka
1	tablespoon lemon juice
1	clove garlic, minced
½	teaspoon **each** salt and ground black pepper
1½	pounds cooked peeled shrimp
1½	cups thinly sliced tender celery hearts, with leaves
	Lettuce leaves

With a toothpick or skewer, pierce each tomato through the middle and through the stem end to the base (this will allow the dressing to penetrate the tomatoes). Lay the basil leaves atop one another. Roll into a tight cylinder. Cut into thin crosswise slices; reserve.

In a bowl, whisk the oil, vodka, lemon juice, garlic, salt, and pepper. Add the shrimp, celery, tomatoes, and basil. Toss gently. Cover with plastic wrap and refrigerate, stirring occasionally, for up to 24 hours.

Allow to sit at room temperature for 15 minutes. Serve on salad plates lined with lettuce leaves.

MAKES 8 SERVINGS

Cooked lobster or cooked scallops may replace all or some of the shrimp.

Half red and half yellow tomatoes, if available, make a pretty salad.

*In Venice, condiments and sauces highlighting the interplay
of sweet and sharp are often used to season fish.*

Sea Bass, Red Onion, Raisin, and Pine Nut Salad

$^1\!/_2$	cup plus 2 tablespoons olive oil, divided
$^1\!/_4$	cup red or white wine vinegar
1	teaspoon sugar
$^1\!/_2$	teaspoon salt
1	medium-large red onion
$1^1\!/_2$	pounds sea bass fillets
2	teaspoons dried thyme leaves
2	dried bay leaves
$^1\!/_2$	cup raisins
$^1\!/_4$	cup minced fresh flat-leaf parsley
$^1\!/_3$	cup pine nuts, toasted

In a 13 x 9-inch glass dish, whisk $^1\!/_2$ cup oil with the vinegar, sugar, and salt. Set aside.

Cut the onion in half from root to stem. Lay each half, cut side down, on a cutting board. Cut into $^1\!/_8$-inch-thick slices running perpendicular to the root end. Set aside.

Heat 1 tablespoon oil in a large sauté pan over medium-high heat. Place the sea bass in the pan and sauté for about 8 minutes, turning once, or until opaque in the center. Place in a prepared dish. It's okay if the fillets crumble into pieces.

Add 1 tablespoon oil to the pan. Reduce the heat to medium-low. Add the onion, thyme, and bay leaves. Stir. Cover and cook for about 5 minutes, or until softened. Spread over the fillets. Sprinkle with the raisins and parsley. Stir gently to coat all ingredients with the dressing. Cover tightly with plastic wrap.

Refrigerate for up to 24 hours, turning the mixture occasionally with a spatula.

Allow to sit at room temperature for 15 minutes. Remove and discard the bay leaves. Sprinkle each serving with pine nuts.

MAKES 8 SERVINGS

A light dusting of dry bread crumbs and herbs
seals in the sweet seafood juices.

Fennel-Crusted Seafood on Skewers

12 ounces medium-large unpeeled shrimp
10 ounces sea scallops
      Salt and ground black pepper
 3 tablespoons olive oil
 2 tablespoons dry white wine
 2 tablespoons plain dry bread crumbs
 2 teaspoons fennel seeds, coarsely ground

Peel the shrimp, leaving the last tail segment on. Place the shrimp and scallops in a 13 x 9-inch glass or ceramic baking dish. Season generously with salt and pepper. Add the oil, wine, bread crumbs, and fennel. Toss to coat the seafood evenly. Thread the seafood onto six or eight 12-inch skewers. Arrange in a single layer in the dish. Cover with plastic wrap and refrigerate for 30 minutes.

Meanwhile, prepare a charcoal or gas grill. Or, preheat the broiler and position an oven rack 4 inches from the heat source.

To grill, place the skewers on the cooking rack directly over the briquettes or burners. To broil, place the skewers in a single layer on a baking sheet with sides. Spread any crumb mixture in the dish evenly over the seafood. Grill or broil for 2 to 3 minutes on each side, or until sizzling and cooked through. Check by cutting into 1 scallop to see if the center is opaque.

MAKES 8 SERVINGS

Two teaspoons minced fresh rosemary leaves or 2 teaspoons crumbled dried oregano leaves may replace the fennel.

Porcini-Stuffed Baby Bello Mushrooms

$^1/_2$ ounce dried porcini mushrooms

$^3/_4$ cup dry white wine

2   tablespoons olive oil

1   small onion, minced

2   large cloves garlic, minced

1   fresh plum tomato, minced

1   teaspoon minced fresh rosemary

$^1/_4$ teaspoon **each** salt and ground black pepper

2   cups soft bread crumbs the size of peas

2   tablespoons minced fresh flat-leaf parsley

36   baby portobello mushrooms (about 1$^1/_2$ pounds)

2   tablespoons ($^1/_2$ ounce) grated Parmesan cheese

A generous pinch of ground red pepper may be added to the stuffing.

The mushrooms may be served at room temperature.

The stuffed mushrooms may be covered with plastic wrap and refrigerated for 24 hours before baking.

Place the porcini and wine in a microwaveable glass measuring cup. Cover with plastic wrap, leaving a vent. Microwave on high for 2 minutes, or until bubbling. Set aside for 10 minutes, or until softened.

Drain the porcini through a fine sieve lined with a coffee filter. Save the liquid. Rinse the porcini and chop.

Coat a large baking sheet with no-stick spray.

Heat the oil in a small skillet over medium heat. Add the onion and garlic. Sauté for 5 minutes, or until softened. Add the tomato, rosemary, salt, pepper, and the reserved porcini and porcini liquid. Increase the heat to medium-high. Cook for about 3 minutes, or until the mixture no longer smells of alcohol. Stir in the bread crumbs and parsley.

Preheat the oven broiler. Remove the stems carefully from the portobello mushroom caps. Reserve the stems for another recipe. With a small spoon, place a dollop of stuffing in the cradle of each cap. Press lightly to help stuffing adhere. Place on the prepared pan, stuffing side up. Sprinkle the mushrooms with Parmesan.

Broil 6 inches from the heat source for about 5 minutes, or until hot and browned.

MAKES 36

First Things First

My husband Walter's close encounter with Italian bureaucracy gave him a surprising insight.

After four years of unwedded bliss, Sharon and I decided to get married. Because Florence was at the core of our relationship, we wanted the ceremony to take place where we had met. So we began to plan a wedding at the church of Santa Croce. It was to take place immediately after we finished the small tour we were conducting through Tuscany.

One would think that lining up a small, modest wedding ceremony—even in Italy—would be an easy task.

No. It was a two-headed monster. We had to work through the imposing bureaucracies of both the Roman Catholic Church and the Italian government.

Anyone who has dealt with Italian authorities will confirm that the Italians have perfected the art, science, and process of bureaucracy. There is a ritualistic formality, a pomposity linking the self-perceived authority of the bureaucrat with the act of officially stamping a document with the appropriate *bollo*, or "stamp" of approval.

When Sharon and I started the process of arranging to marry in Italy, we were astounded by the intricacies. Because we were living in the United States at the time, we had to have all necessary documents translated and stamped for approval by "connected" bureaucrats, both religious and secular, stateside. We accumulated all the necessary documents: birth certificates, baptismal papers, first communion records, confirmation notices, parish affiliations, voter registrations, proof of a felony-free life, on and on. We had them all duly translated and stamped by the designated officials. Of course, there were fees at every turn. When all was said and done, we had assembled nearly two pounds of official documentation. I packed it all for final approval in Florence.

The church stuff was a snap. The clerics at Santa Croce carefully reviewed the information and stamped their approval on the stack of documents.

At the Comune di Firenze——the city hall—the story was different. A week before our wedding, I arrived bright and early at the comune offices housed in the glorious Renaissance Palazzo Vecchio. I must put "bright and early" into the context of a government employee's day. The hours are not exactly grueling. Start at 8:30 A.M. and finish at 1:00 P.M. Monday through Friday; take off the entire month of August, as well as every imaginable civil and religious holiday. Promptly at 8:30 A.M., I took a seat in the waiting room, placing the bulging packet of documents on my lap. The minutes ticked by. Finally, at 8:50 A.M., my guy paced through the waiting room. I swear I could smell the cappuccino on his breath as he boomed "buongiorno" to his administrative assistant.

Another ten minutes passed before I was ushered into his spacious office. His massive desk was as neat as a pin, save for an open briefcase and a three-tiered rack of rubber stamps—there must have been seventy-five of them—poised for action at the front of his desk.

He welcomed me and inquired as to my request. I cheerfully explained about the pending marriage, the Chicago-based official translations of all pertinent documents, and my eagerness to present them all for his kind and authoritative approval.

He motioned for the packet and I handed it over. He opened it, neatly spread the documents across his desk, and carefully perched a pair of reading glasses on the end of his nose. For twenty minutes, he diligently examined the stamps and signatures on each document. Then he gathered them together, put them back into the envelope, slipped off his glasses, looked at me somberly and sighed.

"I'm so sorry," he said. "But you lack a number of critical documents. In their absence, I have no choice but to withhold the city's approval of your wedding."

I was dumbfounded, but I kept my cool. I produced an officially generated checklist of required documents and explained that every document on the list had been presented. A wry smile, a slight shrug, was his official response.

"Very well," I said. "I will return with all the required papers."

There was nothing else to do. The wedding was less than five working days away. I couldn't hope to gather anything from the States within that period. But without the comune's approval, the Church would not allow us to get married.

As the days passed, I grew more and more concerned. Padre Franchi was booked. The food and wine had been ordered. Our friends were all invited.

Planning in desperation to appeal to the bureaucrat's sense of romance, I returned to his office on Friday, the last business day before our scheduled vows. I had spent the morning running errands and arrived at the bureaucrat's door later than I had hoped, at 12:40 P.M. The administrative assistant remembered me and I sought her help in making sure that the official would see me before leaving for lunch.

She ushered me in immediately. The official welcomed me again. The massive desktop was clear, his briefcase packed. He looked ready to make an early exit.

He motioned for the bundle. I presented it. It contained the very same papers—reordered for appearance's sake. Before I could enter my plea for mercy, he had rushed through the stack, not even taking the time to spread them out as he had done before. He looked up at me and beamed. "Very impressive. In fact, you have more documentation than you actually need."

With newfound haste, he stamped and signed all the papers, presented me with an invoice payable at the cashier on the ground level, and ushered me out the door, wishing me a long and happy marriage blessed with many children.

Out in the dazzling sunshine in Piazza Signoria, dazed but triumphant, I bobbed in a river of Florentines flowing by me on their way to lunch. Suddenly I understood.

Nothing, absolutely nothing, is allowed to interfere with mealtime in Italy.

—*Walter Sanders*

Bite-Size Veal and Mortadella Meatballs

$3/4$ cup plain dry bread crumbs

Olive oil

1 pound ground veal

2 ounces mortadella, finely chopped

$1/4$ cup (1 ounce) grated Parmesan cheese

1 tablespoon minced fresh flat-leaf parsley

$1/8$ teaspoon salt

1 egg beaten with 2 tablespoons water

The breaded meatballs may be covered with aluminum foil and refrigerated for 24 hours before baking. Coat with oil before baking.

Preheat the oven to 375°F. Place the bread crumbs on a sheet of waxed paper. Coat a large baking sheet with oil.

Place the veal, mortadella, Parmesan, parsley, and salt in a bowl. Mix with your hands just to combine. Shape into balls the size of large marbles.

One at a time, dip the meatballs into the egg mixture. Lift out and shake off the excess egg, then drop each meatball into the bread crumbs. With the other hand, toss some crumbs over the meatball and roll it to coat. Place on the prepared baking sheet. Continue until all the meatballs are breaded. Coat all sides with oil from a mister or drizzle all the meatballs lightly with oil and roll them gently to coat with the oil.

Bake for about 10 minutes, or until sizzling. An instant-reading thermometer inserted into the center of a meatball should register 160°F.

MAKES 36

Wines for Appetizers and Desserts

Wines poured to enhance appetizers ideally have the fruit and acidity levels, coupled with adequate mouth feel, to mingle with delicate flavors and not overpower the palate. Some fine choices for versatile appetizer white wines include bubbly Prosecco from Veneto, Vermentino di Sardegna, and Arneis from Piedmont.

For wines to grace Italian desserts—whether cream, fruit, or chocolate—choose cherry-nuanced, bubbly Brachetto d'Acqui, or a slightly *frizzante* Moscato d'Asti, with pear and peach aromatics, both from Piedmont. An American raspberry dessert wine is also a splendid match.

—*Carol A. Berman*

vino rosso

Parmesan Soufflé
with Saffron Red Pepper Compote

Compote:

2	large red bell peppers
1	navel orange
	Pinch of saffron threads
	Pinch of ground red pepper
3	tablespoons olive oil
$^1/_4$	teaspoon salt

Soufflé:

$6^1/_2$	tablespoons butter, divided
6	tablespoons plain dry bread crumbs, divided
8	eggs
2	egg whites
6	tablespoons flour
2	cups milk
$1^1/_2$	cups (6 ounces) grated Parmesan cheese
	Salt

The Saffron Red Pepper Compote makes an excellent accompaniment to broiled or grilled seafood.

To prepare the compote: Roast and peel the peppers (page 235). Chop coarsely and place in a bowl.

Grate 1 teaspoon of orange zest. Place in a glass measuring cup. Squeeze the juice from the orange and add to the cup along with the saffron and ground red pepper. Cover with plastic wrap and cook in the microwave for about 1 minute, or until simmering. Add to the bell peppers. Stir in the oil and salt.

To prepare the soufflé: Preheat the oven to 375°F. Rub $^1/_2$ tablespoon of butter on the bottom and sides of a 13 x 9-inch baking pan. Dust with 4 tablespoons bread crumbs to coat, shaking out the excess. Set aside.

Separate the eggs, placing the egg whites in the large bowl of an electric mixer. Place the yolks in a small bowl; set aside. Add the additional 2 egg whites to the mixer bowl.

Melt the remaining 6 tablespoons of butter in a saucepan over medium heat.

Whisk in the flour until smooth. Add the milk and whisk until smooth. Cook, whisking constantly, for about 6 minutes, or until thickened. Add the egg yolks. Cook, whisking constantly, until the mixture bubbles. Remove from the heat. Add the Parmesan and stir. Set aside, whisking occasionally, to cool slightly.

Meanwhile, add a pinch of salt to the egg whites. Whip with electric beaters for about 6 minutes, or until the egg whites hold their shape in peaks. Scoop a large spoonful of beaten whites into the Parmesan mixture. Fold into the mixture to lighten it. Add the Parmesan mixture to the egg whites, pouring it down the side of the bowl so that it doesn't cause the egg whites to collapse. Fold to incorporate. Spoon into the prepared baking pan. Dust with 2 tablespoons bread crumbs.

Bake for 30 to 35 minutes, or until the soufflé is no longer wobbly in the center.

Cut into 12 pieces. Remove the slices with a pancake turner to appetizer plates.

Spoon the compote over or alongside the soufflé.

MAKES 12 SERVINGS

parmigiano-reggiano

Making Crostini

Crostini means "toasts." These little pieces of day-old bread that are spread with vegetables, seafood pastes, cheeses, or chicken livers make delightful nibbles to begin a special meal. The fun is in the combinations. All of the following topping recipes make enough for one loaf of bread, but the amounts may be cut in half or thirds if you choose to make two or three different toppings. Or, prepare a whole recipe and reserve any leftovers for snacks or sandwich fillings.

The Rustic Bread may be replaced with a purchased loaf (about 1 pound) of country-style Italian bread; choose one sturdy enough to hold the toppings.

Basic Crostini

MAKES 36

> 1   loaf Rustic Bread (page 50),
>   preferably 1 day old
>   Olive oil

Preheat the broiler.

Cut off the end crusts of the bread and reserve for bread crumbs (page 247). Cut the loaf into ½-inch-thick slices. Cut the larger slices in half to make pieces that are approximately 2 inches square. Place on a large baking sheet. Broil 6 inches from the heat source for about 2 minutes, just to dry. Remove from the broiler. Turn the pieces over. Spray lightly with olive oil from a mister or dab lightly with a pastry brush dipped in oil. Return to the broiler and cook for about 1 minute, or until the oil is sizzling. Remove.

Fresh Mozzarella, Tomato, and Basil Crostini

MAKES 36

- 36 plain crostini (page 202)
- 3 large cloves garlic, cut in half
- 1 pound fresh mozzarella cheese in whey
- 8 fresh plum tomatoes or small salad tomatoes
- 1 large bunch fresh basil
  Salt and ground black pepper
  Olive oil

Prepare the crostini and place on a serving platter. Rub each crostino with a cut side of garlic.

Remove the mozzarella from the whey. Pat dry. Cut into thin slices. Cut the tomatoes into thin slices. Pick off and reserve several pretty basil sprigs for garnish. Pinch 36 leaves from the stems.

On each crostino, place a slice of mozzarella, a basil leaf, and a tomato slice. Season with salt and pepper. Drizzle a drop of oil on each tomato. Garnish the platter with the reserved basil sprigs. Serve right away.

Pesto Ricotta Crostini

MAKES 36

- 1 carton (15 ounces) ricotta cheese
- $1/2$ cup basil pesto
- 36 plain crostini (page 202)
- $1/4$ cup packed fresh basil leaves

In a bowl, combine the ricotta and pesto. Serve right away or cover with plastic wrap and refrigerate for up to 24 hours.

Prepare the crostini and place on a serving platter. Spread the crostini with the pesto mixture.

Lay the basil leaves atop one another. Roll into a tight cylinder. Cut into thin crosswise slices. Unfurl and sprinkle over the crostini.

Chicken Liver-Rosemary Crostini

MAKES 36

2 tablespoons butter
1¼ pounds chicken livers
1 small onion, minced
1 tablespoon minced fresh rosemary leaves
½ cup dry white wine
⅔ cup ricotta cheese
¾ teaspoon salt
36 plain crostini (page 202)
2 tablespoons minced fresh flat-leaf parsley

The prepared crostini may be covered with waxed paper and refrigerated for up to 2 hours before serving.

In a medium skillet, heat the butter over medium-high heat until the foam subsides. Add the livers and cook, turning occasionally, for 10 minutes, or until no longer pink in the center. Remove and set aside to cool.

Add the onion and rosemary. Cook for 5 minutes, or until softened. Add the wine. Boil for 2 minutes, or until the mixture no longer smells of alcohol.

Meanwhile, chop the livers coarsely.

Return the livers to the pan. Cook over low heat, stirring and mashing with the back of a spoon, for about 2 minutes, or until the mixture is a coarse paste. Transfer to a bowl; set aside to cool.

Add the ricotta and salt. Stir to combine. Serve immediately or cover with plastic wrap and refrigerate for 24 hours.

Prepare the crostini and place on a serving platter. Spread with the liver mixture.

Sprinkle with the parsley.

White Bean, Sage, and Garlic Crostini

MAKES 36

¼   cup olive oil

3   cloves garlic, cut in halves

1   can (19 ounces) cannellini beans, rinsed and drained

2   teaspoons rubbed dried sage

¼   teaspoon salt
     Pinch of ground red pepper

36   plain crostini (page 202)

2   tablespoons minced fresh flat-leaf parsley

In a medium saucepan, heat the oil and garlic. Cover and cook over low heat for 5 minutes, or until the garlic is softened. Add the beans, sage, salt, and red pepper. Cover and cook for 12 minutes, or until the beans are softened. Uncover and cook for about 8 minutes, mashing the mixture occasionally with the back of a large spoon. The mixture should be a coarse purée. Transfer to a bowl. Serve immediately or cover with plastic wrap and refrigerate for up to 24 hours. If the mixture is too thick after refrigeration, stir in 1 to 2 tablespoons of warm water.

Prepare the crostini and place on a serving platter. Spread with the bean mixture. Sprinkle with the parsley.

Tiny pizzas are familiar, yet different enough, to make them a popular choice for casual entertaining.

Mixed Miniature Pizzas

Pizza Dough (page 62)
Cornmeal
Olive oil

Prepare the pizza dough.

Punch down the dough and divide it into 48 balls. Cover with plastic wrap and set aside for 5 minutes.

Preheat the oven to 375°F. Sprinkle several large baking sheets with cornmeal.

On a lightly floured surface, roll or pat the balls into 2½- to 3-inch circles. Place on the prepared pans. Brush or mist each circle with oil. Cover with any of the following toppings.

Bake for 8 to 10 minutes, or until golden and bubbling.

MAKES 48

To freeze pizza crusts: The pizza crusts may be frozen on the cornmeal-dusted baking sheets. Freeze for 2 hours, then remove and stack between pieces of waxed paper. Place in resealable plastic freezer bags. Freeze for up to 1 month. To bake, cover the frozen crusts with the desired topping and bake in a preheated 375°F oven for 8 to 10 minutes.

To freeze cooled, baked pizzas: Pack as above and freeze. Bake in a preheated 350°F oven for 5 to 6 minutes, or until hot.

Toppings:
- Tomato purée, minced fresh basil leaves, finely shredded Fontina cheese
- Basil pesto
- Goat cheese mixed with minced fresh herbs
- Crumbled Gorgonzola cheese
- Grated Parmesan and crushed red pepper
- Ricotta and finely shredded provolone cheese
- Drained roasted bell peppers with drained capers
- Minced garlic sautéed in olive oil, minced rosemary, coarse salt
- Sautéed mushrooms
- Carmelized sautéed onions
- Tapenade (ripe olive purée)

It was the summer solstice at an alfresco dinner at La Pozza when I fell for these light, crispy dough puffs. The caterer, Anna, who was also a professional cellist, shared her recipe with me.

Crescentine

3 to 3½ cups flour, divided
¼ cup cornstarch
¼ teaspoon salt
1 envelope (¼ ounce) active dry yeast (2¼ teaspoons)
¼ cup olive oil
1 cup warm milk (105°F to 115°F)
4 cups vegetable oil (approximately)
   Coarse salt

Coat a large bowl with no-stick spray; set aside.

In a mixing bowl, combine 3 cups flour, cornstarch, and salt. Make a well in the center of the bowl. Set aside.

In a large measuring cup, combine the yeast, olive oil, and milk. Stir to dissolve the yeast. Pour into the well in the bowl. Stir with a fork to make a ball.

Turn the dough out onto a work surface lightly floured with some of the remaining ½ cup flour. Knead for about 6 minutes, using more of the flour as needed, or until the dough feels as smooth as modeling compound. Place in the prepared bowl. Coat with no-stick spray. Cover with plastic wrap and allow to rest for about 45 minutes, or until doubled.

Punch down the dough. Allow to rest for 10 minutes.

On a lightly floured surface, roll the dough into a ¼-inch-thick circle. With a pizza cutter, cut into 2-inch-wide strips, then cut crosswise at 2-inch intervals to make squares. Cover with plastic wrap so the dough doesn't dry out.

Line a large tray with several layers of paper toweling. Heat the vegetable oil in a large heavy pot to 375°F. Test by adding 1 scrap of dough; if the oil bubbles up vigorously, it is hot enough.

Add just enough dough pieces to fill the pan without crowding. Fry for 5 minutes, or until the dough puffs and is golden on all sides. Turn as needed. Some puffs may refuse to turn over. Hold these down gently with a slotted spoon or tongs. With a slotted spoon or tongs, remove to the prepared tray. Sprinkle with salt.

Continue until all the dough is fried.

MAKES ABOUT 36

These puffs of dough are at their most irresistible straight out of the hot oil. For a party, the only sensible thing to do is to invite guests into the kitchen and make the cooking part of the show.

To prepare in a food processor: In the bowl of a food processor, combine the flour, cornstarch, and salt. With the machine running, pour the milk mixture through the feed tube. Process for about 45 seconds, or until the mixture forms a ball. Turn the dough out onto the floured surface and continue with the recipe.

Vino: Chiaro o Scuro?

When my husband Walter shops for wine, he never seems to get beyond the aisle with the Italian reds.

Spend time in Italy—anywhere in Italy—and you'll soon see that wine plays an integral role in Italian life.

It is poured at lunch and dinner. You may occasionally see a morning cappuccino chased with a delicate vin santo. Wine is enjoyed as a pick-me-up at bars and cafes during work breaks. Parents, good parents, even offer it—cut with mineral water or soft drinks—to their children to accompany a meal.

I now perceive wine in Italy as a food. No, even more. Remember the food groups pyramid? Italians would probably name wine as a food group and put it near the base—just above grains.

Perhaps no institution better depicts the integration of wine into Italian life than the *vini*. The word means "wines," but I'm referring to the vest-pocket shops that sell wine and snacks.

The vini are informal gathering places. They provide an opportunity to linger and visit with old friends or stop for a quick snack and a nourishing sip of wine. All in all, vini are a time-honored and textured way to touch the pulse of Italy.

My favorite vini are the Florentine hole-in-the-wall shops. They show up every couple of blocks and are often so unobtrusive that, save for the customers milling in front, you could walk right past them.

The vini present an austere, chest-high wooden counter. On one side of the counter is an assortment of *crostini*: pieces of toasted bread slathered with cooked chicken liver, stacked with salami or prosciutto, or spiked with tuna, onions, olive oil, and pepper. At the other side of the counter is a tower of sturdy glass *gotti*—oversized shot glasses. No fancy stemmed glassware here; these beauties are heavy-duty. Wine in a gotto may be savored sip by sip or gulped to wash down a quick crostino.

Behind the counter is a narrow bin, filled with wine bottles attended to by the ruddy-faced proprietors. No matter which vini I recall, the proprietors are brothers. You can tell they are brothers by their facial similarities, but they are identical twins in their passion for wine.

And behind the brothers: a steep, creaking stairway down to a grotto where the liquid inventory is stored.

The vini serve an array of patrons. The old-timers belly up to the counter and grunt their preference. For these veterans, it is not a matter of a particular vintage, grower, or grape type. A simple *"scuro"* or *"chiaro"* suffices. Scuro, which means "dark," is Florentine slang for *vino rosso*, red wine. Chiaro means "clear" or light—code for *vino bianco*, white wine. I don't see these boys drinking much chiaro.

Other customers are a bit more discriminating, but no less appreciative. They inquire as to what is available. Some even seek recommendations.

Whatever the level of engagement, the proprietors meet it: civil, knowledgeable, but never overbearing.

On a hot summer afternoon during a recent visit to Florence, I stopped at one of my favorite vini near Piazza Signoria. I spotted the familiar knot of patrons: the old-timers, the business types in their suits, some young couples, even a few savvy tourists.

I worked my way up to the counter, fully expecting to greet the old brothers I remembered from the last time I had been here.

Much to my amazement, the old vini was now staffed by a pair of young gentlemen with fresh complexions and quietly efficient manners.

You could tell they were brothers by their facial similarities, but they were identical twins in their passion for wine.

—*Walter Sanders*

Panna cotta, which translates as "cooked cream," is chilled sweetened cream molded with a whisper of gelatin. Think of it as the silk shirt of the dessert wardrobe.

Panna Cotta with Caramel Sauce

Panna cotta:

2	cups whole milk
1	tablespoon plus 1 teaspoon unflavored gelatin (see note)
1¼	cups confectioners' sugar
	Salt
4	cups whipping cream

Caramel:

¼	cup cold water
¼	cup corn syrup
1½	cups granulated sugar
1	cup whipping cream

Any small glass or porcelain container will work for molding the puddings. I use glass punch cups.

Packages of plain gelatin may vary in the amount they contain. For accurate measuring, pour the contents of 2 gelatin packages into a small bowl. With measuring spoons, remove 1 tablespoon plus 1 teaspoon for the recipe. Save any remaining gelatin for another use.

To prepare the panna cotta: Set 12 custard cups (½ cup each) on a tray.

Pour the milk into a saucepan. Sprinkle with the gelatin; set aside for 10 minutes to soften.

Meanwhile, cover the bottom of a Dutch oven with ice cubes. Add cold water to cover; set aside.

Cook the milk over medium-high heat, whisking constantly, for about 5 minutes, or until the mixture is steaming hot but not boiling. Remove from the heat and whisk until no beads of gelatin remain. Check by pouring the mixture into a mixing bowl; if gelatin remains, return the mixture to the pan and heat for 1 to 2 minutes more.

Add the sugar and a pinch of salt. Whisk to dissolve. Gradually add the cream, whisking constantly.

Set the bowl carefully into the Dutch oven. Add slightly more cold water, if needed, to the pan to bring the water up to the level of the mixture in the bowl. Allow to sit, whisking occasionally, for about 15 minutes, or until thickened to the consistency of melted ice cream.

Ladle the mixture into the cups. Refrigerate for at least 4 hours, or until set. (The mixture will jiggle slightly in the center of the cup.)

To prepare the caramel: In a large, heavy saucepan, bring the water and syrup to a boil over medium-high heat. Add the sugar and stir to moisten thoroughly. Cook, without stirring, for about 15 minutes, or until amber-colored. Remove from the heat.

Meanwhile, microwave the cream in a glass measuring cup for 2 minutes, or until steaming.

With oven mitts on both hands, gradually add the cream to the pan, whisking constantly. There will be considerable bubbling and steam.

When the foam subsides, return the pan to low heat. Cook, whisking, for about 2 minutes, or until the mixture is the color of caramel. Remove and pour into a heatproof bowl. Cool. Cover and refrigerate.

To serve the panna cotta: Bring ½ inch of water to a simmer in a small skillet. Run a knife blade around the inside of the cups to loosen the panna cotta. One at a time, dip the bottom of the cup into the water. Bring the dessert plate to the edge of the cup. Gently shake the panna cotta onto the plate. Drizzle with caramel sauce.

MAKES 12 SERVINGS

fragole

The panna cotta may be chilled in a 13 x 9-inch glass dish. To serve, scoop with a large spoon and place, curved side up, on dessert plates.

↩

The caramel sauce may be cooled and refrigerated for up to 1 week. To soften, place in a microwaveable bowl and microwave for 2 minutes.

↩

Strawberry sauce may replace the caramel sauce. In a food processor, process the contents of a 10-ounce thawed package of frozen strawberries packed in syrup with 1 to 2 tablespoons of lemon juice until smooth. Pass through a fine strainer to screen out the seeds.

Peaches and cream in any language equals pleasure.
Reserve this dessert for locally grown, ripe fruit.

Peaches Baked in Pastry Cream

Pastry Cream:

½	cup sugar
2	tablespoons flour
1	egg plus 2 egg yolks
1½	cups half-and-half or whole milk
2	teaspoons vanilla extract

Peaches:

6	ripe peaches, peeled and sliced

To peel peaches, see page 253 (the method for peeling plum tomatoes).

Caramelized almonds (page 213) add a delectable crunch. Sprinkle with some almonds just before serving.

To prepare the cream: In a medium saucepan, whisk the sugar and flour. In a measuring cup, beat the egg, egg yolks, and half-and-half or milk until the egg is incorporated. Whisking constantly, gradually add the egg-milk mixture to the dry mixture. Cook, whisking constantly, over medium-low heat for 4 to 5 minutes, or until the mixture bubbles and thickens. Remove from the heat. Whisk in the vanilla. Set aside to cool slightly, or cool and refrigerate for several hours.

To prepare the peaches: Preheat the oven to 425°F.

Coat a 12 x 8-inch baking pan with cooking spray. Fill with the peach slices in an even layer. Drizzle on the pastry cream. Spread to smooth. Bake for 15 minutes, or until the edges of the pastry cream bubble. Spoon into dessert dishes.

MAKES 8 SERVINGS

pesca

Caramelized Almonds

1   egg white
2   tablespoons water
2   bags (2¼ ounces each) slivered almonds
2   tablespoons sugar

Preheat the oven to 350°F. Coat a baking sheet with no-stick spray.

In a bowl, beat the egg white and water with a fork. Add the almonds and toss to coat. Drain through a fine sieve to remove excess liquid. Scatter the almonds on the baking sheet. Sprinkle with the sugar. Toss to coat. Spread out evenly.

Bake for 10 minutes, or until the almonds at the edges start to brown. Stir the almonds and spread out. Bake for 10 minutes, stirring occasionally, until the almonds are well browned. Remove to a cooling rack. Stir occasionally to speed cooling. Store in a tin in a cool spot for up to 2 weeks.

MAKES ABOUT 1 CUP

If you have access to fresh pine nuts sold in bulk, they are an outstanding replacement for some or all of the almonds in this recipe.

Cocomero is the Italian word for watermelon, but Florentines, who swallow the "c," call it "hohomero." In the heat of a Tuscan summer, vendors peddling cool watermelons seem to appear at every intersection.

Watermelon Wine Granita

1	cup fruity white wine
$1/2$	cup sugar, divided
	4-pound wedge of watermelon

Select a large, shallow, freezer-proof pan, such as a lasagna pan. Clear a spot in the freezer where the pan may sit flat.

In a microwaveable bowl, whisk the wine and $1/4$ cup sugar until most of the sugar granules are dissolved. Cover with waxed paper and microwave for 3 minutes. Whisk until all sugar granules are dissolved. Pour into the reserved pan and allow to cool.

Cut the watermelon from the rind. Cut into chunks. Place in a food processor. Pulse for about 2 minutes, or until the mixture is coarsely puréed.

Add to the wine mixture. Taste; mix in up to $1/4$ cup sugar if mixture is not sweet enough. Place in the freezer for 1 hour. With a spatula, scrape the partially frozen mixture from the sides and bottom of the pan. Return to the freezer for about 2 hours. Every 30 minutes or so, scrape the frozen portions of the mixture to the center of the pan. The mixture is ready to serve when it is frozen in shards.

MAKES 12 SERVINGS

For a sophisticated bittersweet note, add 2 tablespoons of Campari liqueur with the wine.

Once the granita is ready to serve, it can be held for up to a day. Scoop the mixture into a plastic container or resealable plastic freezer bag. Store in the freezer. At serving time, break the granita into chunks and process briefly in the food processor.

cocomero

Fresh Strawberry Tart with Rum Pastry Cream

1	recipe Sweet Pastry Dough (page 217)
$1/3$	cup sugar
2	tablespoons flour
1	egg plus 2 egg yolks
1	cup half-and-half or whole milk
2	tablespoons dark rum, divided
1	tablespoon butter
$1/2$	cup all-fruit apricot preserves
1	quart ($1^1/2$ pounds) fresh medium or small strawberries

Coat a 12-inch round pizza pan with no-stick spray. Prepare the dough. Pat into the bottom and $1/2$ inch up for a border around the edge of the pan. Prick all over with a fork. Refrigerate for 30 minutes.

Preheat the oven to 350°F.

Bake for about 30 minutes, pricking any big air bubbles with a fork, or until the entire surface is lightly browned. Remove to a rack. Store, covered with waxed paper, in a dry place for up to 24 hours.

Meanwhile, in a medium saucepan, whisk the sugar and flour. In a measuring cup, beat the egg, egg yolks, and half-and-half or milk. Add to the pan; whisk until smooth.

Cook, whisking constantly, over medium heat for 4 to 5 minutes, or until the mixture starts to bubble. Cook, whisking vigorously to prevent lumping, for 1 minute. Remove from the heat. Continue whisking until mixture cools slightly. Whisk in 1 tablespoon rum and the butter. Pour into a bowl. Set aside to cool slightly. Cover and refrigerate for at least 1 hour or as long as 1 day.

Place the preserves in a glass measuring cup. Cover with waxed paper and microwave on high for 60 to 70 seconds, or until bubbling. Press through a fine sieve. Discard the solids. Stir in 1 tablespoon rum.

Cut the medium strawberries in halves. Spread the pastry cream evenly over the crust. Top with the strawberries in a decorative pattern. Brush the top evenly with the apricot glaze. Refrigerate, uncovered, for up to 2 hours.

MAKES 10 SERVINGS

This simple tart may be endlessly varied depending upon what seasonal fruits are available. For a pretty effect, create a mosaic of at least three different-colored fruits. The amounts and fruits will vary, but, for example, you could use 2 peaches, peeled and sliced, arranged around the outer edge; 10 medium strawberries, hulled and halved and placed cut-side down, for the next ring; and 1 kiwi, peeled and sliced in circles or lengthwise slices, for the inside ring.

Making Sweet Pastry Dough

Pasta frolla—sweet, tender pastry dough—is easy to prepare. Home cooks in Italy use this versatile confection to make tarts filled with everything from fruits to custards. Although it's primarily a pastry used to line tart shells, sweet pastry dough resembles cookie dough more than it does flaky pie crust. The relatively high proportion of butter to flour, in combination with egg yolks and sugar, ensures a tender result.

With just one basic dough, you can prepare Fresh Strawberry Tart with Rum Pastry Cream, Lattice-Topped Peach and Blueberry Tart, Plum Tart with Honey-Cinnamon Glaze, Roman Cheesecake, and Fig-Walnut Tart with Lemon Glaze. A variation of this dough also provides the base for Orange Sandwich Cookies with Dark Chocolate Drizzles.

The following recipe for Sweet Pastry Dough is flavored with lemon zest, a natural accent for fruit tarts. Orange zest may replace all or part of the lemon zest. With dessert fillings that have a strong citrus component, such as the Roman Cheesecake and the Fig-Walnut Tart, the more neutral Vanilla Pastry Dough is a better choice. Rum or Marsala wine may replace the vanilla.

Keeping Cool

Keeping the butter cold is essential when mixing the sweet pastry dough. Whether preparing the dough by hand or in a food processor, use butter straight from the refrigerator. With a heavy knife, cut it into small chunks so it will incorporate quickly with the dry ingredients. Resist adding more liquid than is called for in the recipe. As the dough sits and the butter softens somewhat, it will absorb more flour.

If you like, you may prepare several batches of dough at the same time and freeze them. Pat each batch of dough into a disk and flour both sides lightly. Lay between 2 sheets of waxed paper. Place on a tray and freeze for several hours or until solid. Pack the disks, separated by the waxed paper, in resealable plastic bags. Store in the freezer for up to 3 months.

Roll Playing

It's true: Rolling pie crust can be intimidating. But with sweet pastry dough, all you have to do is pat the dough into a baking pan. If you find the dough getting too soft and sticky, simply place it in the refrigerator for 5 minutes to firm up the butter.

The faster the dough is spread out, the less time it has to warm up. So, either place a small piece of waxed paper between your palm and the dough or lightly flour your palm to prevent sticking. The pad of your thumb works well for efficiently patting the dough up the pan sides. The crust must be of even thickness so that it will bake evenly. Thin patches may burn before the thicker patches are baked through.

For desserts that call for a top crust or lattice, divide the dough according to the recipe directions. Roll the top portion of the dough on a lightly floured surface or between 2 sheets of lightly floured waxed paper. If it breaks, simply pick up the broken pieces with a spatula and lay them into place. They will melt into each other during baking.

Sweet Pastry Dough

MAKES ONE 10-INCH ROUND CRUST WITH TOP CRUST OR LATTICE, ONE 13 x 9-INCH CRUST, OR ONE 12-INCH ROUND CRUST

- 1¼ cups flour
- ¼ cup cornstarch
- ⅓ cup sugar
- 2 teaspoons grated lemon zest
  Salt
- 1¼ sticks (10 tablespoons) cold butter, cut into small pieces
- 2 egg yolks, beaten with 1 tablespoon water

To prepare by hand: In a mixing bowl, combine the flour, cornstarch, sugar, lemon zest, and a pinch of salt with a fork, pastry blender, or your hands. Add the butter. Cut or break it up into fine bits, mixing well with the dry ingredients. Make a well in the center. Add the egg yolk mixture. Toss to mix. The mixture will look crumbly but moist. Turn the mixture out onto a work surface. With your hands and a dough scraper, work the mixture into a smooth disk.

To prepare in a food processor: In the bowl of a food processor fitted with the steel blade, combine the flour, cornstarch, sugar, lemon zest, and a pinch of salt. Process to mix. Add the butter. Pulse 12 to 15 times to mix. With the machine running, drizzle in the egg yolk mixture. Turn off the machine. Pulse 6 times. The mixture will look crumbly but moist. Turn the mixture out onto a work surface. With hands and a dough scraper, work the mixture into a smooth disk.

Variation
Vanilla Sweet Pastry Dough: Omit the lemon zest. Add ½ teaspoon baking powder to the dry ingredients. Replace the water with 1 tablespoon milk plus ¼ teaspoon vanilla extract.

Lattice-Topped Peach and Blueberry Tart

1 recipe Sweet Pastry Dough (page 217)
1 cup all-fruit apricot preserves
2 tablespoons cornstarch
3 ripe but firm peaches (1 pound), peeled and sliced
½ cup blueberries
1 egg white beaten with 1 tablespoon water
1 tablespoon sugar

Vanilla ice cream or lightly sweetened whipped cream makes a lovely addition to this dessert.

When you separate the eggs to use the yolks in the pastry dough, reserve an egg white for this recipe. Eggs may also be frozen in small containers. Thaw them in the refrigerator.

Coat a 10-inch springform pan with no-stick spray.

Prepare the dough. Cut off one-third of the dough. Pat into a disk; refrigerate for 10 minutes. Pat the remaining dough over the bottom and 1¼ inches up the sides of the pan. Prick all over with a fork. Refrigerate for 30 minutes.

Roll the reserved refrigerated dough between 2 sheets of floured waxed paper into a 10-inch circle. With a pizza wheel or serrated ravioli cutter, cut into 8 strips. Slide the waxed paper onto a baking sheet; refrigerate the dough for 15 minutes.

Preheat the oven to 425°F. In a bowl, mix the preserves and cornstarch. Gently stir in the peaches and blueberries.

Remove the dough-lined pan and the dough strips from the refrigerator. Place the pan on a heavy baking sheet. Spoon the fruit mixture into the pan. Carefully lay 4 strips over the fruit. Place the remaining strips across them. Press the strips to the sides of the bottom crust to join. Brush the lattice with the egg white mixture. Sprinkle the entire surface with sugar.

Bake for 20 minutes. Reduce the temperature to 350°F. Bake for about 40 minutes, or until the juices bubble clear in the center and the lattice is browned. Remove to a rack to cool for several hours.

MAKES 8 SERVINGS

Plum Tart with Honey-Cinnamon Glaze

1   recipe Sweet Pastry Dough (page 217)
1   tablespoon plus 1 teaspoon cornstarch
1   teaspoon ground cinnamon
1   tablespoon plus 1 teaspoon lemon juice
   Honey
20 ripe Italian prune plums (1¼ pounds), halved
   Confectioners' sugar

Coat a 13 x 9-inch baking pan, preferably nonstick, with no-stick spray. Pat the dough over the bottom and 1 inch up the sides of the pan. Refrigerate for 30 minutes.

Preheat the oven to 425°F. In a glass measuring cup, whisk the cornstarch and cinnamon. Add the lemon juice and whisk to dissolve the cornstarch. Add honey to the ⅔-cup mark; whisk to blend. With the back of a spoon, spread half of the mixture over the crust.

Cut tiny slits in the ends of the halved plums so they will lie flat. Arrange the plums in rows, cut-side down. Cut any remaining plums in half and fill in any empty spots. Plums may overlap slightly, but pat them into a level layer. Drizzle with the remaining honey mixture, spreading with the back of a spoon.

Bake for 15 minutes. Reduce the oven temperature to 350°F. Bake for about 40 minutes, or until the glaze starts to bubble in the center.

Remove to a rack to cool. Press the fruit gently with the back of a spoon so the glaze covers it. Cover loosely with waxed paper and store at cool room temperature for up to 24 hours. Dust with confectioners' sugar just before serving.

MAKES 8 SERVINGS

Dark red or black plums (about 1½ pounds) may replace the Italian prune plums. Cut the plums in quarters.

The plums may be replaced with 5 to 6 baking apples (about 2 pounds), peeled, cored, and sliced. Choose Rome Beauty, Gravenstein, Baldwin, Northern Spy, Cortland, Empire, Fuji, Greening, Pippin, Granny Smith, or Golden Delicious apples.

In Florentine slang, a zuccotto is a "stubborn person" with a head as thick as a zucca, or "melon." Zuccotto is also an immensely popular dessert, a dome of cake filled with custard, flavored whipped cream, or ice cream.

Zuccotto

$^3/_4$ cup flour

$^1/_4$ cup cornstarch

6 eggs, separated

  Salt

1 cup granulated sugar, divided

$^1/_3$ cup water

$^1/_3$ cup orange liqueur

$^1/_2$ gallon ice cream, slightly softened

2 tablespoons confectioners' sugar

1 tablespoon cocoa powder

Neapolitan ice cream is a good choice for the filling because you get three different flavors in one package. Or, choose four flavors by selecting 4 pints of ice cream instead of a single half-gallon.

Preheat the oven to 400°F. Coat a 15 x 12 x 1-inch baking pan with no-stick spray. Line with aluminum foil or baking parchment. Coat with no-stick spray. Dust with flour. Set aside.

On a sheet of waxed paper, mix the flour and cornstarch; set aside.

In the bowl of an electric mixer, beat the egg whites and a pinch of salt on medium speed for about 2 minutes, or until foamy. Increase the mixer speed to high. Beat, while gradually adding $^1/_3$ cup granulated sugar, for about 3 minutes, or until the whites hold soft peaks. Set aside.

In a second bowl, without washing the beaters, beat the egg yolks and $^1/_3$ cup granulated sugar at medium-high speed for about 4 minutes, or until the mixture thickens and lightens in color. Fold in half of the beaten egg whites. Repeat folding with the remaining egg whites and the flour mixture until no patches of flour remain.

Pour the batter in a wide swath down the center of the pan. With a spatula, spread the batter to the sides of the pan. Bake for about 8 minutes, or until golden. Remove to a rack to cool for 10 minutes. Lift the foil or parchment from the pan. Gently remove and discard the foil or paper; set the cake on the rack to cool.

Meanwhile, in a microwaveable measuring cup, cook the remaining ⅓ cup granulated sugar and the water for about 2 minutes, or until the sugar dissolves. Add the liqueur. Set aside to cool.

Select an 8- to 10-cup freezer-proof bowl (preferably with no lip around the rim) as a mold. Prick the cake all over with a fork. Brush with the reserved liqueur mixture. Place the bowl, upside down, on the cake. With a sharp knife, cut around the diameter of the bowl to make a circle.

Line the bowl with a large piece of plastic wrap. Cut the remaining cake pieces into sections. Place in the bowl, soaked side down, to completely line the bowl. Trim the pieces as needed to fit like the pieces of a puzzle.

Spoon the ice cream into the bowl, smoothing after each addition. Make sure no air holes remain. Top with the reserved cake circle, soaked side up. Press down gently to seal seams. Cover tightly with plastic wrap. Place in the freezer overnight or for several days.

Thirty minutes before serving, remove the plastic from the top. Place a serving platter over the bowl. Holding tightly with both hands, invert the bowl so the zuccotto slides onto the serving platter. Remove the bowl. Set the zuccotto aside until the cake is softened.

Carefully remove the plastic wrap. Dust with confectioners' sugar and cocoa.

To serve, cut into wedges with a serrated knife.

MAKES 12 SERVINGS

Depending on the season and the type of ice cream used, the dessert plates may be garnished with fresh raspberries, miniature chocolate chips, drizzles of chocolate sauce, candy sprinkles, whipped cream, or toasted nuts.

Raspberry sauce complements a deep dark chocolate ice cream filling. In a food processor, process the contents of a 10-ounce thawed package of frozen raspberries packed in syrup with 1 to 2 tablespoons of lemon juice until smooth. Pass through a fine strainer to screen out the seeds.

Think of this as an Italian orange upside-down cake—it's good for brunch or more casual occasions when a homey, not-too-sweet dessert is in order.

Almond Cake with Caramelized Orange Slices

- 1½ sticks (12 tablespoons) butter, softened, divided
- 2 tablespoons plus ⅓ cup sugar, divided
- 2 navel oranges, unpeeled
- 1¾ cups flour
- ¼ cup cornstarch
- 1 teaspoon baking powder
- Salt
- 1 package (7 ounces) almond paste
- 1 teaspoon orange extract
- 2 eggs
- 1 cup milk

Almond paste, a stiff mixture of ground almonds and sugar, is sold in the baking section of supermarkets. Do not replace it with almond filling, which is a much softer, sweeter mixture.

Preheat the oven to 350°F. Place 2 tablespoons of butter in a 9-inch round cake pan. Place in the oven for 1 minute to melt the butter. Remove and sprinkle with 2 tablespoons sugar. Stir with a fork. Return to the oven for about 5 minutes, or until the sugar bubbles and browns lightly. Remove from the oven and set aside.

With a serrated knife, cut the oranges into very thin slices. Cut some of the smaller slices in halves. With a fork, spread some of the sugar mixture against the sides of the cake pan. Line the sides of the pan with half-circle orange slices, curved side down. Make sure there is sugar between the slices and pan.

Place a whole slice in the bottom center of the pan. Surround with orange slices, squeezing gently to fit in a single layer. Cut a few remaining slices in quarters. Fill in any empty spaces. Press gently to make sure the orange slices are in an even layer.

On a sheet of waxed paper, combine the flour, cornstarch, baking powder, and a pinch of salt. Set aside.

In the bowl of an electric mixer, cream the remaining 1¼ sticks of butter until fluffy. Crumble in the almond paste. Add ⅓ cup sugar and the orange extract. Beat for about 5 minutes, scraping the sides of the bowl when needed, or until smooth. Break up any lumps of almond paste that remain. Add the eggs, one at a time, beating until smooth.

Reduce the mixer speed to low. Add the milk and the dry ingredients alternately, ending with the dry ingredients. Carefully dollop the batter in the pan so the orange slices aren't disturbed.

Bake for about 40 minutes, or until the cake is lightly browned and a tester comes out clean. Remove to a rack for 5 minutes. Place a serving plate over the pan. With both hands in oven mitts tightly holding the pan and plate, invert the cake onto the plate. If any orange slices stick to the pan, remove them with a butter knife and pat into place on the cake.

The cake may be served warm or at room temperature.

MAKES 8 SERVINGS

arancia

A serrated knife works beautifully to cut through the caramelized orange slices.

This torte is stunning when made with blood oranges, which are the color of garnets. Look for blood oranges in some supermarkets in January and February.

*Crunchy biscotti are more than likely the original dunking cookie.
In Tuscany, almond-studded biscotti are dipped into golden* vin santo,
"holy wine," to close a meal on a note that's sweet but not cloying.

Chocolate, Cherry, and Walnut Biscotti

2$\frac{1}{2}$	cups flour
1$\frac{1}{2}$	teaspoons baking powder
$\frac{1}{4}$	teaspoon ground cinnamon
$\frac{1}{4}$	teaspoon salt
1	stick ($\frac{1}{2}$ cup) butter, softened
1	cup packed light brown sugar
2	eggs plus 1 egg yolk
2	tablespoons balsamic vinegar
$\frac{1}{3}$	cup milk
$\frac{1}{2}$	cup walnut halves, toasted and coarsely chopped
$\frac{1}{2}$	cup dried tart cherries
$\frac{1}{2}$	cup semisweet or bittersweet chocolate morsels

Biscotti may be stored in an airtight container for several weeks or frozen in an airtight container for several months.

Dried cranberries may replace the cherries.

On a sheet of waxed paper, combine the flour, baking powder, cinnamon, and salt.

In the bowl of an electric mixer, beat the butter and sugar until light. Add the eggs and egg yolk one at a time; beat until smooth. Add the vinegar and milk. Beat until smooth. Turn the mixer speed to low. Gradually add the dry ingredients, beating just until combined. Stir in the walnuts, cherries, and chocolate morsels with a large spoon. Cover with plastic wrap. Refrigerate for at least 4 hours.

Preheat the oven to 325°F. Coat 2 large baking sheets with no-stick spray. Turn the dough onto a lightly floured work surface. With a pastry scraper, divide the dough in quarters. Roll each piece of dough into a log 1$\frac{1}{2}$ inches in diameter. Place the logs, separated, on the sheets. Bake for 30 minutes, or until golden and set. Remove to racks to cool for 10 minutes. Reduce the oven temperature to 300°F.

On a cutting board with a serrated knife, cut each log into $\frac{3}{4}$-inch-wide diagonal slices. Place the slices, cut sides down, on the baking sheets.

Bake for about 15 to 18 minutes, or until toasted. Remove to racks to cool.

MAKES ABOUT 40

Variation
White Chocolate, Golden Raisin, and Almond Biscotti: Replace the chocolate morsels with white chocolate morsels, the cherries with golden raisins, and the walnuts with toasted slivered almonds. Add $\frac{1}{4}$ teaspoon almond extract with the vinegar.

Chocolate-Hazelnut Cookies

1   cup (5 ounces) skinned hazelnuts, finely ground
1   cup (5 ounces) semisweet chocolate chunks or morsels, finely ground
²⁄₃ cup confectioners' sugar plus some for garnish, divided
3   tablespoons cocoa powder
3   egg whites
    Salt
1   teaspoon vanilla extract

Preheat the oven to 350°F. Coat 2 large baking sheets with no-stick spray.

In a bowl, combine the hazelnuts, chocolate, and ⅓ cup sugar. Stir and set aside. On a sheet of waxed paper, combine the remaining ⅓ cup sugar and the cocoa. Stir with a fork.

In the bowl of an electric mixer, combine the egg whites and a pinch of salt. Beat at medium speed for 2 to 3 minutes, or until foamy. Increase the speed to high. Beat for 3 to 4 minutes, gradually adding the cocoa mixture and the vanilla, until soft peaks form.

Sprinkle half of the hazelnut mixture over the meringue. Stir gently with a fork. Sprinkle with the remaining mixture and stir with a fork just to combine.

Drop in small mounds (2 teaspoons each) onto the prepared baking sheets. Bake for about 12 minutes, or until set. Remove and allow to cool on the pan. Remove to a rack to cool completely.

Sprinkle with confectioners' sugar before serving.

MAKES ABOUT 40

If possible, purchase hazelnuts, sometimes labeled "filberts," that have had their bitter skins removed. If only nuts with skins on are available, follow the directions for toasting hazelnuts (page 250).

Chocolate in bars, cut into small chunks, or chocolate morsels may be ground to a coarse powder in the food processor.

The finished cookies freeze beautifully. Place in a tin layered between sheets of waxed paper. Freeze for up to 6 weeks. Thaw at room temperature for at least 1 hour before serving.

For slightly sweeter cookies, reduce the cocoa powder to 2 tablespoons.

These distinctive little cookies deserve the best bittersweet chocolate you can find. Serve them with ice cream, sliced sweetened peaches, or ripe berries.

Orange Sandwich Cookies with Dark Chocolate Drizzles

1 navel orange
2 cups flour
$^1/_2$ cup sugar
2 tablespoons cornstarch plus cornstarch for dusting
   Salt
1 stick (8 tablespoons) plus 5 tablespoons cold butter, divided
1 egg, beaten
3 ounces bittersweet chocolate, chopped

If a cookie sticks to the glass after it's lifted, slice it off with a small sharp knife and place on the baking sheet.

The wide end of a wooden tart press, sold in cookware shops, works very well for pressing the cookies.

Grate enough orange zest to make 1 tablespoon; set aside. Cut the orange in half. Squeeze the juice from one half of the orange and set aside.

In a mixing bowl, combine the flour, sugar, 2 tablespoons cornstarch, a pinch of salt, and the orange zest. Cut 1 stick plus 2 tablespoons of butter into chunks; add to the bowl. With a fork or pastry blender, cut or break up the butter into fine bits, mixing well with the dry ingredients. Add the egg and 1 tablespoon of orange juice. Toss just to incorporate. The mixture will look crumbly. Pinch the dough to see if it holds together. If needed, add more orange juice, 1 teaspoon at a time, until the dough forms a ball.

Turn the mixture out on a lightly floured work surface. Using your hands and a dough scraper, shape it into a smooth log. Cut the log into 4 equal pieces. With your palms, roll each log, making sure there are no air holes, into an 8-inch-long rope. Place on a flat pan or tray; cover with plastic wrap and refrigerate for about 45 minutes.

Preheat the oven to 375°F. Coat 2 large baking sheets with no-stick spray. Work with one dough rope at a time, keeping the others refrigerated. With a sharp knife, cut into 20 equal disks. Lay the disks down, like coins, on a cornstarch-dusted work surface. With a flat-bottomed drinking glass dipped in cornstarch, press the disks into $1^3/_4$- to 2-inch circles. Transfer to the baking sheets (see note). Twist the glass slightly as you press and lift it off the surface. Dust with cornstarch to prevent sticking. Wipe the glass bottom with a paper towel if the dough starts to stick. Repeat with the remaining dough.

Bake for 8 to 10 minutes, or until the edges are golden. Remove to a rack to cool. Repeat until all the cookies are baked.

In a glass measuring cup, microwave the chocolate and 3 tablespoons butter for 1 minute. Stir. If any lumps remain, microwave for 10 seconds, or until smooth. Set aside for 5 minutes.

Line a large tray with waxed paper. Put a dab of glaze on one cookie and top with another to make a sandwich. Place on the tray. Repeat until all the cookies are sandwiched. Dip a fork into the remaining glaze. Wave back and forth a few inches above the cookies to decoratively drizzle chocolate on the tops. Allow to set before storing in a tin between layers of waxed paper.

To prepare in a food processor: In the bowl of a food processor fitted with a metal blade, combine the flour, sugar, cornstarch, orange zest, and salt. Process to mix. Add the butter. Pulse 12 to 15 times to incorporate the butter. With the machine running, drizzle in the egg and orange juice. Turn off the machine. Pulse 6 times. The mixture will look crumbly. Turn the mixture out on a work surface. Proceed with the recipe.

MAKES ABOUT 40

The finished cookies freeze beautifully. Place in a tin layered between sheets of waxed paper. Freeze for up to 6 weeks. Thaw at room temperature for at least 1 hour before serving.

In a Florentine apartment with terra cotta floors that rippled like waves, I baked brownies in an oven only slightly bigger than the toy ones heated by a light bulb. This is my nod to those treats.

Chocolate Torte

4   ounces unsweetened chocolate, chopped
1   cup flour
1   teaspoon baking powder
    Salt
2   sticks (¹/₂ cup each) butter, softened
1³/₄   cups granulated sugar
4   eggs
2   teaspoons vanilla extract
    Confectioners' sugar

One-half cup of toasted and cooled pine nuts, walnuts, or hazelnuts may be mixed into the batter.

Preheat the oven to 350°F. Coat a 10-inch round springform pan with no-stick spray.

Put the chocolate in a small microwaveable bowl. Microwave for 2 minutes. Stir. If lumps remain, microwave for about 20 seconds. Stir and set aside. On a sheet of waxed paper, combine the flour, baking powder, and a pinch of salt. Stir to mix; set aside.

In the bowl of an electric mixer, beat the butter for about 2 minutes, or until fluffy. Gradually add the granulated sugar, continuing to beat, and scraping the sides of the bowl as needed. Beat in the eggs, one at a time. Add the melted chocolate and the vanilla. Reduce the mixer speed to low. Add the reserved dry ingredients. Mix just to incorporate. Spoon into the prepared pan. Spread evenly.

Bake for about 45 minutes, or until a toothpick inserted into the center comes out clean. Remove to a rack to cool. Remove the outer ring of the pan. Sprinkle with confectioners' sugar just before serving.

MAKES 12 SERVINGS

Variations

Chocolate Torte with Chocolate Glaze: Remove the torte from the oven. Allow to sit for 5 minutes. Remove the outer ring of the pan. Place a serving dish over the torte. Invert the torte onto the dish. Run the blade of a long, thin knife between the torte and the pan bottom to separate. Allow to cool.

Place 4 ounces of chopped bittersweet or semisweet chocolate and 2 tablespoons butter in a microwaveable glass bowl. Microwave for 1 minute. Stir. If lumps remain, microwave for 20 to 30 seconds. Stir until smooth. With the back of a spoon, spread the glaze first over the sides, and then the top, of the cooled Chocolate Torte. Allow to sit for 30 minutes before serving.

Frozen Chocolate Torte with Cappuccino Cream: Remove the torte from the oven. Allow to sit for 5 minutes. Remove the outer ring of the pan. Place a freezer-proof serving dish over the torte. Invert the torte onto the dish. Run the blade of a long thin knife between the torte and the pan bottom to separate. Allow to cool.

In the mixing bowl of an electric mixer, stir 1 tablespoon instant espresso or regular instant coffee with 1 teaspoon cold water to dissolve. Add 2 cups whipping cream. Whip on high speed for 2 to 3 minutes, or until soft peaks form. Add 4 tablespoons of confectioners' sugar. Whip for 1 to 2 minutes, or until peaks hold their shape.

Spread the cream, swirling into peaks, over the top and sides of the cooled torte. Place in the freezer, uncovered, for 2 hours.

For longer storage, freeze uncovered for 2 hours; cover tightly with plastic wrap and then with aluminum foil. Freeze for up to 1 week. To serve, unwrap and allow to sit at room temperature for 15 to 20 minutes.

Bittersweet chocolate shavings may be scattered on top for decoration.

As the torte bakes, it will rise, then fall slightly. The surface may crack, giving it a rustic look. Accompany with a spoonful of whipped cream, a scoop of vanilla ice cream, or a scattering of fresh raspberries.

Adding some cream cheese to the batter helps simulate the creamier ricotta that is found in Italy.

Roman Cheesecake

Vanilla Sweet Pastry Dough (page 217)

1 **lemon**

2 **packages (3 ounces each) cream cheese, softened**

¾ **cup confectioners' sugar, divided**

1 **carton (15 ounces) whole-milk ricotta cheese**

4 **eggs, separated**

Salt

Coat a 10-inch springform pan with no-stick spray.

Prepare the dough. Pat into the bottom and 1¾ inches up the sides of the pan. Prick all over with a fork. Refrigerate for 30 minutes.

Meanwhile, grate 1 teaspoon of lemon zest. Cut the lemon and squeeze 1 tablespoon juice. Set the zest and juice aside.

In a mixing bowl, beat the cream cheese until smooth. Add ½ cup sugar, the lemon zest, and juice. Add the ricotta and the egg yolks. Beat until smooth; set aside.

Preheat the oven to 300°F. Place the egg whites and a pinch of salt in the bowl of an electric mixer. Whip, gradually adding the remaining ¼ cup sugar, for about 4 minutes, or until the whites hold peaks. Stir a large spoonful of the beaten whites into the reserved cheese mixture. Add the cheese mixture to the egg whites, gently pouring it down the sides of the bowl so that it does not make the whites collapse. Fold to combine.

Place the springform pan on a heavy baking sheet. Gently transfer the batter to the prepared pan. Cover loosely with aluminum foil.

Bake for about 1 hour or until a tester inserted into the center comes out clean. Turn off the oven. Open the door. Leave the cheesecake in the oven for 1 hour.

Remove to a rack and remove the foil. Allow to cool completely. Refrigerate overnight.

MAKES 12 SERVINGS

This cake may be served alone or accompanied with fresh seasonal fruit. In summer, choose from raspberries, strawberries, peaches, or nectarines. Clean and slice (if necessary) the desired fruit. Place in a bowl and sprinkle lightly with sugar. Toss. Cover and refrigerate for 1 to 2 hours before serving. In winter, sliced navel or blood oranges drizzled with Caramel Sauce (page 210) are wonderful served with the cake. Look for blood oranges in some supermarkets in January and February.

Choose ricotta that does not contain gelatin or vegetable gums.

Fig-Walnut Tart with Lemon Glaze

Tart:

1	recipe Vanilla Sweet Pastry Dough (page 217)
1	cup (4 ounces) walnut halves, toasted
1	package (8 ounces) dried figs, stems removed, halved
$\frac{1}{2}$	cup raisins
	Grated zest of 1 navel orange
$\frac{1}{2}$	cup honey
$\frac{1}{4}$	cup bourbon whiskey or brandy
$\frac{1}{2}$	teaspoon ground cinnamon

Glaze:

1	cup confectioners' sugar
1 to 2	tablespoons lemon juice

To prepare the tart: Coat a 10-inch springform pan with no-stick spray.

Prepare the dough. Cut off one-third of the dough. Pat into a disk; refrigerate for 10 minutes. Pat the remaining dough over the bottom and 1 inch up the sides of the pan. Prick all over with a fork. Refrigerate for 30 minutes.

Roll the reserved refrigerated dough between 2 sheets of floured waxed paper into a 10-inch circle. Slide the waxed paper onto a baking sheet; refrigerate the dough for 15 minutes.

Meanwhile, preheat the oven to 375°F. In a food processor, grind the nuts finely. Add the figs, raisins, and orange zest. Process into a paste.

Place the honey in a mixing bowl. Whisk in the bourbon or brandy and cinnamon. Add the fig mixture and mix slowly. Spoon into the dough-lined pan, spreading evenly. Remove the dough circle from the refrigerator. Remove the top sheet of waxed paper. Turn the dough circle over on top of the filling. Carefully remove the waxed paper. With a fork, tuck the edges of the top crust inside the edges of the bottom crust. Press to seal.

Bake for about 35 minutes, or until the crust is golden. Remove to a rack to cool.

To prepare the glaze: In a bowl, combine the sugar and enough juice to make a glaze that drips off the spoon. Spread over the tart with the back of the spoon. Allow to set.

MAKES 12 SERVINGS

Toasting the nuts greatly improves the flavor. Spread the nuts in a single layer on a baking sheet. Place in a 350°F oven for about 10 minutes, stirring occasionally, or until the nuts are golden. Remove from the sheet to cool.

For Thanksgiving and Christmas, I prepare this tart up to a week before serving. I cover it with foil and store it in a cool place.

Capturing Summer Flavors for All Meals

Impeccably fresh ingredients are often touted as "the secret" to *la cucina Italiana*. This is true enough, but every coin has a flip side. Turning over this piece of gold, we see the imprint of savory preserved foods: cheese, salami, olives, wine.

Salty, pungent, rich, herbal, or tart, *condimenti* are prepared by methods that date back centuries, to a time when drying and salting were the only viable means of preserving foods. Many condimenti have evolved into delicacies that are integral to la cucina. Imagine Italian cooking without prosciutto, capers, Parmesan, Pecorino Romano, dried chiles and porcini, or roasted peppers in olive oil. Impossible.

Many of these preserved foodstuffs are the province of professionals, but home cooks in Italy, especially in the country, have fashioned their own repertoire of preserves. These aren't viewed as inferior to fresh foods. Neither is better or worse, just different: two sides of the culinary coin.

The tomato, for instance, plays different roles during the year. In the peak of summer, the salad tomato performs immediately, almost impetuously. Plucked off the vine, its sweet, cool flesh and juice revive parched palates. The gratification is instant and direct.

By the end of the growing season, the more reserved plum tomatoes are united in tomato *conserva*, a cooked purée. Throughout the cold months, this distilled essence of summer will flavor ragú, soup, or a braised meat dish. It contributes body, smoothness, and an echo of the garden.

These days, preserving food at home isn't the necessity it once was. But for those who cultivate a summer herb garden or shop at a farmer's market for the ripest fruits and vegetables, there's no better way to prolong the seasonal pleasure than by preparing and freezing homemade basil pesto, caponata, or peaches for *sorbetto*. You're preserving more than food. You're also storing pleasant memories of endless summer days.

Basil Pesto

1   cup olive oil
1   head garlic, cloves peeled
2   cups tightly packed fresh basil leaves, divided
1   cup tightly packed fresh flat-leaf parsley leaves, divided
$1/2$ cup (2 ounces) pine nuts, toasted and cooled, divided
$1/2$ teaspoon salt, divided
1   cup (4 ounces) grated Parmesan cheese
$1/4$ cup (1 ounce) grated Pecorino Romano cheese

In a glass measuring cup, combine the oil and the garlic. Cover with waxed paper. Microwave for 30 seconds. Reduce the setting to low; microwave for 3 minutes, or until bubbly and fragrant. Allow to cool to room temperature.

In a food processor, combine half of each of these ingredients: the basil, parsley, pine nuts, salt, and garlic oil. Pulse 20 times, or until coarsely chopped. Scrape the sides of the bowl. Process for about 2 minutes, or until a paste forms. Transfer to a mixing bowl. Repeat with the remaining ingredients. Transfer to the bowl. Stir in the Parmesan and the Pecorino Romano.

To freeze: Spoon the pesto in 1-tablespoon mounds onto a waxed paper–lined tray. Place in the freezer for several hours, or until solid. Transfer the pesto mounds to a plastic freezer bag. Return to the freezer for up to 6 months.

MAKES 32 TABLESPOONS

Pasta with Basil Pesto: Cook 1 pound pasta until al dente (page 74). Reserve $3/4$ cup cooking water. Drain the pasta and return to the cooking pot. Add 8 tablespoons of frozen pesto and enough of the water to moisten the sauce. Season lightly with salt if needed.

Recipes that call for Basil Pesto:
§ Chicken Noodle Soup with Spinach and Basil, page 32
§ Polenta-Pesto Casserole, page 114
§ Scallop-Tomato-Bacon Kebabs on Romaine with Pesto Dressing, page 136
§ Pesto Potato Salad, page 153
§ Pesto Ricotta Crostini, page 203

At the farmer's market in September, I can buy a bag of red bell peppers for the same price I would pay for a single pepper in January. I roast and peel them in a big batch for the freezer.

Roasted Peppers

12	red, yellow, or orange bell peppers
¾	cup olive oil
1	teaspoon salt

To roast on a grill: Prepare a charcoal or gas grill. Place the peppers in a single layer on the cooking rack. Cover and grill for 8 to 10 minutes. With tongs, turn the peppers as the bottoms char. Cover and grill for 25 to 30 minutes, turning as needed, until charred on all sides.

To roast in the oven: Preheat the oven to 450°F. Coat a large baking sheet with no-stick spray. Cut the peppers in half. Remove the cores and seeds. Lay the peppers on the pan, cut-side down. Bake for about 20 minutes, or until the skin puffs up like a blister. (The skin won't be charred.)

To peel the peppers: Remove the peppers from the grill or the oven. Place in a large bowl. Cover tightly with plastic wrap. Set aside for 20 to 30 minutes, or until the peppers are cool enough to handle.

Set a fine sieve over a large bowl. Have some loose paper towels at hand. One at a time, pull the core from the pepper and let the juice run through the sieve. Peel away the charred skin and scrape away the seeds. Use a paper towel to remove any stubborn bits of skin and to keep hands clean. Tear the peppers in half. Place in the bowl with the reserved juice. Add the oil and salt. Cover and refrigerate for several hours to chill.

To freeze: Spoon the peppers into seven 1-cup containers. Store in the freezer for up to 6 months.

To thaw: Place the peppers in the refrigerator for 1 to 2 days. Or microwave on the defrost setting for 10 minutes.

MAKES 7 CUPS

These peppers may be used in any recipe calling for roasted peppers. For a simple salad or side dish, they may be seasoned with minced herbs, chopped olives, or drained capers.

A Cook's Ransom

"The dispensa, or larder, was a gastronomic Aladdin's cave," writes Kinta Beevor in *A Tuscan Childhood* of the pantry at Poggio Gherardo, her aunt's country estate overlooking Florence. Beevor recorded her World War I–era experiences more than seventy years after they occurred, yet her account glows with immediacy.

"Rows of jars contained preserves in every form: dried tomatoes, tomatoes in oil and artichokes in oil (*sott'olio*), pickled vegetables, capers, pine nuts, bread crumbs, juniper berries for ground game and saffron for risotto. There was also a large terra-cotta jar full of olives."

I, too, have had the pleasure of experiencing such a larder, many decades after Beevor did, at the farm of Mario and Anna Maria Gaggio in the hills east of Florence. Anna Maria, retired from a career as a cultural guide, maintains a pantry that would put some restaurants to shame. "Food is culture," says Anna Maria, who should know; she holds a doctorate in ancient Greek and Latin.

Her pantry is a cook's ransom of foodstuffs either cultivated or foraged from the surrounding countryside. Jade-green oil pressed from the family's olives. Jars of whole tomatoes canned with basil. Brown bottles of tomato *conserva*, a concentrated purée also seasoned with basil. Walnut-size artichokes pickled with sage leaves. Marmalade made from both plums and peaches. Home-dried rosemary, thyme, basil, and sage. Dried red onions and hot chiles.

The freezer is a chest filled with edible treasures: bag upon bag of cannellini beans, sliced porcini mushrooms, rabbit, duck, and guinea hens. There's even wild boar, which Mario hunts in the mountains.

As Anna Maria proudly serves me a Tuscan tradition—a dish of stewed tomatoes, onions, basil, and bread called *pappa al pomodoro*—she adds the final seasoning with her words. "Our tomatoes, our bread, our oil." ✍

A classic Sicilian vegetable relish, caponata is a versatile condiment to have in the freezer. Spread it on toasted bread slices to make crostini *(page 202). Or serve it as a relish with sliced roasted pork, turkey breast, or chicken.*

Caponata

2	medium eggplants, peeled and cut into 1-inch cubes
2	tablespoons salt
10	tablespoons olive oil, divided
1	whole celery heart, cut into $^{1}/_{4}$-inch slices
1	large onion, coarsely chopped
8	ripe plum tomatoes, peeled and coarsely chopped
2 to 3	tablespoons sugar
2 to 3	tablespoons red or white wine vinegar
$^{1}/_{2}$ to $^{3}/_{4}$	teaspoon crushed red pepper
$^{1}/_{4}$	cup drained capers
$^{1}/_{3}$	cup green olives, pitted and cut into slivers

Place the eggplant cubes in a large colander. Sprinkle with the salt. Toss to coat. Set the colander in the sink for 30 minutes. Rinse the eggplant under cold water. Pat dry.

In a large sauté pan over high heat, heat 4 tablespoons oil. Add the eggplant. Cook, stirring occasionally, for 5 minutes, or until browned. Remove to a platter.

Heat 2 tablespoons oil in the pan. Add the celery and onion. Reduce the heat to medium. Cook, stirring, for 5 minutes, or until the onion is golden. Add the tomatoes and the reserved eggplant. Cook, stirring occasionally, for 5 minutes, or until the tomatoes soften. Add 2 tablespoons sugar. Cook for about 10 minutes, or until the eggplant is very soft. Stir in 2 tablespoons vinegar and red pepper to taste. Remove from the heat. Stir in the capers, olives, and 4 tablespoons oil. Cover and refrigerate for 24 hours for flavors to blend.

Taste the caponata. Add more sugar and vinegar if needed to adjust the sweet-sharp balance.

To freeze: Spoon into 1-cup plastic freezer containers, leaving $^{1}/_{2}$ inch of head room. Store in the freezer for up to 6 months.

To thaw: Place the caponata in the refrigerator for 1 to 2 days. Or microwave on the defrost setting for 10 minutes.

MAKES ABOUT 8 CUPS

To reuse the freezer containers, spray the interior with no-stick spray. When the caponata is frozen solid, release it from the container by running a butter knife down the side. Transfer the frozen caponata to plastic freezer bags. Seal tightly and return to the freezer.

Use $^{1}/_{4}$ to $^{1}/_{2}$ cup caponata per serving as a condiment with grilled meat, poultry, or cheese. To use as an antipasto, spread 1 to 2 tablespoons caponata on a thin slice of toasted rustic bread.

Zesty onions are always welcome with grilled or roast pork, chicken, or beef—or to dress up un panino, *an Italian sandwich.*

Sweet and Sharp Onions with Raisins

3   tablespoons olive oil, divided

7   large sweet onions, peeled, each cut into 8 wedges

1   cup raisins

1   cup water

¼   cup plus 2 tablespoons red or white wine vinegar

2   tablespoons sugar

2   teaspoons salt

2   teaspoons dried thyme leaves

In a large sauté pan, heat 1 tablespoon oil. Add one-third of the onion wedges, cut side down, and cook over medium-high heat for 5 minutes, turning once, until browned. Remove to a platter. Repeat with remaining oil and onions in 2 batches.

Return the browned onions to the pan. Add the raisins, water, vinegar, sugar, salt, and thyme. Cook, stirring, for 10 minutes, or until the onions are softened and glazed. Remove from the heat. Cover and refrigerate for several hours to chill thoroughly.

To freeze: Spoon the onions and sauce into seven 1-cup containers, leaving ½ inch of head room. Seal tightly. Store in the freezer for up to 6 months.

To thaw: Place the onions in the refrigerator for 1 to 2 days. Or microwave on the defrost setting for 10 minutes.

MAKES ABOUT 10 CUPS

To reuse the freezer containers, spray the interior with no-stick spray. When the relish is frozen solid, release it from the container by running a butter knife down the side. Transfer the frozen relish to plastic freezer bags. Seal tightly and return to the freezer.

Pickles—Italian style! Serve these as a garnish with Flank Steak Carpaccio-Style with Spinach and Shaved Parmesan (page 177), with cheese or salami sandwiches, or simply as part of an antipasto spread.

Hot and Garlicky Pickled Zucchini

12	small zucchini (2½ pounds), cut into ¼-inch rounds
⅓	cup kosher or canning salt
	Water
1½	cups red or white wine vinegar
¼	cup plus 2 tablespoons sugar
1	teaspoon crushed red pepper
6	cloves garlic

In a large bowl, combine the zucchini and salt. Cover with cold water. Stir to partially dissolve the salt. Cover and refrigerate for 3 hours.

In a large bowl, combine 2½ cups water with the vinegar, sugar, and red pepper. Whisk to dissolve the sugar. Cut the garlic cloves into thin slices, then into slivers. Add to the vinegar mixture.

Drain the zucchini and rinse well with cold water. Add to the vinegar mixture. Stir well. Place a salad plate over the zucchini to submerge it. Refrigerate, stirring occasionally, for 24 hours.

With a slotted spoon, transfer the zucchini, garlic, and crushed red pepper into seven 1-cup jars. Pour on the vinegar mixture to cover, leaving ½ inch of head room. Close tightly and refrigerate for up to 2 months.

MAKES ABOUT 7 CUPS

Select small, uniformly sized zucchini—about 5 inches long and 1 inch wide—for this recipe so the finished pickles will be evenly sized.

Canning or pickling salt contains no anti-caking agents—as free-flowing table salt does—that would make the brine cloudy.

zucchina

Vodka really makes fresh tomato sauces taste exceptional.
The alcohol, which evaporates during cooking, dissolves certain flavor
compounds that neither oil nor water can release.

Plum Tomato Purée with Vodka

| 10 | pounds very ripe plum tomatoes, cut in lengthwise quarters |
| $^{1}/_{2}$ | cup vodka |

Pack a large, non-aluminum pot with as many tomatoes as will fit, pressing with clean hands or a large spoon to squash the tomatoes to release some juice. Set on medium-high heat. Cook, stirring occasionally, for 10 to 12 minutes, or until the tomatoes start to release more juice. With the back of a large spoon, press the tomatoes. Gradually add the remaining tomatoes until they all fit in the pot. Reduce the heat to medium-low. Cook, stirring occasionally, for 25 to 30 minutes, or until the tomatoes are very soft.

Set a food mill over a large, non-aluminum pot. Working in batches, ladle the tomatoes and juice into the food mill. Pass the tomatoes through the mill to purée. With a rubber spatula, lift out and discard the skin and seeds after each batch.

Set the purée over high heat. Stir in the vodka. Bring to a boil; reduce the heat to medium and cook at a brisk simmer for 5 minutes. If the purée is too thin, continue to cook until it is reduced to the desired thickness. Skim and discard any light-colored foam that rises to the surface. Refrigerate for several hours to chill thoroughly.

To freeze: Ladle into 1-cup containers. Store in the freezer for up to 6 months.

To thaw: Place the amount needed overnight in the refrigerator, or thaw in the microwave on the defrost setting for 10 minutes. Heat the sauce in the microwave for 6 to 8 minutes or transfer to a saucepan set over medium heat.

MAKES ABOUT 12 CUPS; 3 CUPS WILL SAUCE 1 POUND PASTA, COOKED

Pasta with Plum Tomato Purée with Vodka: Cook 1 pound pasta until al dente (page 74). Heat 3 cups of Plum Tomato Purée with Vodka. Season with 1$^{1}/_{2}$ teaspoons salt. Drain the pasta and return to the cooking pot. Add 1 tablespoon butter; toss. Add 2 cups heated tomato sauce; toss. Spoon into pasta bowls. Top each portion with some of the remaining 1 cup sauce. Garnish with grated Parmesan cheese.

SERVES 6 TO 8 AS A SIDE DISH OR FIRST COURSE

This purée may be used as an ingredient in any recipe calling for plain tomato sauce or purée.

Pasta with Tomato Cream Sauce: Cook 1 pound pasta until al dente (page 74). Heat 2 cups of Plum Tomato Purée with Vodka, combined with ¼ cup whipping cream or half-and-half and 1 teaspoon salt. Drain the pasta and return to the cooking pot. Add the tomato cream sauce; toss. Garnish with grated Parmesan cheese.

SERVES 6 TO 8 AS A SIDE DISH OR FIRST COURSE

Pasta with Tomato Pesto Sauce: Cook 1 pound pasta until al dente (page 74). Heat 2 cups of Plum Tomato Purée with Vodka with 1 teaspoon salt. Drain the pasta and return to the cooking pot. Add 2 tablespoons frozen Basil Pesto (page 234). Toss to coat. Add the tomato sauce and toss.

SERVES 6 TO 8 AS A SIDE DISH OR FIRST COURSE

pomodori pelati

Don't salt the purée because it is a base sauce that may be used in many dishes such as tomato soup, sauce for cooked pasta, or stew.

A food mill, an old-fashioned hand-cranked sieve, makes quick work of puréeing cooked tomatoes while screening out the skins and seeds. Food mills are sold in cookware departments and some hardware stores. The tomatoes may also be pushed with the back of a large spoon through a fine sieve set over a bowl. This method, however, is more work.

Keeping Herbs

I've dabbled at growing vegetables, but the truth is, they require actual work. Herbs, on the other hand, don't seem to mind being ignored. Also, they are almost impossible to kill. They make me look like a brilliant gardener.

Whether you raise herbs or buy them in big, cheap bunches at summer markets, preserving them is the natural conclusion. You'll have top-quality seasonings all winter long at a fraction of the price of bottled dried herbs or fresh bunches from the supermarket.

Herbs can be kept by drying or freezing. Which method better preserves flavor, color, and texture seems, to me, to vary with each herb. Some herbs shouldn't be kept at all, but rather enjoyed fresh in their season. Chives from the garden are as much about sprightly texture as they are about mild onion flavor. Frozen, they go limp; dried, they fade in flavor. The best way to enjoy the essence of chives in the off-season is to chop scallion greens.

One herb that I don't bother to dry is oregano. Perhaps I haven't found the right variety of this plant, but the oregano I grow tastes too strong, a bit bitter. I look for oregano imported from the Mediterranean that has been dried on the branch. Its sweet flavor is incomparable.

Drying Herbs

Rosemary, thyme, and sage are the herbs I like to dry. I cut branches from the plants, one variety at a time, and tie the ends together with kitchen string. With a paper towel I brush off any visible loose dirt. (If you haven't grown the plants yourself, wash them in cold water and dry thoroughly before proceeding.)

I place each bundle in a clean, large brown grocery bag and fold the top so no light penetrates. I store the bags in the garage for three to four weeks. (A dark, cool closet works well, too.) From time to time I check the herbs. When the leaves crumble when I rub them between my fingers, they are ready to store. With scissors or fingers, I trim the leaves away from the woody branches and put the leaves into a labeled resealable plastic bag for storage in the pantry. (The branches I toss onto hot charcoal briquettes on the grill.)

This technique may also be used to preserve leftover herbs from a supermarket bunch. When you buy rosemary, thyme, or sage for a recipe and don't use all of it, place the leftover branches in a small brown paper bag, label it, and place in the pantry to dry.

Freezing Herbs

Bay leaf, basil, and parsley may be frozen.

I like to freeze bay leaves because they remain supple and hold their color and flavor better than if they're dried. I harvest the leaves from my tiny potted bay laurel tree at the end of every summer. (The tree spends a dormant winter in the garage.) After wiping the leaves clean with a paper towel, I place them in a labeled resealable plastic bag.

Because fresh basil leaves are so fragile, processing them into pesto is the best way to capture their magic. The olive oil actually traps the volatile flavor compounds that would be lost if the leaves themselves were frozen. Adding chopped fresh flat-leaf parsley to the pesto helps maintain the color.

Flat-leaf parsley is, no contest, the hardest-working herb in the Italian kitchen. When it comes to parsley, I break my own "don't buy fresh herbs in the winter" rule because parsley perks up so many dishes.

Parsley can be frozen successfully. The color will darken somewhat, but it is still useful for adding to soups and stews. Just chop the parsley and store in a resealable plastic bag.

To use frozen herbs, remove the desired amount from the bag—no need to thaw.

This sauce adds a lively summertime note to baked or sautéed
chicken breasts, turkey scaloppine, or fish fillets.

Chunky Plum Tomato Sauce

5	tablespoons olive oil, divided
1	onion, chopped
1	rib celery heart, chopped
1	carrot, chopped
$1/4$	cup minced fresh flat-leaf parsley
2	dried bay leaves
$4^{1}/_2$	pounds very ripe plum tomatoes, cored, skinned, and coarsely chopped
$1^{1}/_4$	teaspoons salt

In a large sauté pan, warm 3 tablespoons oil over medium heat. Add the onion, celery, carrot, parsley, and bay leaves. Cook, stirring occasionally, for 5 minutes, or until the onion is translucent. Reduce the heat if necessary, but do not allow the vegetables to brown.

Increase the heat to high. Add one-third of the tomatoes. Cook, stirring occasionally, for 2 to 3 minutes, or until the tomatoes start to soften. Add half of the remaining tomatoes. Cook, stirring occasionally, for 2 to 3 minutes. Reduce the heat to medium. Add the remaining tomatoes and cook, stirring frequently, for 5 minutes, or until a chunky sauce forms. Stir in the salt and the remaining 2 tablespoons oil. Refrigerate to chill.

Because plum tomatoes sometimes have tough skins, it is best to peel them (page 253) before cooking in recipes in which the sauce won't be strained.

To freeze: Remove and discard the bay leaves. Ladle the sauce into 3-cup (or 1-cup) plastic freezer containers or large resealable plastic bags. Store in the freezer for up to 6 months.

To thaw: Place the sauce overnight in the refrigerator. Or microwave on the defrost setting for 10 minutes. Heat the sauce in the microwave for 6 to 8 minutes or transfer to a saucepan set over medium heat.

MAKES ABOUT 6 CUPS; 3 CUPS WILL SAUCE 1 POUND OF COOKED PASTA

Pasta with Chunky Plum Tomato Sauce: Heat 3 cups of Chunky Plum Tomato Sauce. Cook 1 pound pasta until al dente (page 74). Drain the pasta and return to the cooking pot. Add 1 tablespoon butter and toss. Add 2 cups of warm sauce; toss to coat. Spoon into pasta dishes. Top with the remaining 1 cup sauce.

SERVES 6 TO 8 AS A SIDE DISH OR FIRST COURSE

Enjoy the intense summer flavors of fruit sorbetti *by freezing the fruit and syrup in resealable plastic bags, making it easy to break the sorbetto base into chunks to purée in the food processor.*

Strawberries for Sorbetto

2½   cups water
2½   cups sugar
 2   pounds strawberries, sliced
 3   tablespoons lemon juice

In a microwaveable bowl, whisk the water and sugar until most of the granules are dissolved. Cover with waxed paper and microwave for 3 minutes, or until the water is warm. Whisk until all the sugar granules are dissolved. Set aside to cool.

Add the strawberries and lemon juice. Cover and refrigerate for several hours to chill thoroughly. One at a time, place four 1-quart resealable plastic bags on a freezer-proof tray. Ladle 2 cups of the berries and syrup into each bag. Squeeze out air and seal the bags tightly.

To freeze: Place in the freezer for several hours, or until solid. Remove the bags from the tray and return to the freezer for up to 6 months.

To prepare the sorbetto: Remove 1 strawberry-syrup bag from the freezer to sit for 10 to 15 minutes. Place the bag on a heavy cutting board. With a rolling pin or other heavy object, hit the bag several times to break the mixture into pieces the size of ice cubes. Pour the pieces into a food processor. Process for 2 to 3 minutes, scraping the sides of the work bowl frequently, until very smooth. Serve right away or scoop into a freezer-proof bowl. Cover and place in the freezer to ripen flavors for up to 24 hours.

MAKES 8 CUPS; 16 SERVINGS

fragole

Variation
Peaches for Sorbetto: Replace the strawberries with 3 pounds ripe peaches, peeled and pitted (page 253, the method for peeling plum tomatoes). Cut the peaches in quarters. Trim any fibers where the pits were attached. Slice the quarters. Replace the lemon juice with 3 tablespoons dark rum.

MAKES 8 CUPS; 16 SERVINGS

Selected Bibliography

Beevor, Kinta. *A Tuscan Childhood*. London: Penguin Books, 1995.
   Beevor lived in Italy, in a Tuscan castle and a country estate overlooking Florence with her British parents, long before Tuscany became the new Provence.

Bittman, Mark. *How to Cook Everything: Simple Recipes for Great Food*. New York: Macmillan, 1998.
   Bittman's reassuring prose is a joy to read even if you never cook a thing from this masterful book.

Boni, Ada. *Italian Regional Cooking*. New York: Bonanza Books, 1964.
   For informative text and inspiring location photographs of each region's dishes, I turn to this book again and again.

Bugialli, Giuliano. *The Fine Art of Italian Cooking*. New York: Quadrangle, 1977.
   On my shelf since 1977.

Bugialli, Giuliano. *Giuliano Bugialli's Foods of Italy*. New York: Stewart, Tabori & Chang, 1984.
   Crammed with beautiful location photographs by John Dominis.

David, Elizabeth. *Italian Food*. New York: Penguin Books, 1999.
   With a foreword by Julia Child, this is a reissue of the 1954 classic celebration of pan-Italian cooking by a revered British food writer.

Field, Carol. *The Italian Baker.* New York: Harper & Row, 1985.
   This work is as sweet as *pasta frolla* and as satisfying as *pane rustico*.

Forster, E.M. *A Room with a View*. New York: Dover Publications, 1995.
   Published in 1908, the insights in this novel remain startlingly modern.

Harrison, Barbara Grizzuti. *Italian Days*. Atlantic Monthly Press, 1998.
   At once intimate and expansive, Harrison's journey through the landscape of Italy and her own emotions is compelling reading from start to finish.

Hazan, Marcella. *Essentials of Classic Italian Cooking*. New York: Alfred A. Knopf, 1992.
   A fully revised and updated compendium of Hazan's *The Classic Italian Cook Book* and *More Classic Italian Cooking*.

Jenkins, Nancy Harmon. *Flavors of Tuscany: Traditional Recipes from the Tuscan Countryside*. New York: Broadway Books, 1998.
   American author Jenkins lives part-time in Cortona, Italy.

Kamman, Madeleine. *The New Making of a Cook*. New York: William Morrow, 1997.
   For my money, the finest reference on the art and the science of cooking. Kamman is French, not Italian, but nobody's perfect.

Kasper, Lynne Rossetto. *The Splendid Table: Recipes from Emilia-Romagna, the Heartland of Northern Italian Food*. New York: William Morrow, 1992.
> This graceful volume is the definitive work on the cuisine of the cities of Bologna, Modena, Parma, and the region that cradles them.

Luongo, Pino. *A Tuscan in the Kitchen: Recipes and Tales from My Home*. New York: Clarkson N. Potter, 1988.
> A noble foray into writing recipes without exact amounts.

Mariani, John. *The Dictionary of Italian Food and Drink*. New York: Broadway Books, 1998.
> *The* reference for Italian food terms, from *abbacchio* to *zurrette*.

May, Tony. *Italian Cuisine: Basic Cooking Techniques*. New York: Italian Wine & Food Institute, 1990.
> This book is a thorough reference on the Italian kitchen.

Parks, Tim. *Italian Neighbors, or a Lapsed Anglo-Saxon in Verona*. New York: Fawcett Columbine, 1992.
> A British expatriate's wry scribblings on Italian social mores and more.

—————. *An Italian Education: The Further Adventures of an Expatriate in Verona*. New York: Avon Books, 1995.
> Becoming a father draws Parks even further into the Italian culture.

Raris, Fernando e Tina. *I Funghi: Cercarli, Conoscerli, Cucinarli*. Milano: Gruppo Editoriale Fabbri, 1973.
> An Italian reference on hunting, identifying, and cooking mushrooms.

Romer, Elizabeth. *The Tuscan Year: Life and Food in an Italian Valley*. San Francisco: North Point Press, 1989.
> A meticulous account of twelve months with a Tuscan farm family.

Tropiano, Joseph. *Big Night*. St. Martin's Griffin, 1996.
> With this novelization of the film, written by Tropiano and Stanley Tucci, I can revisit Primo and Secondo's Paradise trattoria.

Willinger, Faith Heller. *Eating in Italy*. New York: William Morrow, 1998.
> Don't leave home for a trip to Italy without this informative volume.

Articles

"Cooking School: Pasta Frolla." *The Magazine of La Cucina Italiana,* October 1999.

Ferri, Edgarda. "I Buoni Ristoranti Italiani: Gran San Bernardo." *La Cucina Italiana,* November 1966.

Kummer, Corby. "Corby's Table: True Taste of Tuscany." *The Atlantic Monthly,* May 1998.

Rentschler, Kay, with Collin, Julia. "The Secrets of Panna Cotta." *Cook's Illustrated,* July and August 2000.

Wells, Patricia. "Florence for Food Lovers." *Travel & Leisure,* July 1992.

A Glossary of Basic Ingredients, Techniques, and Tools

Eating well every day is a pleasure we all deserve. An intelligently stocked, well-integrated pantry of Italian ingredients—in a kitchen equipped with solid pots and pans—makes this pleasure a continual possibility. Turn to page 254 for a chart about "Setting Up a Pantry."

Consult the following entries on an as-needed basis: when you want more information about selecting ingredients at the supermarket and storing them in your kitchen; when you need to learn basic useful techniques such as roasting bell peppers, toasting nuts, and peeling tomatoes; and, finally, when you need to know which pots, pans, and utensils really cook.

Bread

Italian Rustic Bread (page 50), is made from only flour, water, yeast, and salt. When you buy bread, select a full-flavored type, with a dense crumb and pronounced crust. Frozen sliced bread, wrapped in plastic and aluminum foil, is convenient to have on hand. To use a few slices, simply remove and thaw in a toaster or toaster oven. To thaw an entire loaf, place the unwrapped slices, separated slightly, on a large baking sheet. Bake in a preheated 350°F oven for about 10 minutes, or until warm.

Unseasoned, fine dry bread crumbs add interest to a wide array of dishes. Crumbs may be purchased but are easily made at home with leftover good-quality bread.

To prepare bread crumbs: Break or cut leftover slices into chunks. Allow to dry for several days on a large tray covered with a paper towel, or dry in a 350°F oven for about 30 minutes and then cool completely. Process bread in a food processor until finely ground. Or, place bread in a resealable plastic bag. Close the bag and lay flat. Crush the bread with a rolling pin. Store in a resealable plastic bag in the freezer. No need to thaw before using.

Broth

Homemade Basic Broth (page 38), homemade Chicken Broth (page 39), or canned reduced-sodium chicken broth may be used in this book's recipes. If unsalted homemade broth is used, increase the amount of salt called for in the recipe, to taste. If regular canned chicken broth is used, reduce the amount of salt called for in the recipe. Vegetarians may replace chicken broth with canned vegetable broth or porcini Mushroom Broth (page 38).

Butter

Salt preserves butter, and it can mask "off" flavors in old butter. Unsalted butter is best for pastries, desserts, and occasional sautéing. If salted butter is used, reduce the amount of salt called for in the recipe. Stock up when butter is on sale; it freezes beautifully for up to a year.

Cheeses

In ingredient lists, the amounts of cheeses are given in dry measure and by weight. Measures are for shredded or grated cheeses packed lightly in nesting measuring cups; cooks who have the cheese on hand may grate and measure. Cooks who don't have the cheese on hand may purchase the weight specified. Wrap cheeses loosely in plastic and keep them in a paper bag placed in the vegetable crisper of the refrigerator.

- Fontina: Cow's milk cheese produced in the Val d'Aosta in far northwestern Italy. Creamy, with a slight acidic tang, excellent for melting.

- Gorgonzola: Blue-veined cow's milk cheese named after the town of Gorgonzola in Lombardy. Gorgonzola *dolce* is younger and sweeter than *naturale*, *piccante*, or *stagionata*, which are aged longer.

- Gruyère: Cow's milk cheese with a nutty, complex flavor. Select Swiss or French Gruyère, or *groviera* from Italy, if available. Extremely versatile, a beautiful melting cheese.

- Mozzarella: Fresh mozzarella made from the milk of water buffaloes originated in southern Italy. Today, most mozzarella is made with cow's milk and is called *fior di latte*. Many supermarkets carry fresh mozzarella in whey; check for the freshest available. Store in the refrigerator and use as soon as possible. Remove from the whey and pat dry before slicing.

- Parmesan: Cow's milk cheese formed in huge wheels before aging from eighteen months to five years. A billboard on the road into the city of Parma proclaims "Welcome to the Home of the King of Cheeses, *Parmigiano-Reggiano.*" In this case, civic boosterism is no exaggeration. Parmesan's sweetness and complexity are incomparable. When shopping, select cheese in a wedge with the rind showing the legal pin-prick stamp "Parmigiano-Reggiano." The interior should be pale yellow and crumbly but not hard. Renowned as a grating cheese, a young Parmesan is also wonderful to eat with fruit and bread, or as part of an antipasto spread.

- Pecorino Romano: Aged sheep's milk cheese used for grating. Piquant and assertive, this cheese is used sparingly as a flavor accent.

- Tuscan Pecorino: Tuscan sheep's milk cheese is increasingly available in supermarkets. Younger than Pecorino Romano and more yellow, it is pleasantly piquant with a smooth texture. It adds spunk to many dishes or can be eaten with fruit and bread. Manchego cheese from Spain, which is slightly sharper, is a good substitute.

- Provolone: Cow's milk cheese originally produced in Campania, but now made in many other regions. Sharp and feisty, it delivers a characteristic "pan-Italian" taste. The flavor sharpens with age.

- Ricotta: "Recooked" cow's milk whey, a by-product of cheese production, is the base for this fresh soft cheese. Select ricotta with no gums, gelatin, or other additives; store in the refrigerator and use well before the pull date.

Condiments

Mostly pickled or cured vegetables, Italian condiments add savor to sandwiches, composed salads, antipasti, pastas, and more.

🍴 Capers: Pickled buds of the caper bush packed in brine. Store the opened jar in the refrigerator and drain the liquid before adding capers to a dish.

🍴 Giardiniera: Literally means "garden-style"; a pickled mixed vegetable relish often seasoned with hot chile. Store the opened jar in the refrigerator.

🍴 Olives: Select olives that are loose-packed in the delicatessen or bottled (not canned) from Italian, French, Moroccan, or Spanish sources. Ripe (dark) olives that have been dry-cured in salt and/or olive oil—often seasoned with garlic, rosemary, or other herbs—are shriveled and chewy. Ripe (dark) olives cured in brine are tender, smooth, and plump. Think of the textural difference between dried raisins and dried raisins after being plumped in warm water. Gaeta, either brined or dry-cured, is a versatile ripe Italian olive. Moroccan dry-cured ripe olives make a good replacement for dry-cured Gaetas. The Ligurian olive or French Niçoise brine-cured ripe olive is excellent for salads and snacking. Green olives usually have a firmer texture than ripe olives. Look for green Cerignola or Sicilian colossals.

🍴 Peperoncini: Pickled chiles packed in brine. Store the opened jar in the refrigerator.

🍴 Bell peppers, roasted: Homemade and frozen (page 235) or purchased from the delicatessen. Avoid bottled roasted peppers, which are often bitter.

Cornmeal

Yellow cornmeal is used to make polenta, the Italian version of cornmeal mush. Quaker brand cornmeal is universally available.

Eggs

Select Grade AA large eggs, the fresher the better. Store in the refrigerator and use well before the pull date on the carton.

Fruit

In summer, select fresh, locally grown fruits: blueberries, blackberries, cantaloupe, cherries, grapes, honeydew melon, nectarines, peaches, plums, raspberries, strawberries, watermelon. Serve whole fruits to end a meal or dice several fruits into a *macedonia*, a mixed fruit salad, sweetened with sugar and spiked with lemon juice or chilled white wine.

Store berries and grapes in the refrigerator. Melons and stone fruits may be ripened in a brown paper bag with some bananas (which hasten ripening). Chill before serving these ripened fruits.

Fall through winter, select long-keeping fruits such as apples and pears. In winter, select citrus fruits. Oranges are the tomatoes of the winter kitchen. I often add bright, sweet navel orange slices to winter salads. Clementines, loose-skinned seedless members of the mandarin orange family, keep beautifully in a cool garage. Blood oranges, with flesh the color of garnets, are a special treat in late winter. Lemons should be in the refrigerator always. Both lemon zest (the colored peel) and juice are indispensable in Italian cooking.

Store apples and citrus in a cool garage or in the refrigerator's vegetable crisper. Pears may be ripened in a brown paper bag with some bananas and chilled before serving.

Commercially frozen loose-packed fruits, such as strawberries and sliced peaches, are convenient to have on hand when nothing looks good in the supermarket.

Meats, cured

Used in moderation, spicy, rich cured meats add character to many dishes. Many cured meats, including the incomparable *prosciutto di Parma,* are now imported. Some good domestic products are also prepared Italian-style. The generic category of salami includes uncooked types such as *salsicce* (pork sausage in casings seasoned with fennel and hot peppers); cooked sausages such as *mortadella* (finely ground pork seasoned with spices, often studded with pistachios and peppercorns); and dry-aged salami, such as Genoa-style (made with ground pork and sometimes beef).

Milk, half-and-half, and whipping cream

For best results, use the liquid dairy product called for in the ingredients list. If no specific type of milk is called for, any type will work in the recipe. Select whipping cream, if possible, that is not ultrapasteurized or stabilized with gums or other additives.

No-Stick Spray

Plain vegetable oil spray is convenient for coating baking pans and baking dishes.

Nuts

Almonds, pine nuts, walnuts, and hazelnuts (filberts) are sprinkled throughout savory and sweet recipes in this book. If possible, buy nuts in bulk from a store with a brisk turnover; they're generally less expensive and are likely to be fresher. I heartily recommend toasting nuts to deepen the flavor. Store nuts, either raw or toasted, in resealable plastic bags in the freezer for up to a year.

To toast almonds and pine nuts on the stove top: Choose a heavy skillet in which the nuts cover the bottom in a single layer. Add the nuts and cook over medium-high heat for about 5 minutes, stirring frequently, until golden. Pour onto a plate to cool.

To toast walnut halves and hazelnuts in the oven: Place the nuts in a single layer on a heavy baking sheet in a preheated 350°F oven for about 10 minutes, stirring occasionally, or until walnuts are fragrant and the skins of hazelnuts start to split. Pour onto a plate to cool. To peel hazelnuts, rub off the skins with fingers or a kitchen towel.

Olive Oil

Extra-virgin olive oil is cold-pressed from ripe olives. Lush with flavor, it is indispensable for the recipes in this book. Because these meals are pared down to a minimum of ingredients, using the best flavored oil is very important. I'm not advising an expensive boutique oil. Many fine imported Italian extra-virgins are in supermarkets in reasonably priced containers. I buy extra-virgin olive oil in 2-liter (2 quart, 4 ounce) plastic bottles from a warehouse market. I store it in a cool, dark cupboard. Because I use it quickly, it never goes rancid. To gauge your needs, purchase a smaller bottle and keep an eye on how long it takes to use it up.

An airtight pouring can (sold in housewares shops) filled with about a cup of oil is convenient to have near the range top. Also, a refillable mister (sold in housewares shops) is handy for lightly coating ingredients: sliced vegetables for grilling; bread for garlic bread or soups.

Pasta

Dried: See pages 74 and 75.
Fresh: See pages 86 and 87.

Rice

Stored in a cool, dry cupboard, rice keeps well for up to one year. For risotto, select arborio, carnaroli, or other rice labeled "superfino." Long- or medium-grain rice is the choice for rice salads, soups, and stuffings.

Seasonings

- Dried red chiles: Select whole dried red chiles to crumble by hand, or commercially packed crushed red pepper.
- Ground cinnamon: The warm and fragrant flavor of cinnamon enhances winter fruit, dried fruit dishes and pastries.
- Fennel seeds: Lightly toasting the seeds before crushing them—in a mortar and pestle, under a scaloppine pounder, or in a spice grinder—releases their sweet, delicate anise flavor.
- Garlic: Select plump, firm bulbs and store them in a basket in a cool pantry so air can flow around the garlic.
- Herbs: For a discussion of herbs, see page 242.
- Ground nutmeg: Adds a subtle nutty essence to cream and cheese sauces, as well as dishes made with spinach or other greens.
- Black Tellicherry peppercorns: Grind to order in a pepper grinder.
- Saffron: Select dried threads (crocus stigmas) as a once-in-a-while indulgence when making Fusilli with Spicy Clams (page 79), Risotto alla Milanese (page 111) or Saffron Red Pepper Compote (page 200).
- Salt: Kosher, flaked, or coarse sea salt for savory cooking; finely ground sea

salt, because it dissolves more quickly, for baked goods and breads. Any pure salt, without the addition of free-flowing additives, is fine. Adjust amounts to your own taste.

§ Pure vanilla extract: Its vibrant floral notes are a necessity with cream dessert sauces.

Tools

Substance, not style, is my mantra for pots, pans, and utensils. Investing in a few key pieces can make a huge difference in the quality of the meals you cook.

§ Gas range top. Simply the best for adjusting heat *instantly*. I realize you can't change your stove top as readily as your socks, but if you're buying a stove in the near future, or moving to a new home, consider a gas stove top. Some manufacturers of home ranges offer burners that fire up to 12,500 BTUs—hot enough to bring a pot of water to a boil in less than five minutes and to truly sauté meats and vegetables.

§ Sauté pan: If you invest in just one cooking pan that you'll hand down to the grandchildren, make it a 10- or 12-inch sauté pan made from anodized aluminum, enameled cast iron, or stainless coated heavy-gauge aluminum for superior heat conduction that browns the food surfaces evenly. A large rolled steel wok, preferably with a flat bottom, is a decent, and usually less expensive, alternative. Remember that, depending on your stove top and your equipment, cooking temperature and times may have to be adjusted slightly. Be flexible.

§ Pasta pot: I have two medium-quality 6-quart pots, neither of which will outlive me. They're fine for boiling water, though. For stews, which require long and even cooking, I turn to my twenty-five-year-old enameled cast iron Dutch oven.

§ Utility baking pan: I have two 16 x 10-inch speckled blue enamel pans, the kind the hardware store sells. They're good for baking vegetables and roasting meats. An enameled cast iron lasagna pan is also a versatile piece.

§ Large nonstick skillet: I love my enameled cast iron skillet for frittatas and pan-fried potatoes.

§ Scaloppine pounder: See page 148.

§ Springform pan: A pan about 10 inches in diameter is useful for a variety of savory tarts, sweet pastries, and tortes. Removable sides ensure the dessert will look as pretty as it tastes.

§ Colander: For draining pasta and washing vegetables; the larger and sturdier the better. Stainless steel with a ring base works well.

§ Knives: At the minimum, you need a 4-inch paring knife for peeling and trimming and a large (8-inch or so) chef's knife or cleaver for chopping. Keep them sharpened.

§ Four-sided metal cheese and vegetable grater: Use the sharp-toothed side for grating hard cheeses such as Parmesan. Use the side with the small shredding holes for semisoft cheeses, such as Fontina and provolone, because the finer the shred, the more evenly the cheese melts.

- Instant-reading digital thermometer: Worth the small investment of money because it eliminates guesswork in determining doneness for poultry and meat. Also useful for checking water temperature when making bread or pizza dough.

- Utensils: Large wooden fork to stir pasta; several large stainless steel cooking spoons; hand whisks in several sizes from tiny to large; a plastic dough scraper; pastry brush.

- Olive oil mister: A refillable pump spray can, which can be purchased in cookware stores or catalogs, is handy for lightly coating foods. Brushing foods with a pastry brush dipped in olive oil is also an option.

- Waxed paper: Saves mightily on clean-up if you use it for breading foods, grating cheeses, rolling pastry crusts, and more. Place the waxed paper, curl-side down, on a work surface, and it will lie flat.

Vegetables

If you cook with the seasons, you'll be rewarded with better-tasting meals. Many supermarkets showcase regional farm produce, and that is the stuff to buy: asparagus and scallions in May; tomatoes, bell peppers, and corn in August; squashes in late September. When selecting a vegetable, use your senses. Does the vegetable look lively and feel firm? Does it *look* good enough to eat?

Be flexible in making choices and try some vegetables that are now supermarket standards but may be unfamiliar to you: savoy cabbage, bulb fennel (often labeled anise), portobello mushrooms, kale, rucola (rocket, often labeled arugula), radicchio.

- Beans: For a discussion of canned and dried beans, see page 102.

- Bell peppers: The sweet meaty flesh of red or yellow bell peppers enhances appetizers, frittatas, soups, pastas, and main dishes. The grassier-tasting green bell peppers play a more limited role.

To roast and peel bell peppers: See page 235 for basic method; if preparing only one or two peppers, place in a plastic bag, instead of a large bowl, to steam.

- Tomatoes: There are two basic types, salad and sauce. Two recipes for freezer sauces in "Capturing Summer Flavors for All Meals" call for fresh plum tomatoes. When these are not available, commercially canned diced tomatoes are convenient for making sauces. Dry-pack, recipe-ready sun-dried tomatoes (some are pre-cut) sold in cellophane bags are convenient because they don't have to be reconstituted in hot water before adding to a dish.

To peel plum tomatoes: Bring 1 quart of water to a boil in a medium saucepan. Fill a sink with cold water. Working with about 6 tomatoes at a time, drop into the boiling water for 30 seconds. With a slotted spoon, transfer to the cold water for several minutes. With a small sharp knife, cut out the tomato core. The skin should slide right off. Cut or chop according to recipe directions. Use the same method to peel peaches.

Vinegar

Stock a good-quality, unflavored wine vinegar, either red or white, as well as a decent-quality commercially produced balsamic vinegar, preferably imported from Modena. Although not as rare, refined, or costly as a true *aceto balsamico* produced by artisanal methods, mass-produced balsamic is a versatile condiment in its own right.

Water

If your tap water doesn't taste good enough to drink, don't use it in soup or bread, either. Use filtered or bottled water instead.

Wine and Liquor

Stock decent red and white wine (consult Carol A. Berman's accessible recommendations throughout the book or the wine buyer at your local store for bargains bought by the case) to have on hand for cooking and daily meals. Other cooking wines and liquors to consider are Marsala, a fortified wine from Sicily; vodka, which is magic for tomato sauces; orange liqueur for pastries; dark rum for desserts.

Setting Up a Pantry

To make many of the recipes in this book—with minimal additional shopping—stock your kitchen with the following foods:

In the Cupboard
canned beans, cannellini or Great Northern, chick-peas (garbanzo beans)
canned reduced-sodium chicken broth
garlic cloves
dried porcini mushrooms
extra-virgin olive oil
yellow and red onions
dried pasta, in a variety of shapes
red or white potatoes
raisins
long-grain and superfino rice
seasonings: kosher or sea salt; Tellicherry black peppercorns in a grinder; dried rosemary, oregano, thyme, fennel seeds, crushed red pepper
canned diced tomatoes

wine vinegar (red or white) and balsamic vinegar
table wine, white and red

In the Refrigerator
large eggs
carrots
celery hearts
cheeses: Parmesan, Gruyère, and Pecorino Romano
lemons
green and ripe olives
fresh flat-leaf parsley

In the Freezer
rustic Italian bread
plain dry bread crumbs
yellow cornmeal
pine nuts and walnuts
frozen baby peas
basil pesto

High-Altitude Cooking Tips

Most of the recipes in this book will need to be adjusted only slightly, if at all, by cooks living at altitudes of 3,500 feet and above. There are some general tips that may come in handy, however:

- When boiling pasta, use either less water (4 to 5 quarts per pound of pasta) or a larger pot, so that the water fills the pot only about halfway. Because of the lower atmospheric pressure at high altitudes, liquids have a tendency to boil over. Also, because water boils at a lower temperature, allow a little extra cooking time for boiled or simmered foods such as pasta and vegetables.

- Long-simmered foods such as beans and stews may take quite a bit longer to cook—as much as an hour longer at 5,000 to 6,000 feet. If you live above 7,000 feet, either buy canned beans or cook beans in a pressure cooker.

- Breads and pizzas rise very quickly at higher altitudes. While this saves time, it has two disadvantages: The flavor does not have time to fully develop, and because of all the air in it, the dough can easily collapse if the bread or pizza is jostled too much before baking. To counteract this, I recommend cutting the amount of yeast in half and adding just a bit more flour (anywhere from 1 to 4 teaspoons) to the dough to strengthen the structure. Raising the oven temperature by 25°F may help as well. A higher oven temperature helps form a crust faster, stabilizing the dough.

- For light cakes (such as the sponge cake used in the Zuccotto, page 220), make sure the ingredients are cool, and do not overbeat the eggs. In fact, it's better to underbeat the eggs by a few seconds. Add 1 tablespoon additional flour and 2 tablespoons water for each cup of flour or flour-cornstarch mixture called for in the recipe (at 5,000 feet). You might try raising the oven temperature by 15°F to 25°F, especially if you live at altitudes above 5,000 to 6,000 feet, but check on the cake a few minutes before the end of the allotted baking time to make sure it does not burn. The Chocolate Torte (page 228), heavier cakes such as the Almond Cake with Caramelized Orange Slices (page 222), and crisp cookies such as biscotti (page 224) usually need little, if any, adjustment.

- Because water evaporates quickly, caramel sauces (such as the one with Panna Cotta, page 210) can be tricky. You may want to just buy a good-quality caramel sauce, especially if you are cooking at an altitude above 5,000 feet. Otherwise, add an additional tablespoon of water to the sugar mixture and allow extra time for the sugar to melt. The sugar may crystallize into lumps before melting and may take up to 20 to 30 minutes (at 5,000 feet) to turn into caramel.

International Conversion Information

The recipes in this book were tested using standard American utensils that measure by volume:

- An 8-ounce (1 cup) fluid measuring cup with a pour spout for liquids.
- A set of four nesting cups (1 cup, ¾ cup, ½ cup, ¼ cup) for sugar, flour, cornmeal, rice, and other dry ingredients.
- Standard tablespoon and teaspoon measures (1 tablespoon = 3 teaspoons) for smaller amounts of liquid and dry ingredients.

Butter is listed in sticks or tablespoons, which are often marked with lines on the wrapper (1 stick = 4 ounces or 8 tablespoons).

Measures are given in weight (ounces or pounds) for meat, cheese, and other solid ingredients, as well as canned beans, tomatoes, and other packaged foods. Manufacturers sometimes change the weights of packaged foods. Use the size that's closest to the one given in the recipe.

When specific dimensions are important, pan sizes are indicated in inches.

Cooks outside the United States may choose to purchase a set of American cup measures, sold in major stores around the world and through cookware stores on the Internet. Another option is to consult the chart (page 257) for either the metric or imperial equivalents. The list is selective, including the measures used most often in the recipes. The figures are rounded (usually down) to the nearest even measure. This will present no problem with most of the recipes in this book. In a recipe calling for 16 ounces (1 pound) of green beans, using 450 grams instead of 453.6 grams (the precise equivalent) will make no difference in the outcome of the dish. Amounts in recipes for baked goods, however, must be converted precisely for best results. Also, please note these items in converting recipes:

- An imperial pint measures 20 fluid ounces, compared with an American pint, which measures 16 fluid ounces. An imperial cup measures 10 fluid ounces; an American cup, 8 fluid ounces.
- In Australia, 1 tablespoon = 4 teaspoons, or 20 ml.
- In England, Australia, and New Zealand, 1 dessertspoon = 2 teaspoons.
- Lukewarm liquid is 100° Fahrenheit or 45° Celsius.
- One large egg weighs 50 grams.
- All-purpose (plain) flour is used throughout the book, measured by volume in dry nesting cups. To measure accurately, spoon the flour into the cup and level the top with a knife.
- Confectioners' sugar is icing sugar.
- Cornstarch is cornflour.
- Half-and-half is 12-percent fat milk.
- Whipping cream is double cream.
- Zucchini and yellow squash are courgettes.

Volume measurements

U.S.	Imperial	Metric
$1/8$ teaspoon	$1/8$ teaspoon	0.5 ml
$1/4$ teaspoon	$1/4$ teaspoon	1 ml
$1/2$ teaspoon	$1/2$ teaspoon	2 ml
$3/4$ teaspoon	$3/4$ teaspoon	4 ml
1 teaspoon	1 teaspoon	5 ml
1 tablespoon	1 tablespoon	15 ml
$1/4$ cup	$1/4$ cup	60 ml
$1/3$ cup	$1/3$ cup	75 ml
$1/2$ cup	$1/2$ cup	125 ml
$2/3$ cup	$2/3$ cup	150 ml
$3/4$ cup	$3/4$ cup	175 ml
1 cup	1 cup	250 ml

Weight measurements

U.S. and Imperial		Metric	
Ounces	Pounds	Grams	Kilos
1		25	
4	$1/4$	115	
6		170	
8	$1/2$	225	
12	$3/4$	350	
16	1	450	
18		500	$1/2$
36	$2^{1}/4$	1000	1

Oven temperatures

Fahrenheit	Gas Mark	Celsius
300°	2	150°
350°	4	180°
400°	6	200°
450°	8	230°

Cookware and baking pan sizes

U.S.	Metric
6-quart pot	5 to 6 L
5-quart sauté pan	4 to 5 L
12 x 8-inch baking pan	30 x 20 cm
13 x 9-inch baking pan	33 x 23 cm
15 x 10-inch baking pan	38 x 26 cm
9 x 5-inch loaf pan	23 x 13 cm
10-inch springform pan	25 cm
9-inch round cake pan	23 cm

Can and package sizes by weight

U.S.	Metric
6 ounces	170 g
15 ounces	425 g

Index

Note: <u>Underscored</u> page references indicate recipe introductions and marginal notes.